The Enthusiastic Employee

Ideas. Action. Impact.
**Wharton School
Publishing**

In the face of accelerating turbulence and change, business leaders and policy makers need new ways of thinking to sustain performance and growth.

Wharton School Publishing offers a trusted source for stimulating ideas from thought leaders who provide new mental models to address changes in strategy, management, and finance. We seek out authors from diverse disciplines with a profound understanding of change and its implications. We offer books and tools that help executives respond to the challenge of change.

Every book and management tool we publish meets quality standards set by The Wharton School of the University of Pennsylvania. Each title is reviewed by the Wharton School Publishing Editorial Board before being given Wharton's seal of approval. This ensures that Wharton publications are timely, relevant, important, conceptually sound or empirically based, and implementable.

To fit our readers' learning preferences, Wharton publications are available in multiple formats, including books, audio, and electronic.

To find out more about our books and management tools, visit us at whartonsp.com and Wharton's executive education site, exceed.wharton.upenn.edu.

The Enthusiastic Employee

How Companies Profit by Giving Workers
What They Want

David Sirota
Louis A. Mischkind
Michael Irwin Meltzer

Ideas. Action. Impact.
**Wharton School
Publishing**

Library of Congress Publication in Data: 2004112244

Vice President, Editor-in-Chief: *Tim Moore*
Executive Editor: *Jim Boyd*
Editorial Assistant: *Richard Winkler*
Development Editor: *Russ Hall*
Marketing Manager: *Martin Litkowski*
International Marketing Manager: *Tim Galligan*
Cover Designer: *Alan Clements*
Managing Editor: *Gina Kanouse*
Senior Project Editor: *Sarah Kearns*
Copy Editor: *Sheri Cain*
Indexer: *Larry Sweazy*
Compositor: *Kim Scott*
Manufacturing Buyer: *Dan Uhrig*

Ideas. Action. Impact.
Wharton School Publishing

© 2005 by Pearson Education, Inc.
Publishing as Wharton School Publishing
Upper Saddle River, New Jersey 07458

Wharton School Publishing offers excellent discounts on this book when ordered in quantity for bulk purchases or special sales. For more information, please contact U.S. Corporate and Government Sales, 1-800-382-3419, corpsales@pearsontechgroup.com. For sales outside the U.S., please contact International Sales at international@pearsoned.com.

Company and product names mentioned herein are the trademarks or registered trademarks of their respective owners.

Printed in the United States of America

First Printing

ISBN 0-13-142330-4

Pearson Education LTD.
Pearson Education Australia PTY, Limited.
Pearson Education Singapore, Pte. Ltd.
Pearson Education North Asia, Ltd.
Pearson Education Canada, Ltd.
Pearson Educatión de Mexico, S.A. de C.V.
Pearson Education—Japan
Pearson Education Malaysia, Pte. Ltd.

Ideas. Action. Impact.
**Wharton School
Publishing**

C. K. Prahalad
THE FORTUNE AT THE BOTTOM OF THE PYRAMID
Eradicating Poverty Through Profits

Yoram (Jerry) Wind, Colin Crook, with Robert Gunther
THE POWER OF IMPOSSIBLE THINKING
Transform the Business of Your Life and the Life of Your Business

Scott A. Shane
FINDING FERTILE GROUND
Identifying Extraordinary Opportunities for New Ventures

Bernard Baumohl
THE SECRETS OF ECONOMIC INDICATORS
Hidden Clues to Future Economic Trends and Investment Opportunities

Sayan Chatterjee
FAILSAFE STRATEGIES
Profit and Grow from Risks that Others Avoid

Robert Mittelstaedt
WILL YOUR NEXT MISTAKE BE FATAL?
Avoiding the Chain of Mistakes That Can Destroy Your Organization

Mukul Pandya, Robbie Shell, Susan Warner, Sandeep Junnarkar, and Jeffrey Brown
NIGHTLY BUSINESS REPORT PRESENTS LASTING LEADERSHIP
What You Can Learn from the Top 25 Business People of our Times

Oded Shenkar
THE CHINESE CENTURY
The Rising Chinese Economy and Its Impact on the Global Economy, the Balance of Power, and Your Job

Lawrence G. Hrebiniak
MAKING STRATEGY WORK
Leading Effective Execution and Change

This work is dedicated to our families:

Our wives: Barbara, Carol, and Janet.

*And our children: Rima and Abigail,
Samson and Eden, Rachel and Daniel.*

Our enthusiasm at its source.

Contents

Acknowledgments

As the saying goes, "it takes a village"…to do any number of things. Well, in our case, it took the efforts of an entire company over many years to make this work possible. We refer, of course, to our colleagues, past and present, at Sirota Consulting. Over the years, Sirota Consulting has been fortunate to have some of the best minds in the field of industrial and organizational psychology using attitude research methods to study human behavior in the workplace and assist in the improvement of organization effectiveness. Many of our colleagues provided research and statistical analysis; others offered the value of their experience and insights. Still others gave freely of their time to review and professionally critique our work.

In particular, this book would not have been written without the encouragement, assistance, and generous support of Jeffrey Saltzman and Douglas Klein, the principal owners of Sirota Consulting. Not only did they freely offer their own expertise, but they provided us with the full support of the company to undertake the work. Others at Sirota Consulting played equally important roles: Martin Brockerhoff, Ph.D. and Shawn Del Duco provided key statistical analyses. Patrick Hyland, Joyce Chan, and Jeanine Andreassi were extremely helpful in tracking down supporting evidence. John Sherman, Ph.D. offered thoughtful insights while Cynthia

DeMarsh and Susan Mancini helped in preparing the manuscript, fixing the messes we created in the document. Bruce Segall added his own talents at the end of the process and helped us finish.

Our work greatly benefited from the participation of many accomplished senior executives. In the course of writing this book, these leaders allowed us to test our observations and conclusions against their real-life experiences and, simply, to learn from them: Ed Finn (Barron's), John Goff (Crescent), Paul Weidman (Wabco), Charles R. Larson (Admiral, U.S. Navy (Ret.), Bill Taylor (Mercedes), Trip Welch (Mayo Clinic), Ewout Durieux (Shell Oil), Tom Rauzi (Dell), and Craig Ramsay (Intuit). We also benefited greatly from the suggestions of Yoram (Jerry) Wind, Ph.D. and his colleagues at the Wharton School.

We also wish to express our appreciation to our publishers and the team that worked so hard on bringing *The Enthusiastic Employee* to fruition: Jim Boyd, our senior editor, supported the project early on and always provided reliable guidance and just the right dose of urgency and common sense. Ruth Mills, an early reviewer, Russ Hall, who provided important comments on the work, and Sarah Kearns, who labored over the copy and patiently corrected our syntax and hyphens.

Each of us also has personal acknowledgments to make, and we do so here:

David Sirota: I'd like to thank Dr. Harold Weissman, a friend who for many years has been a sounding board for, and a provider of, ideas and who suggested the title for this book; my sister, Shirley Sirota Rosenberg, who taught me a lot about writing, albeit not entirely successfully; and my wife, Dr. Barbara Sirota, who, in addition to her patience and support, provided invaluable advice in matters dealing with individual psychology. A major theme of this book is the importance of teamwork in accomplishing objectives and I acknowledge the terrific cooperation of my two team members during the long time it took to get this book written. We had many debates but no arguments and, best of all, many laughs. It was truly a pleasure working with Lou and Michael.

Louis Mischkind: I'd like to thank the scholars I encountered when I was a callow graduate student at NYU. The wisdom of people such as Lewin, Argyris, and Likert always rang true to me. After thirty-eight years as a practitioner and working on this book, I am thoroughly convinced they had hit the mark. David, Michael, and I were of like mind. We had controversy over the uses of dashes and brackets but never over fundamental concepts, so I echo David's sentiments. I also want to thank my wife Carol for putting up with me while writing this book and my sister Ruth Kolbe, my intellectual mentor. I am also grateful to my teachers (too numerous to name), who consist of my professors, executive clients, and the thousands of workers I have met who led me to understand what the workplace is all about.

Michael Meltzer: First and foremost, I very thankfully acknowledge my co-writers, David Sirota and Lou Mischkind. David and I had discussed the idea of him writing a book some years ago; little did I know that I would have the opportunity to participate in its creation. I have David to thank for that, and I am grateful indeed. Not only was it great fun to work on the book with David, but I also had the opportunity to work closely with Lou, and I have never enjoyed anything more in my career. His seeming vast store of knowledge is as inspiring as is his repertoire of humor engaging. While the three of us quickly melded into a team, I say without hesitation that I often felt like the student among them; I came away knowing much more than when I started. Others also helped me in a variety of ways and I gratefully acknowledge and thank them here: Mary O'Neil Berry, Ph.D., J. Nicholas Starritt, and David A. Mader, colleagues and friends, who offered kind words, lots of encouragement, and many helpful ideas; my good friend and former law partner, Howard W. Segal, Esq., whose astute insight into human nature sharpened my own; and Rabbi Isidoro Aizenberg, my teacher for life. My son Daniel Meltzer focused me on the sum not the parts, and my daughter Rachel Meltzer—who is actually the best writer I know—said years ago the very thing I needed to hear; how grateful I am to them both. And of course last, but not least, to my parents, Helen and Seymour Meltzer, whose fault I am.

About the Authors

David Sirota has two abiding professional interests: organization behavior and survey research. Both of these interests took hold at the University of Michigan, where he received his doctorate, and which, in that university's Institute for Social Research, was a leading center for applying survey methods to the study of organizations, their employees, and their effectiveness.

Upon receiving his doctorate, he was recruited by the International Business Machines Corporation to help initiate behavioral science research there. He stayed at IBM for 12 years in a variety of management and research positions, leaving in 1972 to set up his own firm, Sirota Consulting. Sirota Consulting specializes in the diagnosis and improvement of the relationships of organizations with all of their key constituencies: employees, customers, suppliers, investors, and communities. In 1996, David became Chairman Emeritus of the firm, after completing his own succession plan with key employees. He continues to consult with selected clients, primarily on matters of teamwork within and between organizations.

Parallel to his career as a consultant, David has had an academic career, having taught at the School of Industrial and Labor Relations of Cornell University, the School of Industrial Administration of Yale University, the Sloan School of the Massachusetts Institute of Technology, and the Wharton School of the University of Pennsylvania.

David is married with two children and lives in New York City.

Louis A. Mischkind is a Senior Vice President of Sirota Consulting and the first appointed Fellow of the David Sirota Research Foundation for the Social Sciences. He has been associated with the firm for over fifteen years.

Lou's work has spanned the public, private, and government sectors. He specializes in multi-constituency research such as the teachers, principals, students, and staff members of the Dallas Independent School District and the trade affected workers, employers, training providers, and staff of the Trade Adjustment Program of the Department of Labor. His other clients are quite varied and include the Mayo Clinic, the New York Times Company, General Mills, the Computer Science Corporation, and the Bank of America.

Before joining Sirota, Lou was Program Director of Executive Development for IBM. One of his duties included running the executive assessment center for the IBM technical community. Lou also spent ten years as the "Plant Shrink," as it was affectionately called, in the IBM General Products Division San Jose site in California. He oversaw the employee survey, ran team development programs, and was a teacher in management and professional development programs.

He holds a Masters Degree in Experimental Psychology from Columbia University and a Ph.D. in Organizational Psychology from New York University. He lives in Irvington, New York, with his wife, Carol. He is the father of two grown children.

As a practicing attorney in a Manhattan law firm for over 25 years, **Michael Meltzer** has seen a startling assortment of business environments. From financial consultancies to real estate developers, from sales and distribution juggernauts to professional practices and entertainers, Michael has had the benefit of extensive experience in dealing with people and businesses. His practice ultimately transcended legal issues alone and Michael has had the opportunity to also focus on key business issues: organizational governance, business strategy, and personnel policies.

In the course of his general practice, Michael represented Sirota Consulting and in 1990 was named as the company's outside general counsel while he continued his private practice. In 2001, he became Sirota Consulting's first in-house counsel. He now serves as the firm's Chief Operating Officer and its General Counsel.

In the early part of his career, Michael was also an Adjunct Assistant Professor at Pace University in New York, teaching business organizations, real estate law, and trusts and estates. He holds a B.A. from The George Washington University, in Washington, D.C., and a J.D. from Brooklyn Law School.

Michael lives in White Plains, New York, along with his wife, Janet, who is a nursery school teacher and who continues to teach him the truly important lessons. Michael has learned to play well with others but still cannot draw a straight line. They have two grown children.

Introduction

The impact shook everything for blocks. Fire, charged by thousands of gallons of jet fuel, sucked so much oxygen out of the air around the impact zone that windows in nearby buildings blew out as the towers of the World Trade Center began to wither and then collapse. On the 32nd floor of the World Financial Center, the offices of *Barron's Magazine* shook. Computers, office supplies, and equipment flew out the windows. Stunned workers held on for dear life. Then, they carefully made their way out of the building to safety. The editorial and business offices of *Barron's Magazine* had been almost instantaneously decimated. The damage was so great that it took more than a year to refurbish the offices.

Yet, on September 11, 2001, as people fled the building, *Barron's* employees had already turned their attention to the task of publishing the magazine on time. Months later, Ed Finn, *Barron's* Managing Editor, recalled that the attack had not prevented his employees from publishing a full edition of the magazine three days after their offices were destroyed. In fact, the idea of not publishing never even came up; the only question any employee asked was how the team would accomplish it. None of us would want to face the challenges that *Barron's*—and many, many others—faced that day, but we can all appreciate what the *Barron's* employees did. We can all agree that most organizations would love to have employees who display that level of enthusiasm for their jobs, their companies, and their colleagues.

This is a book about enthusiastic workers.

Managers at all levels often spend an inordinate amount of time with "difficult" individual employees—employees who are angry, uncooperative, or perhaps neurotically demanding of attention. In fact, the task of dealing with such behavior problems is often perceived as a significant human resources cost. But, the reality is even worse, because the bigger problem is the vast number of workers who are not openly troublesome, but who have become largely indifferent to the organization and its purposes. This is the greater problem because the troublemakers can be identified and dealt with; the "walking indifferent," however, are silent killers. They have learned to expect not too much and to give not too much. Yet, these workers are normal people with reasonable human wants. Somehow, their human needs are only marginally satisfied, if at all, by the companies for which they work. In return, they give to the companies a mere fraction of what they are capable of contributing. The economic cost of this under-utilization to the affected businesses is enormous.

How does a company tackle this problem? One approach is to more closely supervise employees, pressuring them to do more. On a more positive note, other managers treat their workers to a procession of "motivational" speakers, rah-rah events, and programs. Neither approach will do much good—in fact, the former will likely exacerbate the problem. We need to get to the root of the matter, the source of employee indifference, and we need to address it. The real challenge is to turn indifferent workers into enthusiastic workers. The solution might surprise you.

First, we must understand what workers want. Then, we must give it to them!

This may sound absurd to some, a sure road to insolvency. On the contrary, it is a powerful path to business success. Why do we say this?

1. Many years of research have established that, surprisingly, little real conflict exists between the goals of the overwhelming majority of workers and those of their employers.

   It is a common, but harmful, misconception that people and their organizations are in a natural state of conflict. This book starts by setting the record straight, examining the source of this confusion, and providing a fresh start to understanding what workers really want. We show that the key question is not how to motivate employees, but how to sustain—and prevent management from destroying—the motivation that employees naturally bring to their jobs.

2. Workers have basic human needs that management can and should work to address. Creating an environment in which these needs are met results not just in satisfied employees, but enthusiastic employees.

   What is the basis of human motivation in the workplace? We discuss three key factors of worker motivation and what they mean. We also show the extraordinary effect of successfully addressing all three of these key factors.

3. Employee enthusiasm—a state of high employee morale that derives from satisfying the three key needs of workers—results in enormous competitive advantages for those companies with the strength of leadership to manage for real long-term results.

Our proof is the numerous cases that we have collected over 30 years of survey research into the effect of employee attitudes on organizational effectiveness. We explore what the data show, illustrating our data with case histories and comments drawn from our extensive research, and we connect the data to business outcomes.

Asking the Questions

How do we claim to know what workers want? It is not by untested hypothesis, imagination, or philosophy. It is not by thinking "out of the box" as the vogue term goes, nor is it by generalizing based on a series of anecdotes. The only real way to learn what's on workers' minds is to *ask them*! This involves asking them simply and directly using inquiry methods that assure that the results are representative and valid.

Real data are the best antidote against jumping to conclusions based only on personal biases, the latest fad, or anecdotes. By using real data, we know what workers want, why they want it, and what it means.

We have been asking workers questions for more than 30 years...or, more accurately, a talented group of industrial organizational psychologists at Sirota Consulting, along with the authors, have engaged in employee-attitude research for more than 30 years. In that time, we collected over 4 *million* survey responses from employees around the word. The data have been collected on various general topics or dimensions of attitudes. Over the course of time, we organized those dimensions into a model that aligns employee attitudes with bottom-line business outcomes.

Asking the Right Questions

Although it is certainly a positive thing that we have collected extensive attitudinal data by actually asking workers about their opinions, we imagine that a few readers are now wondering how we know which questions to ask. The answer to that question requires a little background.

In 1972, David Sirota organized a small business to pursue his mission of improving organization performance through the systematic assessment and management of employee, customer, and community relations. From 1959 through 1972, David was a director of behavioral science research and application for IBM. There, David's activities included the establishment of IBM's worldwide employee-attitude survey program.

David has a broad industrial and academic background. With a doctorate from the University of Michigan, he was a study director at that University's Institute of Social Research. He now serves on that institute's Board of Advisors. He has taught at the School of Industrial and Labor Relations of Cornell University, at Yale University, the Sloan School of Management of the Massachusetts Institute of Technology, and as associate professor of management at the Wharton School of the University of Pennsylvania. He is now Chairman Emeritus of Sirota Consulting.

Co-author Louis Mischkind is, likewise, steeped in survey research, with over 35 years of experience in the field. Prior to joining Sirota Consulting, as Senior Vice President, Lou was the program director of executive development at IBM, advisor on human resources to the president of the General Products Division, and in charge of opinion surveys and management assessment for IBM's technical community. He has taught courses in social and organizational psychology at NYU. He holds a master's degree in experimental psychology from Columbia University and a Ph.D. in organizational psychology from New York University.

Co-author Michael Meltzer comes to the subject from a different background. Michael is a lawyer, practicing business and related law since 1976. He has been an advisor to diverse businesses, including financial consulting, real-estate development, sales and distribution, labor law, construction, and business management companies. Michael also served as an adjunct assistant professor at Pace University, teaching business organizations, real-estate law and trusts and estates, and he has served as a New York City civil court arbitrator. Michael received a B.A. from The George Washington University in Washington D.C., in 1972, and a J.D. from Brooklyn Law School in 1975. He joined Sirota Consulting in 2001 as Managing Director and General Counsel.

As David's reputation grew, both for superior research and for an ability to collect meaningful data that could be used for real business improvement, the small business expanded into an internationally known and respected consultancy. Sirota Consulting is now one of the larger independent privately owned companies in the U.S. that specializes in organization survey research. Sirota consultants have conducted a wide variety of surveys for hundreds of organizations around the world. The company's mission remains much the same as it was when David first started it: to use survey data to help organizations build strong, productive relationships with its key constituencies such as employees, customers, suppliers, communities, investors, opinion leaders, and the public at large.

Our experience, although extensive, is not the only basis for the statement that we have asked the right questions. The research done by Sirota Consultants over the years has followed a widely accepted protocol for attitudinal research: individual interviews, focus groups, and reliability and validation testing. You can find more detailed information on our methods in Chapter 2, "Employee Enthusiasm and Business Success," in Appendix A, "Survey Administration and Population Composition," and Appendix B, "Reliability and Validity of the Data."

Our years of research, experience, and testing have resulted in an enormous pool of responses from which the data for this book have been drawn.

Questions Result in Data

What are our survey data made of? Regarding the kinds of questions we ask, our approach, as we have indicated, is to ask simple and direct questions. You will see that we "psychologize" neither in the interpretation of the answers to our surveys nor in the way we ask our questions. If we want to know how employees feel about their pay, we ask them how they feel about their pay. We don't use "projective" techniques (such as asking them how they feel *others* would rate their pay) on the assumption that they would be hesitant to tell us how they feel but would "project" their views onto others. Although some debate exists among survey researchers about the use of direct versus indirect techniques, the evidence is clear: when administered correctly, such as with guarantees of confidentiality, almost all employees answer direct questions honestly. Furthermore, there is no confusion when the responses to such questions are reported to management: when employees say that they are happy or unhappy with their pay, that's exactly what they mean. You can find a detailed discussion of this matter and examples of the numerous reliability and validity tests we have applied to our data methods in Appendix B.

How about the kinds of people we survey? This is an important question because we need to know just how representative and recent our evidence is. First, the analyses in this book are based on the employee survey data collected just from 1994 to 2003; therefore, the data are relatively recent. Second, although the data come from many organizations and are representative of them, we do not claim that they are representative of all workers everywhere over that period. That would be an over-generalization. Yes, a wide variety of industries is represented, but our evidence comes predominantly from the private sector, with just 5 percent of the organizations surveyed being government agencies and 12 percent not-for-profit organizations, such as hospitals. Because survey efforts of this type are not typically done in small organizations for various reasons, large corporations predominate in our sample. Many participating companies are multinational corporations; most are headquartered in North America and 78 percent of the employees we surveyed work in the U.S. or Canada. The majority of the others work in Europe. See Appendix A for further details on the composition of the surveyed populations.

Obviously, our data come only from organizations that asked us to survey their employees. To the casual reader, it might seem that this fact might make the participating organizations unrepresentative because the sample would be made up of companies that are probably more interested in employee satisfaction than the average company. Although that's theoretically true, the reality is that the overwhelming majority of large organizations in all sectors have conducted surveys, so this is not significant.

Another issue concerns the types of organizations that would commission this particular firm, Sirota Consulting, to conduct the survey. Sirota

Consulting employs a rather intensive data-feedback and action-planning process that requires more management time than is true of the typical employee poll. Agreeing to this process might mean that management is more serious about morale than is the average company and, therefore, possibly has higher morale than elsewhere. We have collected and reviewed the data from many surveys performed by others—both external and internal consultants—and we find a great similarity between their results and ours. This, therefore, is not an important problem, either. Appendix D contains a comparison of our data with those from research done by others.

The main issue, then, is the skewed nature of our sample with respect to organization size and geography. But, although the company's clients as a whole may not be perfectly representative of the universe of all organizations, there still is considerable diversity among them: in size, type of industry, types of occupations, average ages of the workforce, and the like. This book shows that the basic patterns of results we describe hold across all these differences. In statistical terms, therefore, having a sample more representative of all organizations, for example, with more small companies, would likely have little impact on our conclusions.

We can bring together the results from many different organizations because, although the surveys are geared toward the needs and conditions of individual clients, a core set of questions is appropriate and is asked just about everywhere. The core questions permit a broad, reliable depiction of worker attitudes across many varied organizations, and an analysis of those attitudes determines their causes and their business consequences. These data and analyses—amply supplemented by the systematic studies and thoughtful observations of others—form the research basis of this book.

The data are also liberally supplemented throughout by "qualitative" and "anecdotal" data. The quantitative information and analyses provide *scientific rigor*; the qualitative information helps to give *meaning* to the numbers. One source of qualitative information is the "open-ended" questions in our surveys to which employees are asked to respond in their own words (rather than check an answer to a multiple-choice question). When, say, 73 percent of employees in a company respond negatively to a multiple-choice question about their ability to get their jobs done, the answer to an open-ended question can tell us why they feel that way. For example, in answer to the open-ended question, "What do you like least about working here?" an employee in that company wrote:

> *The biggest problem here is the maze of bureaucracy and red*
> *tape. I frequently see long e-mail chains that show very clearly*
> *how often people have spent days, if not weeks, just trying to*
> *track down the proper person or department to contact for assis-*
> *tance or approval. Why do we need so many approval levels? I*
> *often feel this company cannot get out of its own way, not unlike*
> *the ill-fated Titanic.*

Numerous similar comments about "bureaucracy" appeared in that company's survey.

Our other major sources of qualitative information are:

- Focus groups, conducted before just about every survey with
  small groups of randomly selected employees from throughout
  the organization. We use these free-wheeling discussions to help
  determine the unique issues that need to be addressed in that organization's questionnaire and to help in the interpretation of the
  quantitative data that the questionnaire generates.

- In-depth interviews and case studies from clearly identified high-
  morale, high-performing client organizations to give greater
  insight into what those managements do. These are both total
  organizations and segments of them (such as *Barron's Magazine*,
  which is a division of Dow Jones).

- Our own informal observations and discussions over the many
  years we have been doing this work. For example, we have
  observed how managers struggle with a variety of pay-for-
  performance plans, seeking the one that will best reward and most
  motivate employees (or, at least, will result in the least dissatisfaction). As we move from company to company, we observe which
  plans seem to work best and which least well, and we share these
  observations with the reader. When sound research on these issues
  is available, we bring it to bear on our conclusions.

Therefore, the data in this book consist of a *combination* of quantitative
and qualitative data.[1] While disputes rage in the social sciences between
proponents of the two kinds of information, *both* kinds of data are
important—neither stands well by itself. One provides statistical reliability and proof, the other provides meaning—it brings the dry statistics to

life and can also provide direction for dealing with the issues uncovered by the survey. Most of the underlying framework for our book, however, comes from the quantitative data—the percentages of employees that report satisfaction or dissatisfaction on our surveys and the way those numbers relate statistically to each other and to management practices and measures of performance. As will be seen in this book, our results, as well as the survey results of others, repeat themselves in similar basic patterns in study after study. This is the great benefit of quantitative research: its results can be *tested* through replication using scientific methods. Qualitative information—such as anecdotes—don't have that power: one can "prove" or "disprove" anything through a selected anecdote or write-in comment. Their power lies in their giving depth to the statistics.[2]

In conclusion, Sirota Consulting has been studying the attitudes of people at work—and the business consequences of those attitudes—for more than three decades. Since 1994 alone, we have surveyed approximately 2.5 million employees in 237 private, public, and not-for-profit client organizations in 89 countries. Sirota Consulting's database of responses is extensive and, supplemented by our sources of rich qualitative data, provides insight into what workers want and why smart managers give it to them!

After the Honeymoon

It is a well-known phenomenon that the overwhelming majority of people begin a new job with a sense of enthusiasm. As they enter a job, people are naturally excited about their work and their organizations, eager to be part of a productive team of co-workers, and reasonable in how they expect to be treated. This is true for about 95 percent of any worker population; the other 5 percent—largely those who might be described as "allergic" to work—should never have been hired and, while at work, can be managed only with continuing close supervision and credible threats of dismissal. A major problem is that, in many organizations, management generalizes the behavior of this small group to just about every worker, which makes the work environment oppressive for all and suppresses the natural enthusiasm that most people bring to their jobs.

For that reason and others, usually starting about six months after being hired, something happens to the great masses of employees who begin work enthusiastically. We find significant declines in morale in 9 out of 10 companies after the "honeymoon" period. It is not just that the novelty wears off; the decline—and its deleterious impact on performance—is a consequence of management practice. In fact, one can say that, often, it is *management* that kills enthusiasm!

Yet, we find that in about 10 percent of organizations, worker enthusiasm does not materially diminish. What accounts for this difference? That is a central topic that this book explores and answers.

A Quick Look at "Old-Fashioned" Theories

Some people might see this book as having an old-fashioned point of view because our thinking flies in the face of the currently vogue theory that "loyalty is dead." The "loyalty is dead" crowd suggests that new economic conditions have made untenable the previous paternalistic pattern of lifetime careers in "caring" companies. In short, the new theorists argue that it's every person for himself or herself in a brutal new environment where the employment relationship becomes no more than a transaction.

We argue that loyalty between workers and management is, indeed, dead if it derives from the old parent-child model of paternalistic organizations. That's not what we talk about when we argue for satisfying workers' wants. We think of most workers as mature and independent adults, not children.

However, the paternalism of the past does not have to be replaced with a value-neutral transactional system where, in essence, employees "are owed nothing but a paycheck" and are removed from the payroll as soon as they are no longer needed. (In fact, if at all possible, they are not put on the payroll and are instead employed as "independent contractors.")

The gains from a transactional relationship are usually temporary, in part because such organizations receive from most of their workers little beyond what is absolutely required and monitored. For example, can a company expect its employees to treat customers with individual care and concern—the care and concern that create loyal customers—when the employees themselves are treated as invisible, interchangeable and expendable parts? A transactional relationship is therefore often a prescription for short-term success (in terms of cost reduction) and long-term mediocrity.

We therefore maintain that neither a paternalistic nor a transactional relationship is the most effective way to create high levels of long-term organization performance. The policies and practices we describe in this book represent, in their sum, a third alternative, which we call *partnership*.

The loyalty in a partnership relationship is not the kind that parents and children have toward each other, but rather the bonds that develop among adults *working collaboratively toward common, long-term goals and having a genuine concern for each other's interests and needs.* As we use the term, partnership is a business relationship *plus*—the plus being the human dimension, the trust and goodwill, that allows people to perform above and beyond what is required by monetary calculations, formal contracts, and very short-term interests. Partnership has not been used often to describe the actual or even ideal employee-management relationship, but in our view, it most accurately captures the spirit of the policies and practices we find repeatedly in enthusiastic and high-performing organizations.

This book is old-fashioned in other ways as well. For one, there is a strong tendency for modern authors in our field—the field of organization psychology—to focus almost exclusively on what they term higher-order employee needs, such as "self-actualization." There is less written about the fact that people also work for a living! Ignoring or downplaying matters such as pay, benefits, and job security is an error of monumental proportions. As we show in this book, management can do little to maintain high employee morale if workers harbor a fundamental sense of unfairness as to how they are treated on these basic issues.

A related error is made by "new economy" theorists who disparage what they consider characteristics of "old economy" companies and older workers, such as the need for work direction and structure. At the extreme, these theorists seem to advocate extraordinarily fluid organizations, almost chaos, as what today's workers want and what organizations need to survive in a rapidly changing business environment. Nonsense! Many classical dictums about direction and structure are as applicable today as they were before the "information age." We wonder how much of the implosion of companies in the hi-tech sector was a consequence of their inattention to the basics (the "blocking and tackling") of management. And we think that workers themselves have not changed that much. Although frustrated by micromanagement, they certainly don't want an absence of management, no matter what their industry or their age.

Solid Theory, Research, and Management Practice to Which We Are in Debt

We therefore find ourselves in sharp disagreement with those in our field whose views are supported neither by research evidence nor business results—these are pet nostrums and fads that fade away after a burst of publicity and experimentation. But there has also been a great deal of substantial and illuminating research and theory that, while generating less publicity, has had a significant and steady impact on management practice and has been immeasurably important to our own work and to this book. For one, we are indebted to the seminal work of five giants of our field: Douglas McGregor (his "Theory X—Theory Y" paradigm), David McClelland (the needs for "achievement" and "affiliation"), Abraham Maslow (the "hierarchy of needs"), Elton Mayo (the importance of social relationships at work), and Rensis Likert (management systems and styles).[3] A good deal of what we ask in our surveys is strongly influenced by the concepts of these five, as are our interpretations. For example, our repeated assertion of the desire of most workers to do their work and do it well is a direct descendent of McGregor's Theory X—Theory Y.

We are also greatly indebted to a number of contemporary researchers and we reference their relevant studies throughout the book. Among the more important for us have been Jeffrey Pfeffer, Edward Lawler, James Collins and Jerry Poras, Fredrick Reichheld, and Wayne Cascio. Their work is distinguished by solid research and thoughtful interpretation and while they cover somewhat different areas than we do, there is, where we overlap, considerable congruence between their findings and conclusions and ours.

How This Book Is Organized

This book's organization is straightforward. Chapter 1, "What Workers Want—The Big Picture," and Chapter 2, "Employee Enthusiasm and Business Success," elaborate on the general ideas of employee enthusiasm and its consequences for performance. They also contain a description of and an introduction to the Three Factor Theory—the three key needs of employees whose satisfaction is the basis for an enthusiastic workforce.

Chapters 3 through 10 break the Three Factor Theory into specific practices that organizations can and should deploy to maintain employee enthusiasm. Understanding and applying these specific practices within an organization results in marked improvements in employee commitment and performance and in long-term business success. Chapter 11, "The Partnership Organization," and Chapter 12, "Translating Partnership Theory into Partnership Practice," provide the wrap-up, where we show how the various policies and practices add up to a "partnership" culture and provide practical guidance on the necessary steps to achieve genuine cultural change.

The conclusions and recommendations are at both the broad policy level (for senior management) and for individual managers at all levels working day-to-day to achieve the highest possible performance from their own employees.

Finally, the appendixes describe our research methods and provide additional data and statistical analyses. Appendix E contains a Readiness Questionnaire to assist with cultural change.

PART I

Worker Motivation, Morale, and Performance

CHAPTER 1

What Workers Want—
The Big Picture

> *"Human capital will go where it is wanted,
> and it will stay where it is well treated. It
> cannot be driven; it can only be attracted."*

—Walter Wriston, Former Chairman,
Citicorp/Citibank

An accurate understanding of motivation in the workplace is more than an academic pursuit. The effectiveness of critical business policies depends on the extent to which our assumptions about human motivation are accurate. If they are not accurate, they either have no impact at all, or worse, they boomerang and damage the organization. Accuracy depends not only on wisdom and experience, but on *systematic research*. Research protects us from personal bias, seeing what we want to see instead of what is there. Research also protects us from the lure of fads and fashions.

The problem with many theories in this field is not that they have nothing to say, but rather that they:

- Focus on just *one* aspiration as *the central* motivator (and, therefore, the central explanation) of employee morale and performance.

- Claim that most people are frustrated with the achievement of that aspiration (the "sky is falling" scenario) and that dealing with that single frustration will solve all problems.

- Typically assert that what the theorist has uncovered characterizes a "new generation" of workers and is therefore novel.

It is helpful to look at a few of the more prevalent management fads before we review the results of real research.

Blame It on the Young

For reasons that we will soon show are misguided, popular theories of what employees want change continually, and the change is often couched in terms of "new generations" of workers whose needs and expectations somehow magically differ from their predecessors. We are told that there are important differences between the "baby boomers" and "GenX." Don't look now, but here comes Generation Y, followed almost immediately by Generation D (for digital!). It is theorized that they all need to be dealt with differently because they are all different.

These seemingly significant differences make for interesting reading, and the business media have surely accommodated us. Numerous stories have been published on generational change and its implications for management practice. Generation X, for example, is widely assumed to put maximum emphasis on individual freedom and minimum emphasis on company loyalty. A few years ago, the author of a *Fortune* article on GenX advised that, "If your competitor lets employees keep a birdbath in the office, you will have no choice but to follow suit."[1] A *Time* columnist summed up the generation as one that, "...would rather hike in the Himalayas than climb a corporate ladder."[2]

These observations are seductive; managing people is a difficult and complicated job filled with many headaches, and most managers want to learn all they can about human motivation. Furthermore, the answers provided by the theories on generational change seem intuitively correct. When a certain age in life is reached, people almost inevitably begin to talk about "that new generation" in a way that means, "What's this world coming to?" The new generation is not only "not like us," but they are "not like we were at that age." This discussion has been going on forever.

The fact that young people are so often viewed with apprehension by their elders should make us think about the validity of assertions about genuine generational change. It may be just a matter of age, but even more importantly, it may be a confusion of what's apparent, such as the clothes and music preferences of young people, with what is real, such as their basic goals as they enter the workforce.

An example of this tendency to confuse youthful tastes with human needs became most dramatically apparent in the early 1970s. As the tumultuous '60s ended, a deluge of books, television specials, and newspaper articles spotlighted a new generation of workers. These young people were (supposedly) severely discontented with work. Even worse, it was popularly suggested that the traditional sources of worker grievances (unhappiness with pay, benefits, hours, and working conditions) were no longer the primary causes of worker dissatisfaction. We were told that the very nature of work itself drove the "new" worker to near distraction. This worker was shown as a product of the '60s, when rebellion against "over 30" adult materialistic values appeared widespread, and freedom and self-actualization were the goals. These workers, it was claimed, would not settle for their fathers' routine and mind-numbing jobs.

The concern about workers and work at that time was perhaps best summarized in a 1973 study sponsored by the U.S. Department of Health, Education, and Welfare (HEW), titled *Work in America*. In describing the profoundly negative impact work seemed to have on so many young employees, the study's editors reported the following:

> The discontent of trapped, dehumanized workers is creating low productivity, increasing absenteeism, high worker turnover rates, wildcat strikes, industrial sabotage, poor-quality products and a reluctance of workers to give themselves to their tasks.

> Work-related problems are contributing to a decline in physical and mental health, decreased family stability and community cohesiveness, and less "balanced" political attitudes. Growing unhappiness with work is also producing increased drug abuse, alcohol addiction, aggression, and delinquency in the workplace and in the society at large.[3]

That statement was quite an indictment, and one that the media repeated endlessly. Of course, when a single factor (in this case, "dehumanizing" work content) is presumed to be responsible for so many business, social, and personal ills, rest assured that a single cure would soon follow. In the case of the HEW report, the cure (or, more accurately, the cure-all) was seen as the magic of "job enrichment."

The Lordstown Strike and Job Enrichment "Solution"

Based on Frederick Herzberg's "motivator-hygiene" theory, job enrichment was seen as an attempt to reinvigorate work with the prospect for real achievement, thus creating genuine satisfaction and motivation. In brief, the motivator-hygiene theory states that the work itself—the challenge of doing a job from start to finish, and so on—is the true motivator of workers, while the work environment—"hygiene" factors such as pay, benefits, and human relations—cannot positively motivate workers but, when adequate, temporarily prevent them from feeling unhappy. Therefore, the key to true motivation and lasting satisfaction is job enrichment, structuring work so it provides workers with a sense of achievement and accomplishment.[4]

The motivator-hygiene theory and the job-enrichment solution were extraordinarily popular in management thinking and teaching for much of the 1970s, but have since faded from view. That is not surprising because, for one thing, cure-all solutions for cause-all problems are seldom real. Despite its academic trappings, the hullabaloo smacked of patent-medicine salesmanship. In fact, considering that so much of the expressed concern was about blue-collar workers on assembly lines, no labor unions had placed demands for more meaningful work on their collective-bargaining agendas. Indeed, many labor leaders explicitly declined to join the rising chorus of voices concerned with job content.

The attention given to a 1972 workers' strike in the Lordstown, Ohio, assembly plant of General Motors (GM) reinforced the skepticism about job enrichment and its claims. This strike was widely interpreted to be the result of the dehumanizing nature of assembly-line work. However, the reality of Lordstown vastly differed from the way the strike was generally portrayed in the media and academia.

The GM Lordstown plant was a sprawling complex of factories. In the 1960s, GM built a new factory at Lordstown that was specially designed to assemble Vega passenger cars that GM hoped would prevent foreign manufacturers from eroding GM's margins in the compact-car arena. By 1966, GM was hiring workers for the factory, eventually employing about 7,000 people. This new plant, built by GM with advanced robotics, represented a $100-million investment by the company. GM recruited younger, better-educated workers who, it was claimed, were products of the ethos of the 1960s. Many of them even had long hair, so this was indeed a "new generation." Then, GM adopted a variety of efficiency rules designed to increase the production of the new Vega plant from 60 cars every hour (or

1 every minute) to 100 cars in the same time (or one every 39 seconds). The company did not increase the work force or decrease the number of procedures each worker was responsible for. It just required its workers to increase their pace. The workers fell behind, reasonably not being able to keep up with the line's speed.

If the pace was maddening, the results were disastrous. Workers tried various self-help remedies, such as letting cars go by, doubling up (surreptitiously doing an additional procedure for a short period of time—usually very poorly—so that a friend could rest). Absenteeism increased, and harsher work rules were imposed that violated many traditional but unspoken shop-floor conventions.

The workers went on strike. The primary reason for the strike was the workers' view that the company was engaged in a speed-up, which is hardly a novel issue in the history of labor-management conflict. It was not a sense that the work itself had become dehumanizing, but that the company's demand for faster work was impossible to reasonably satisfy. As one writer put it, "The main principle of Lordstown technology is the speed-up as developed by Henry Ford."[5]

What People Actually Say About Work

Employee surveys regularly ask people specifically how they feel about the kind of work they do, as opposed to other aspects of their employment, such as pay or the relationship with their supervisors. Our job satisfaction "norm" is 76 percent. This means that, on average, 76 percent of all workers across all the organizations surveyed generally enjoy the work they do. Although a 76-percent average satisfaction rate may not approach unanimity (although it would be considered a landslide in an election), it appears to belie the notion that work for most employees is somehow intrinsically unsatisfying, or "dehumanizing."

Contrary to the variety of unsupported theories about worker attitudes, such as the GenX and job-enrichment fads, we find that the overall satisfaction of workers with the type of work they do is strong and constant over a wide variety of industries and occupations. For example, on the high end, the job-satisfaction figure for healthcare and hospital workers is 79 percent. At the low end is the job satisfaction of oil and gas workers, which is at 71 percent. That's not much of a difference. Management across all industries is a bit more positive than non-management (83 percent versus 74 percent on the average), and the higher the management level, the more positive; non-management professionals (such as engineers, accountants, and sales-people) have a slightly higher satisfaction rate than other salaried employees (such as clerical workers) who, in turn, are higher than hourly (mostly blue-collar) employees. But 72 percent of hourly employees are still positive! Therefore, the percentage of people satisfied with their work is high for every group; most of the remaining employees are neutral, and a small percentage express dissatisfaction. The differences among the various groups are small and, by and large, in line with what you might expect.

Also, there is no evidence that younger workers are more (or less) disenchanted than their elders. Although individuals are rarely asked to state their age in surveys, we do obtain data on tenure, which is a reasonable surrogate measure. Racial and gender differences are also small or nonexistent, as are those by regions of the world. (North America and Europe are the two regions for which we have sufficient data.) Appendix C, "Job Satisfaction: Demographic, Occupational, and Regional Breaks," details the job-satisfaction data for the various demographic, occupational, and regional groups.

Our results on job satisfaction may seem counterintuitive to those unfamiliar with employee attitude survey findings. However, as noted in the Introduction (and summarized in Appendix D, "Comparisons with Other Norms"), our data are similar to those collected by other researchers. Furthermore, going back to 1972 when Sirota Consulting began its surveys, we find hardly any change at all. The average level of job satisfaction on our surveys in 1972–1982 was 73 percent and in 1983–1993 it was 79 percent.

If, contrary to popular social myth, people generally like the work they do, why is it that some workers nonetheless appear more highly motivated than others, that workforces in some companies routinely perform better than others, and that workers are often unmotivated to do their jobs well, despite apparently liking what they do? In other words, if people generally like the work they do, why are they often unhappy with their work situations? Are they being irrational? What accounts for this apparent disparity?

Let's Ask

What can you learn by asking workers about their goals and views in a simple and direct way? First, that identifying what *most* motivates employees—such as the work itself—is a waste of time. The vast majority of employees want a *lot* of things "most." Indeed, it is a psychological illness to want just one thing, such as money to the exclusion of everything else, or affection to the point that one is willing to sacrifice anything for it, including fair compensation for one's labor.

Three Factors

We assert that there are three primary sets of goals of people at work: *equity, achievement, and camaraderie*. We call this our *Three Factor Theory of Human Motivation in the Workplace* and we maintain that:

1. These three sets of goals characterize what the overwhelming majority of workers want.

2. For the overwhelming majority of workers, no other goals are nearly as important as these.

3. To our knowledge, these goals have not changed over time and they cut across cultures, at least the cultures of the economically developed sectors of societies (the only sectors we studied).

4. Understanding these sets of goals, and establishing organization poli cies and practices that are in tune with them, is the key to high workforce morale and firm performance. There is no conflict between the goals of most workers and the needs of their organizations.

Note

Keep in mind that our focus is on the goals of people *at work*. There is more to life than work, and our theory is not meant to cover all human motivation.

What is the evidence on which our assertions about human motivation are based? For one, we have been in the business of observing and querying employees for more than four decades. After all this time and the literally tens of thousands of employees with whom we have had direct contact and the millions we surveyed by questionnaire, we see certain themes repeating themselves time and again. They repeat themselves no matter what the occupation—from assembly-line workers to research scientists—no matter what the region of the world (North America or Europe), and no matter what the sex, race, or age. The specifics vary, of course, but everywhere we worked, people want to be proud of the work they do. They want to be paid a fair wage for their efforts and have job stability. Their co-workers—their cooperation and congeniality—are important to them. There is no escaping these fundamental needs of people at work and the enthusiasm they experience and express when the needs are satisfied (and the frustration when they are not).

Having trained as behavioral scientists, we are also aware that these impressions—no matter how impressive and convincing to us—must be buttressed by evidence gathered through systematic research. The evidence we have is derived from numerous analyses of survey data:

- Statistical analyses of the answers to the multiple-choice questions in our questionnaires invariably show that the questions that correlate most highly with employee morale and performance are those that measure the three factors (equity, achievement, and camaraderie).

- When we directly ask employees what they want from their jobs and their companies, they mention several goals, and the bulk of their answers fall into the three factors.

- When we ask employees, in focus groups and in the "write-in" questions at the end of the questionnaire, what they like and dislike most about working for their company, a careful analysis reveals that their likes and dislikes almost always reflect the three factors.

- In our research on employee turnover, we learn that the major reasons people stay with or leave an organization—other than personal reasons, such as a spouse getting a job in a different geographical area—almost always reflect the three factors.

To summarize, the evidence—both impressionistic and systematic—is overwhelming. We review a portion of this evidence later in this chapter. But first, here is our description of the three factors and the degree of satisfaction of employees with them in their work lives.

Equity. To be treated justly in relation to the basic conditions of employment.

Certain basic conditions are expected simply by virtue of the employment relationship. They are unrelated to position in the company or to performance. They are defined by generally accepted ethical and community standards and, while the basic goals do not change over time, a number of the standards that define what is acceptable do change. The basic conditions are as follows:

- Physiological, such as having a safe working environment, a workload that does not damage physical or emotional health, and reasonably comfortable physical working conditions.

- Economic, such as having a reasonable degree of job security, satisfactory compensation, and satisfactory fringe benefits.

- Psychological, such as being treated respectfully, having reasonable accommodation made for personal and family needs, having credible and consistent management, and being able to get a fair hearing for complaints.

Are those things surprising? Of course not. What is surprising is how little we hear of them in many modern theories of management. *But, enlisting the willing cooperation of a workforce in achieving the aims of an enterprise is impossible unless people have a sense of elemental fairness in the way they are treated.*

We use the term "reasonable" frequently in our definitions because employees do not expect a level of perfection unrelated to the realities of our world. For example, the desire for job security does not mean that employees expect a lifetime-employment guarantee. They are not naïve; they understand that such a guarantee is virtually impossible in a capitalist economy. But, they are angry when they (or their co-workers) are laid off without the company having a pressing need to let them go (when, for example, it is already highly profitable or when it has not exhausted other more obvious ways to reduce costs). Their anger is magnified by insensitive handling of layoffs, such as when layoffs are done without adequate notice or financial and job-placement assistance.

In other words, employees become angry when, in their view, elementary considerations of fairness are completely submerged by the company's pursuit of its short-term business interests, such as the anticipated immediate impact of an announced layoff on a company's stock price.

Similarly, consider compensation. Most people know that becoming tremendously rich is more fantasy than reality. So, the common assumption that "employees will never be happy with their pay" is fallacious. Our norm on our satisfaction-with-pay survey question is 46 percent favorable and 23 percent unfavorable. (The rest are neutral about their pay.) Although pay satisfaction is among the lower-rated aspects of work, it is hardly very negative. Furthermore, those are the averages across many organizations, and the range of responses is large: the most positive company response is 69 percent favorable and the least positive is 16 percent.

Contrary to "common sense," people can view their pay as fair. Our research shows that perceived fair compensation is a function of a number of variables, including perceptions of what other organizations pay for similar work, the relationship of pay to employee contribution, and the company's profitability. Chapter 4, "Compensation," elaborates on these variables. The underlying attitude that these results reflect is simply whether the organization tries to be fair with its salary policies or whether it tries to squeeze every last nickel from its employees. And "fair" does not mean wildly generous. Everything else being equal, we find employees pleased with "competitive" pay and *very* pleased with compensation that is even a few percentage points above other companies' pay.

Similar observations can be made about other elements of the equity factor, such as benefits. But there are elements where the ultimate is expected, such as the following:

- **Safety.** Where loss of life or limb is at stake, perfection has become the goal, and understandably so.

- **Respect.** People want to be treated like responsible adults, but many workers—primarily in factories but also in many white-collar settings—are, as they see it, treated like children or criminals, subjected to strict monitoring of their work and other behavior to coerce performance and conformity to the "rules." The response to this kind of treatment is that anger builds up in workers over time, and this has always been a major element in the more severe industrial relations conflicts we have studied. Even when the reaction is not explosive, this mode of management is self-defeating for the company. It is based on false assumptions about the great majority of workers (e.g., that they are irresponsible) and becomes a self-fulfilling prophecy: management that expects the worst from people gets it.

- **Management credibility.** A basic need of human beings from childhood through adulthood is to be able to trust the word of those whose actions have significant impact on them. A major source of discontent among many workers is information about important matters that is incomplete, unclear, contradictory, or simply absent. When workers assume that the company is deliberately withholding information, the void is filled with paranoid thoughts about what is really going on. This is a sure way to poison the relationship between management and its workforce.

How do workers feel about the degree to which their equity needs are being met? Our research indicates that the highest degree of average satisfaction concerns how people feel about safety at work, while the lowest relates to the failure of the organization to effectively deal with favoritism. There is a large difference in response from the highest to the lowest; in this case, from 79 percent favorable for safety to 43 percent favorable for favoritism. This demonstrates that employees make sharp differentiations among the various aspects of their work.

See Table 1-1 for a sample of the normative data relating to equity. We show in that table the average percentage satisfied across all our surveys for each question and its range: the lowest score we have ever obtained on the question (the "minimum") and the highest (the "maximum").

Table 1-1   1994–2003 Norms and Ranges for a Sample of Equity Questions

		Range	
Question	**Norm**	**Min**	**Max**
Safety	79%	33%	94%
Treated with respect and dignity	67%	32%	91%
Supervisor's human-relations competence	66%	35%	82%
Benefits package	65%	12%	97%
Physical working conditions	62%	24%	94%
Job security	60%	6%	90%
Amount of work expected	58%	17%	77%
Company interest in employee well being	52%	5%	98%
Company communication on important matters	52%	10%	80%
Sr. management's actions consistent with words	51%	37%	70%
Pay	46%	16%	69%
Favoritism (lack of)	43%	21%	70%

The overall ranking of items is similar within most of the individual organizations that we survey. When we discover an exception to the pattern, it is cause for particular attention. Take safety, for example. In general, safety is highly rated in our surveys, but there are a few organizations, especially in heavy manufacturing, where it is one of the lower-rated items. But, there are exceptions to that, too. As an example, see Chapter 6's discussion of Paul O'Neill (the former Secretary of the Treasury) and his work on safety when he was chairman of Alcoa. These "exceptions to the exceptions" are particularly noteworthy and illuminating because from them we learn that in management practice, little is foreordained. Much can be done if there is a will to do it.

Although this pattern tends to hold up across organizations (with exceptions, as noted), the *levels* of satisfaction—within the same broad pattern—vary widely. Thus, for example, employees in companies A and B can rate safety among the highest and pay among the lowest of all the equity items, but company A employees can be much higher than those in company B on both of these (and on just about every other equity item).

The great variations among organizations can be seen in the ranges in Table 1-1, and they are extremely important. First, they lend the lie to the commonly held assumption that people, no matter where they work, are similar to each other in their disgruntlement with their employment conditions. What management does is critical and the differences among organizations in management behavior—and therefore employee response—can be huge. Second, the variability allows us to answer the "So what?" question about employee attitudes: does satisfaction matter for business success? In Chapter 2, "Employee Enthusiasm and Business Success," we show how business performance varies markedly among organizations with different degrees of employee satisfaction.[6]

Achievement. To take pride in one's accomplishments by doing things that matter and doing them well; to receive recognition for one's accomplishments; to take pride in the organization's accomplishments.
A sense of basic equity in the employment relationship serves as the foundation on which high employee morale can be built: the powerful need to feel proud of one's accomplishments and the accomplishments of the organization is then freed to drive behavior toward high performance. Pride comes both from the employees' own perceptions of accomplishment and from the recognition received from others.

That is why the often-asked question, "How do you motivate employees?" is foolish. Most people enter a new organization and job with enthusiasm, eager to work, to contribute, to feel proud of their work and their organizations. Perversely, many managers then appear to do their best to *demotivate* employees!

You may reject that argument if you believe that people (other than a few saints, overachievers, or neurotic workaholics) are basically greedy and lazy when it comes to work. The reverse is true: most people are reasonable in what they expect in terms of treatment and are eager to perform in a way that makes them feel good about their performance. When we observe the opposite in an employee, it is either an atypical case (see the following discussion on individual differences) or, most commonly, because management has damaged that employee's motivation.

Our statistical analysis shows that a sense of achievement has six primary sources:

- **Challenge of the work itself.**   The extent to which the job uses an employee's intelligence, abilities, and skills.

- **Acquiring of new skills.**

- **Ability to perform.**   Having the training, direction, resources, authority, information, and cooperation needed to perform well.

- **Perceived importance of the employee's job.**   The importance to the organization, to the customer, and to society.

- **Recognition received for performance.**   Both non-financial (such as a simple "thank you" from the boss or a customer) and financial (compensation and advancement that are based on performance).

- **Working for a company of which the employee can be proud.** Because of its purpose, its products (their quality and their impact on customers and society), its business success, its business ethics (treatment of customers, employees, investors, and community), and the quality of its leadership.

As with the equity items, the surveys reveal a mixed picture regarding achievement. A sample of the normative data relating to achievement is shown in Table 1-2. We ask many questions about this area, and these are discussed in relevant chapters. But, for now, we note that among the most positive ratings are those focused on two opposite organization poles: the macro and the micro. Employees, on the average, are most favorable toward the overall characteristics of the organization (such as the quality of the organization's products and services, its profitability, and its ethics) and, at the other pole, toward the immediate work environment (such as the job, co-workers, and the technical ability of the immediate supervisor). The least positive ratings tend to be about efficiency at a "middle" level (such as bureaucracy, consistency of direction from management, and, as will be seen later, cooperation across units) and also about reward. There are some apparent contradictions, such as the view of many employees that the amount of work expected of them hurts quality and yet the very positive feeling about the quality of the products and services the organization delivers to its customers. These matters are all discussed in detail in the book. Where we have comparisons with other surveys, the results are similar to ours (see Appendix D).

Table 1-2   1994–2003 Norms and Ranges for a Sample of Achievement Questions

		Range	
Question	**Norm**	**Min**	**Max**
Clear idea of results expected	84%	7%	95%
High-quality products/services for customers	80%	16%	100%
Supervisor's technical competence	78%	38%	91%
The work itself	76%	52%	95%
Pride in organization	74%	48%	96%
Company profitability	72%	13%	97%
Corporate citizenship	67%	11%	100%
Tools and equipment to do job	64%	23%	94%
Information to do job	62%	29%	88%
Training	57%	9%	83%

Question	Range		
	Norm	**Min**	**Max**
Company overall is effectively managed	57%	24%	92%
Employees treated as important	57%	40%	73%
Feedback on performance	53%	21%	79%
Recognition for good job	51%	16%	86%
Decisions without undue delay	49%	30%	85%
Participative environment	44%	21%	81%
Not a lot of wasted time and effort	44%	24%	71%
Don't receive conflicting instruction from management	43%	25%	65%
Solve problems rather than blame	41%	16%	69%
Merit salary results from performance	40%	5%	91%
Bureaucracy (lack of)	39%	12%	72%
Balance of praise vs. criticism	38%	11%	71%

Camaraderie. To have warm, interesting, and cooperative relations with others in the workplace.
Human beings are social animals: positive interaction with others is not only gratifying, but essential for mental health. We often neglect the extent to which an organization functions not only as a business entity, but also as a *community* that satisfies social and emotional needs of its members.

We offer respondents an opportunity to write comments on the survey. One typical question asks, "What do you like most about working here?" One of the most frequent and consistent responses to this question involves the people with whom they work. That is because co-workers are important and because, by and large, people get along well with each other within their work units. We receive considerably fewer positive comments about relationships with other units in the organization; those comments are often in response to what employees like *least*. For example, note the following:

- From an employee in a real estate company (what employee likes "most"): "My team is full of intelligent people who are friendly and constantly want to do better and help each other. We work beautifully together."

- From an employee in a factory (likes "most"): "The people I work with." Simply this phrase, or variations of it (such as "the great people I work with"), appears repeatedly in almost every survey in response to the question about what respondents like most.

- From an employee in a hospital (likes "least"): "Cooperation and communication between physicians and nurses needs to be much better. Nurses truly know the patients. We are at the bedside dealing with families and the patient. Many times, we are ignored. It's like we're the physicians' servants and we should jump when they say so."

- From an employee in an information-technology group in a bank (likes "least"): "What gets me most upset is the way the departments we have to service are absolutely clueless about how busy we are and short handed we are. We can't do everything just when they want it. They don't care and when they complain to our V.P., he doesn't support us."

The quality of interaction in organizations is obviously greatly affected not just by friendliness and mutuality of interests, but also by co-workers' competence and cooperation. In that environment, a friendly slacker is an oxymoron: being unhelpful to co-workers is, by definition, unfriendly. This is another example of the way employees' needs—in this case, for positive interpersonal relationships in the work setting—are congruent with the organization's needs for high performance.

The camaraderie concept is somewhat less complex than equity and achievement, and we came to an explicit realization of its importance somewhat later in our work. Therefore, in our surveys, fewer questions have asked about camaraderie and these are shown in Table 1-3. However, we can state that the most favorably rated aspect of camaraderie is simply the relationship between co-workers, followed by teamwork within the workers' unit, teamwork across departments in a given location, and finally, teamwork and cooperation across the entire company.

Table 1-3   1994–2003 Norms and Ranges for a Sample of Camaraderie
            Questions

Question	Norm	Min	Max
Relationship with co-workers	83%	37%	97%
Teamwork within work unit	73%	51%	93%
Teamwork across departments in location	51%	23%	89%
Teamwork across company as a whole	49%	5%	88%

As previously mentioned, teamwork is not just a camaraderie issue. It also
has a major effect on achievement. And we said that attitudes toward
teamwork are more positive at the *micro* level—within units—than at
what we have termed the *middle* level—across units. The differences
between companies, however, are large, which shows that familiarity and
proximity do not always breed contentment or distance antagonism. For
example, although the norm for teamwork within the unit is 73 percent,
the range varies from 51 to 93 percent. Also, the norm for teamwork
across units is 51 percent, but the range varies from 23 to 89 percent!

   Chapter 10 discusses camaraderie, its impact on performance, and
ways of enhancing it. That chapter also discusses the way camaraderie can
sometimes work against organization goals. For example, solidarity in a
workgroup might develop in opposition to a management whose practices
are considered unjust by employees. Management becomes the "enemy
camp" and, in those situations, equity issues must be dealt with first.

   That summarizes the key sets of goals of the overwhelming majority
of employees. Other than extreme cases where our theory does not apply
(which will soon be discussed), we assert that a manager does not need to
know much more about human motivation at work. That is quite an assertion, but we challenge anyone to suggest other motivators that are as powerful, relevant in the workplace, and widespread. We further claim that a
genuinely high-morale, enthusiastic, and highly productive workforce is
impossible if those needs go unsatisfied.

   The three goals we propose are distinct needs that, unfortunately, cannot be substituted for each other. For example, enriching the content of a
job does not increase satisfaction with pay or cause an employee to

minimize the importance of his pay dissatisfaction. Discontent with pay can be ameliorated only by more pay! Similarly, unhappiness with a boring job can be solved only by restructuring the job or transferring the employee to work that is more interesting. Paying the employee more won't solve the issue. Each goal—and most every subgoal—must be dealt with individually. There are no panaceas.

The Evidence

We make rather strong claims—some might say startling and unbelievable—about the pervasiveness of the three sets of goals. We claim that they are nearly universal, applying to roughly 85 to 90 percent of a workforce (that's just about any workforce).

Our assertions might appear to be counterintuitive—they go against common observation and common sense. Managers and employee-relations experts talk endlessly about differences: the differences between individual workers and between categories of workers (such as males and females, older and younger workers, professionals and non-professionals) and between workers in different countries. Are we saying that this is hogwash? Yes, in part.

We already discussed what we consider to be distortions about generational differences—the belief that younger workers are not interested in working as hard as their elders and that they are not concerned about job security. We have solid evidence for our assertion that generational differences are greatly exaggerated as are other purported differences and we will soon provide that evidence.

First, however, consider the following questions in relation to the three factors: do you believe that an entire category of workers—demographic (age, sex, race, and so on), occupational, or national—does not consider being fairly treated by their employer—say, in wages—to be of very high priority? Do you believe that a category of workers exists in which the overwhelming majority does not want to take pride in their work and in their organization? Do you believe that there is a category of workers for whom having congenial and cooperative co-workers is unimportant? Of course, there are *individuals* to whom these rules do not apply—even individuals who willingly allow themselves to be exploited economically by their employers—but never more than a very small minority in any category.

Are there no major demographic, occupational, or national differences in these needs? Not in the fundamentals we have described (the desire for equitable treatment, achievement, and camaraderie). The differences emerge largely in *what* will satisfy these needs, which varies because of differing objective conditions and expectations. Let's consider a few examples of this:

- **The work itself.**   In Chapter 8, "Job Challenge," we discuss the satisfaction people seek from the kind of work they do. We say that workers want to be proud of their work. Pride in work has numerous sources, among them the employees' feelings that their intelligence and skills are being used; that, in turn, is partly a function of the latitude they have to exercise judgment in doing their jobs. We know that the latitude given to, say, the average engineer is normally going to be much greater objectively than what's given to a blue-collar machine operator. *Despite this difference, they may experience the same degree of subjective satisfaction with their job autonomy.* The machine operator doesn't expect—indeed, would consider it inappropriate—to have the engineer's latitude. But he doesn't want to be treated as an automaton; that is, he wants to exercise the judgment that makes sense *for that job and for his skills*, and that latitude can be considerable (as you will see in Chapter 8). People at work are not stupid and do not have outrageous expectations. They—no less than engineers—have a need to be treated on the job as intelligent human beings, but the standards by which this is judged are obviously somewhat different.

- **Job security.**   Chapter 3 discusses job security. How an organization treats employees in this regard is a key source of employee morale, but what is considered fair has greatly shifted in the United States over the last few decades. Although employees in many organizations previously expected lifetime job security, employees today rarely expect that. They understand that the business world has changed, but this does not mean that their desire for security has diminished. *The change has been in the criteria that employees use to judge the fairness with which the issue is handled by organizations.* Organizations differ greatly in this respect—for example, in whether layoffs are treated as a last resort instead of the first action taken—and these differences have a profound impact on the morale and performance of a workforce.

- **Vacations.** A concrete and visible example of a cultural difference is that between the vacations received by workers in the
  countries of Western Europe compared to those in the United
  States. On average, Western European countries have much
  longer vacations; even new employees receive at least a full
  month of vacation. (Vacation time is five weeks in France,
  Sweden, Austria, Denmark, and Spain.) This certainly is a major
  difference, with profound cultural meaning and probably significant economic effect, but what are its implications for our argument regarding the commonality of the major needs? Are
  European workers lazy? Are they less interested in doing a good
  job? Do they find their jobs less interesting? *There is absolutely
  no evidence for any such an assertion.* By virtue of broad historical and social trends, different countries evolved different patterns
  of labor relations. Even within the United States, different industries have different patterns, including the amount of vacation
  time employees receive. These differences result in different subjective standards of what is "fair," but in no way undercuts our
  proposition regarding the fundamental goals of workers.

Similar comments could be made about the satisfaction of many other goals
and subgoals: employee expectations in the United States regarding the
fringe benefits an organization provides—especially medical insurance—
have greatly changed, and what might have been considered unfair a decade
or so ago, such as an organization not paying full medical-insurance premiums, can be entirely satisfactory today; operating in the opposite direction is
equipment, where the tools people use on their jobs *improve* continually, so
what was satisfactory before is rarely satisfactory today.

Our argument, then, is not that there are no demographic, occupational, or cultural differences or that the differences are unimportant. It comes
down to this: when we say that workers want to feel pride in their work,
we mean almost all workers, whoever they are, whatever they do, and
whenever or wherever they do it. The fundamentals are constant, but
knowing how to satisfy those fundamental needs often requires knowledge of the expectations of particular groups of workers. To cite an
extreme example, if an organization decided to halve the vacation time of

European workers based solely on the assumption that their fundamental need to do a good job and to be treated fairly are the same as American workers, that organization is in for big trouble.

But don't make the opposite error, namely, to assume that the obvious cultural, occupational, and demographic differences in expectations and standards signify major differences in basic goals. For example, treat a blue-collar worker as if all that interests him is his wages—that exercise of his judgment on the job doesn't matter—and you wind up with an indifferent or hostile employee. At the other extreme, treat engineers and scientists as if wages don't matter—that all they want is an opportunity to be creative—and you wind up with hostile engineers and scientists (if they stay with the organization at all).

Table 1-4 summarizes a representative portion of the strong quantitative evidence on which we base these claims. As we will explain, the table shows that employee morale strongly relates to the degree to which each of the three needs is satisfied, *and that the relationships are extraordinarily similar across all demographic, occupational, and national groups*. There are no differences in the strengths of the goals to speak of; they are, indeed, nearly universal.

How do we know, in a systematic, quantitative way, whether a goal is important and how universal it is? One way is to correlate satisfaction with it with employees' *overall* satisfaction with the organization. Table 1-4 does this within a number of groups. Overall satisfaction is a product of the degree to which employees feel their specific goals are being met, so the higher the correlation between satisfaction with a specific goal and overall satisfaction, the more important we can assume the goal to be. If an employee doesn't care much about something—say, the color of the walls where she works—liking or not liking it would have no impact on how she feels about the organization as a whole. Compare that to the importance of how she feels about her pay or boss. This reasoning is identical to how the performance approval rating of the president of the United States—determined from political-opinion polls—is a function of how Americans feel about specific aspects of the president's performance, such as his handling of the economy, of national security, and so on. The stronger the correlation is between a specific aspect and the overall approval rating of the president's performance, the more important that aspect is.

Table 1-4 Evidence for the Near Universality of the Three Factors

Correlations with Overall Satisfaction			
	Equity	**Achievement**	**Camaraderie**
Total	.59	.43	.36
Within Racial and Ethnic Groups			
White	.60	.45	.34
Black	.57	.45	.34
Hispanic	.58	.47	.41
Asian	.63	.45	.41
Native American	.54	.44	.37
Within Tenure Groups			
0–2 yrs	.60	.48	.35
2–5 yrs	.60	.45	.33
5–10 yrs	.58	.42	.33
10–20 yrs	.59	.44	.36
> 20 yrs	.56	.39	.36
Within Genders			
Women	.59	.42	.35
Men	.59	.45	.37
Within Levels			
Mgt	.58	.44	.33
Non-Mgt	.58	.43	.36
Within Positions			
Professional	.60	.46	.36
Non-Professional	.55	.39	.30
Within Regions			
North America	.60	.45	.37
Europe	.58	.40	.32

The relationship between variables (such as between overall satisfaction and satisfaction with pay or the color of the walls) can be assessed in various ways. In our analysis, it is measured by a statistic called the *correlation coefficient*, which has a symbol of "r." The higher r is, the stronger is the relationship. r can range from .00, which means no relationship, to 1.00, which means a perfect relationship. (r can also be negative, in which case, the relationship is inverse: the higher on one variable, the *lower* on the other.)

Our basic finding is that highly significant positive correlations exist between the questions on our surveys that tap the three needs and overall satisfaction. These correlations hold up in *all* demographic, occupational, and national groups *and at approximately the same level.* Illustrations of these correlations are shown in Table 1-4 where the following questions are used to tap the three needs:

- **For equity.**   "How would you rate your organization on taking a genuine interest in the well-being of its employees?"

- **For achievement.**   "Do you agree or disagree: my job makes good use of my skills and abilities."

- **For camaraderie.**   "How would you rate the cooperation and teamwork within your work unit?"

The question measuring overall morale is "Considering everything, how would you rate your overall satisfaction in [organization] at this time?"

The correlations shown in Table 1-4 were calculated using data from 135,000 employees in 40 organizations surveyed over the last 5 years. All four questions were asked in identical ways for each organization. For those readers interested in tests of statistical significance, all the correlations are highly significant, beyond the .00001 level!

This table contains the correlations for three demographic breaks: race/ethnicity, gender, and tenure, and for occupation and regions of the world. Those familiar with correlational data, will, we trust, be amazed at just how similar the patterns are. In *every* instance, the item measuring the equity goal correlates in the .50s or .60s with morale, that measuring achievement in or near the .40s, and that measuring teamwork in the .30s and .40s. The possible reasons for the differences in sizes of the correlations—why equity should be the highest and teamwork the lowest— are discussed later in this chapter. For now, suffice it to say that not only are all the correlations highly significant, which verifies the importance of the goals, but to all intents and purposes, they are also the same in all categories of employees.

Which aspects of work do we find *not* correlated with overall employee morale? They tend to be about what might be termed the "frills" of work. Although senior management often spends much time on them, they don't really touch on workers' basic goals and what goes on in important ways in their daily workplace activities. We refer to matters such as the aesthetics of the physical work environment (such as the wall color), recreational activities (such as holiday parties), various formal "programs" (such as suggestions programs), and formal communication mechanisms (such as a company newsletter). It's not that employees don't care about these at all, but that they matter much less than other more fundamental concerns. It matters much less to them, for example, that there be a well-designed company newsletter or a suggestions program than that their immediate supervisors communicate and listen to them. We are in no way suggesting that the frills be dropped—almost everyone likes a holiday party—but that they be seen as supplements to, not substitutes for, the more basic policies and practices that we discuss throughout this book.

Similar findings are obtained in analyses of answers to the open-ended questions. This type of analysis shows that the things employees spontaneously write in about what they "like most" and "like least" about their organizations almost invariably involve the three factors. These findings are given as examples throughout this book. The frills are almost never mentioned.

How the Three Factors Work in Combination

Our analysis shows that the three factors interact with each other in an interesting way. The Three Factor Theory asserts that employees seek to satisfy three needs—equity, achievement, and camaraderie—in any employment situation. It further asserts that, when all three needs are met, it results in enthusiasm directed toward accomplishing organizational goals. As we discuss in Chapter 2, enthusiasm is not just about being happier or more content—it is employees feeling that they work for a great company, one to which they willingly devote time and energy beyond what they are being paid for or what is expected and monitored. A great company for employees is one that largely meets *all* of their needs for equity, achievement, and camaraderie. Until that happens, it is no more than a "good" company.

Statistical support for this idea can be seen in the way individual satisfaction of the three needs interact to produce overall satisfaction. They just
don't add to one another in their impact, but *multiply* each other's impact.
Figure 1-1 shows how employees respond to the question, "Considering
everything, how would you rate your overall satisfaction in [organization]
at this time?" The percentages shown are just those saying "very satisfied," the highest possible response to the question. The percentages are
shown for four categories of employees: those whose satisfaction with all
three needs is relatively low (labeled "None"), those who have just one
need being satisfied, those who have two, and those for whom all three
needs are being satisfied (labeled "All Three"). The questions used to
assess satisfaction with the three needs are the same as in the correlational
analysis shown in Table 1-4, namely, "How would you rate your organization on being concerned about the well-being of its employees?," "My job
makes good use of my skills and abilities," and "How would you rate
cooperation and teamwork within your immediate work unit?"

It can be seen that as more satisfied needs are added, the percentage of
very satisfied employees increases *exponentially*. When all three needs are
being satisfied, the percentage is 45! What would you think of as a great
company in which to work? It's probably not just having very good pay
and benefits, or challenging and enjoyable work, or having terrific co-
workers. It involves *all* these needs, and when all these needs are satisfied,
something unique happens to many employees and their relationship with
the organization… It is what we call enthusiasm.

Figure 1-1   The exponential impact of the Three Factors.

There is one more wrinkle, namely, the special effect of equity. More in-depth analysis suggests that although all the needs are important, equity has a certain basic importance. That is, if people are not satisfied with the fairness with which they are treated, satisfaction of either of the other two needs has a relatively minor effect on morale. On the other hand, feeling fairly treated does have a major impact even when one or both of the other needs are not being satisfied. That is the reason the correlations of overall satisfaction with the equity need are consistently higher than the correlations with the other two factors.[7]

The moral of the story is that it can be difficult to get employees excited about a company that, say, gives them challenging work to do (part of the achievement need) when they have a basic sense of inequity as to how they are treated. But equity alone is not enough to create enthusiasm: the impact of fair treatment is greatly magnified when all three needs are being satisfied.

These analyses and conclusions hold up in an amazingly consistent way across demographic groups, occupations, and world regions.

Individual Differences

We repeatedly refer to the goals of "the overwhelming majority of the workforce." But, of course, individual differences exist in the strengths of needs. Some people are less socially oriented than others; some are more prone to see injustice in their treatment than are others; for some, work can be less important as a source of pride, perhaps because of fulfilling outside activities. The differences between individuals that are of most practical relevance to managers are the employees at the extremes, people who with regard to the equity need, for example, see injustice at every turn or, at the other end, never see it. We estimate these extremes to constitute approximately 12 to 15 percent of a population of workers, 5 percent who are almost invariably negative and about 7 to 10 percent who are almost invariably positive. Our theory, and its practical implications for management practice, is much less relevant for these workers at the extremes.

Where do we get these estimated percentages of people at the extremes?

At the most general level, when employees are asked about their overall satisfaction with their organization, even the most positive organizations in our database (over 85 percent satisfied) still have 6 to 8 percent of workers rating themselves as dissatisfied. (The rest are neutral.) Some portion of these people are not invariably unhappy, but might be unsuited to their particular positions in that organization, or to a particular manager, or even, perhaps, to an enthusiastic culture. But, we do know that, by nature, some people are cranky and won't be positive about their employment anywhere. Our rough estimate, based on largely informal assessments over the years, is that these constitute about 5 percent of most every workforce.

At the other end of the continuum, even in very low morale companies, 12 to 15 percent will express satisfaction. Some of this is no doubt due to a fortuitous fit, albeit unusual for those organizations, between themselves and their jobs, their managers, or the culture. (Some of them are likely to be the ones making everyone else unhappy!) But, we also know that there are people who, no matter how bad the environment is, come across as happy souls, the proverbial optimists who try to see the bright side and usually give management the benefit of the doubt. It takes an enormous amount to frustrate or anger these people and our rough estimate is that they constitute about 7 to 10 percent of an average workforce.

That's the general condition of the exceptionally and persistently dissatisfied or satisfied individuals. Our theory has less relevance for them because their satisfaction (or lack of it) will not be much affected by management's actions. At a more specific level relating to the three factors, consider the exceptions to what we said about the achievement goal. We asserted that most people want to work and be proud of their work. But, we know that there are employees who are, in effect, "allergic" to work—they do just about anything to avoid it. For them, our question, "How do you keep management from demotivating employees?" is nonsense. They *are* unmotivated and a disciplinary approach—including dismissal—is about the only way they can be managed.

At the opposite extreme are those employees who are just about impossible to *de*motivate, namely workaholics. They work through any and all obstacles that the organization puts in their path, perhaps even secretly relishing the obstacles because these provide an excuse for spending additional time at work. For them, too, the motivational issue that we are discussing is largely irrelevant.

In a workshop one of the authors of this book conducted on recognition practices, managers were asked to describe their experience with "unintended effects" of recognition. One spoke of her experience with two employees who were, by far, the most productive people in her department and among the most productive she had come across at any time. She already had given them several large salary increases but wanted to do more. She called them into her office and announced that she was granting them two additional paid days off as a token of her appreciation. They frowned, so she asked them what was wrong. Were two days not enough? Their response was extraordinary: for them, days off from work were a punishment, not a reward. Such was the level of involvement in their work. She replaced the days off with dinner-for-two rewards and they expressed their appreciation.

Similar extremes can be found on the equity and camaraderie dimensions. For example, some people feel unfairly treated no matter what ("collectors of injustices," if you will), and those who never see injustice no matter what management does. Also, there are social isolates for whom social interaction appears to be unimportant (or even distasteful) and those for whom it is all-consuming.

Obviously, managers must be sensitive to these extremes and adjust their behavior accordingly. But, a major problem is the tendency of many organizations and individual managers to mistake the extreme for the whole. This is especially obvious, and dysfunctional, with regard to the achievement goal. Many organizations and managers assume that the desire of an employee to do something that matters and do it well is the exception rather than the rule. So, when an isolated problem occurs, control systems and supervisory styles are applied to everyone, and that has the effect of demotivating the great majority who come to work eager to contribute.

In summary, this chapter presented what is essentially a positive view of the nature of people at work. That view is supported by the mountain of evidence we gathered over many years of research, by the thinking and systematic research of others, and by observation of the success of organizations whose policies and practices reflect such optimism.

We say that the essentials of human motivation have changed very little over time. If significant change is observed, it is not that workers' goals have changed, but that management is acting differently and is reaping the consequences of its actions.

For example, treat workers as disposable commodities, which began to happen with the downsizings of the late '80s and the '90s, and—surprise!—employees are no longer "loyal." Why would they be? Most people are eager to strongly identify with an organization of which they can be proud and that treats them well. But, it would be irrational for people to be loyal to organizations that show no interest in them other than as, essentially, temporary "hands" to get the work done.

Nothing is very complicated about what we have proposed. Although the detailed implications for management practice are reserved for future chapters, those are not complicated, either. Let's call them the "blocking and tackling" of an enlightened management, enlightened in its understanding that what the overwhelming majority of people seek from work doesn't conflict with management's objectives and, in fact, usually strongly supports them. Satisfying these goals—fairness of treatment, pride in work and company, and a sense of camaraderie with fellow employees—is to everyone's advantage. The results will be outstanding. Let's now look in more detail at the evidence for the business implications of employee enthusiasm.

CHAPTER 2

Employee Enthusiasm and Business Success

"...there is one key to profitability and stability during either a boom or bust economy: employee morale."

—Herb Kelleher, Southwest Airlines Founder

"Only people who want to, work this hard."

—Jim Mittelhouser, Netscape Founding Engineer, commenting on the 70-hour workweek norm at Netscape

Having explored the question of what workers want in the previous chapter, we now must ask the obvious and legitimate business question: so what? Simply put, what does employee enthusiasm have to do with business success? Because, from the organizations' perspective, unless there is a connection between what workers want and what organizations need (bottom-line results), there is little reason to pursue the subject.

Making the Connection

Over the years, many of our clients have been notable for their long-term success. These clients include companies such as Starbucks, Intuit, American Express, Bank of America, *Barron's Magazine*, and the Mayo Clinic. These organizations share little in common; there is no concentration of a particular industry, geographical area, or business model. However, they share one thing: the morale of their workers, as measured in our surveys, is much higher than most other companies. We believe that this is one of the key characteristics of most every company that has experienced long-term success. We posit that the high morale of their workers is a result of specific policies and practices that engender enthusiasm in their employees about their jobs and their companies.

What these organizations specifically do to achieve enthusiastic employees is detailed in future chapters. For now, let's closely examine what we mean by worker enthusiasm and show how it relates to business success.

Employee morale is measured on a continuum, but we make a rough distinction between four levels of morale: enthusiasm, satisfaction, neutrality, and anger. These levels are operationally defined simply by asking workers to consider everything that can affect how they feel about an organization and then to rate their overall satisfaction with it. This is the same question we used in Chapter 1, "What Workers Want—The Big Picture," to test the universality of the Three Factor Theory. It asks workers, in effect, to provide a summary measure of their morale. What goes into this mental calculus is left up to that individual (for example, how much weight an employee gives to pay, to her boss, to advancement opportunities, and so on). By not characterizing satisfaction or setting conditions or comparisons, we are most likely to get a clear and unbiased picture.

We have asked about overall satisfaction using that formula since 1972, and some striking differences emerge between organizations. Before we review the specifics, let's define organizations with enthusiastic employees: these are organizations that generally have more than 75 percent of their workers indicating overall satisfaction and less than 10 percent of workers indicating dissatisfaction. That, of course, leaves about 15 percent of neutral participants. Based on this construct, we find that of all the many organizations we have surveyed, only 13.8 percent can be categorized as having an "enthusiastic" workforce. The focus in much of this book is on the very important difference—a difference rarely commented on—between organizations with moderately satisfied employees, which make up the bulk of our surveyed employees, and those organizations with enthusiastic employees. (The small minority of companies with truly discontented and angry workforces is discussed later in this chapter.) That is, there is a world of difference between working for a "pretty good" company and a "terrific" company.

Organizations, especially very large ones, are complex entities that, although having distinct cultures and practices and, therefore, morale levels significantly different from each other, nevertheless exhibit quite a bit of internal variability.

For example, in one of our companies with the highest morale—a very large corporation with hundreds of departments the bulk of the departments show high overall satisfaction, but the range across departments is 100 to 41 percent. In one of our lowest scoring large corporations, the range across departments is 65 to 30 percent. These ranges are typical and there are many reasons for them—the most important being differences in the styles of individual managers within those organizations.

Why do we call organizations with superior overall satisfaction scores—whether total companies or units within them—enthusiastic? Why not simply call them "highly satisfied?" Because something going on at these elevated ranges is much different from what we find in organizations where employees are just moderately satisfied. And, as we show in the next section, on average, organizations with enthusiastic employees are much *higher performing* organizations than the rest.

Tell Us in Your Own Words

Not only do these high-enthusiasm/high-performing organizations look different in the statistical data, but their people literally sound different when giving "write-in" comments. At the end of most surveys, we ask employees to summarize their views in their own words instead of responding to a multiple-choice question. As mentioned in the previous chapter, employees are usually asked, "In your own words, what do you like most about working here?" and "What do you like least?" (or occasionally, "What do you most want to see improved?"). We categorize the answers into various content categories.

Listen to what some workers in enthusiastic organizations say. First, the responses from a very positive organization (one characterized, remember, by having more than 75 percent of its employees satisfied and less than 10 percent dissatisfied). Here's a sampling of what they say they most like:

> *We are totally committed to our customers. This is the passion of this company from the executive suite to my colleagues on the front line. I know from first-hand experience that customers believe they are the primary focus of our business and greatly appreciate the level of service and attention we provide them.*

We are a dynamic company with first-class leadership. Our boss is the best. Her word is her bond. It may sound corny, but I would go into battle with her as my leader. We, almost to a person, are always striving to be the best. We are...able to move quickly in a rapidly changing marketplace because we have business-savvy leaders. But, I feel our greatest strength is managers with high levels of integrity.

The bottom line isn't everything here, employees count, too.

We really work together like a team. Everyone listens with respect to your ideas. I've never worked at a place like this. It's almost never who you know or your background that matters but what you know. We can speak our minds and tell it like it is. Nobody points fingers—if there's a problem, we roll up our sleeves and fix it.

I mean it, I feel like I've died and gone to heaven here. If things stay this way, I'd like to spend the rest of my working life for this company. You feel like a real person, not just a number.

It is instructive to look at the nature of enthusiastic employees' concerns. Here are some responses from various companies to the question, "What would you say are the organization's key areas for improvement either as an employer or a business?"

Keep the improvements in communication with [a certain group] going! We do read those e-mails and I have been surprised how much it means to my staff to feel like they are included in what is going on.

The company spends too much on legal bills. Why does the company have an internal legal staff, but has high outside legal bills? The company could save a lot of money by changing how it does business in this aspect.

It would be helpful to help people understand "the big picture." What I mean by this is that sometimes corporate will ask something of the divisions and we do not understand "the big picture" on why it is needed. Maybe a flow chart to show how reporting is put together. It could make everyone see how they fit into the puzzle.

Eliminate redundancy and unnecessary paperwork to speed up the approval process in all aspects of their business. It's gotten better, but it's not good enough.

Develop better internal relationships between departments. I still feel there is a power struggle between certain areas of the [department name] management group and the [department name] group. Maybe it only involves the employees at my level. This area could benefit from improved personal relationships and communication.

My team knows what it's doing. We just have to get [a higher-level manager] off our backs. He means well, but he's too damn nervous.

Most of the concerns are business oriented as opposed to personally oriented. Even these employee frustrations demonstrate their commitment to the company because they want to see the organization become even more successful.

Enthusiastic employees, as is the case in many organizations, have concerns about pay. Here are some typical comments:

Increase in pay or make offers more competitively.

Increases in base pay to keep up with market in order to attract and retain key employees.

At my pay level, the rates may be a little below industry standards.

Re-evaluate the pay scale from time to time. We might start losing people.

Notice that these issues are about industry standards and not about internal equity (such as favoritism and inconsistency). Also, the tenor of the comments indicates no concerns about exploitation of employees or greediness of senior management; they just simply want somewhat higher wages to keep up with the market.

The moderately satisfied employees, on the other hand, tend to express a liking and appreciation for the organization, but with little sense of active enthusiasm or involvement. Take these comments, for example:

The pay is not bad and the benefits are competitive. I especially appreciate the tuition refund program.

This is a company that has been around for a long time. This gives me a comfortable feeling about my job security.

My manager is a considerate person and I like her. She is flexible when a family problem arises.

They seem to understand that everyone makes an error now and then, and the world doesn't come crashing around you when you have a bad day.

I love the location.

Here is what employees in the moderately satisfied companies say about what they'd like to see improve. Now, many personal gripes are expressed with little confidence in management:

The pay is not keeping up with the cost of living, and please explain why new hires doing the same job are making as much as the people who have been here for years, like me. Doesn't loyalty count?

At my location, there is a lack of structure, and the qualifications and experience of people with the same jobs are different and varied. Nobody will explain to me why this is so and why the pay should be so different from person to person.

The endless changes that happen at every moment without any rhyme or reason as far as I can tell. Doesn't management know what it's doing?

There is an undue emphasis on systems and procedures that interfere with the delivery of services.

There is little opportunity for people like me because I don't have the sheepskin. It's very discouraging since my evaluations are always very positive, my co-workers come to me for advice, but I can't get ahead because I don't have a degree.

I rarely ever see my manager. He stays in his office and only shows up when there is a crisis. Also, it wouldn't be a bad idea if the people at the top would visit now and then.

There's a lot of favoritism in who gets overtime.

Enthusiastic employees are caught up in the organization and identify with it, so its successes and failures become, in effect, the employees' successes and failures. This is above and beyond a pragmatic calculation, such as the impact of the company's performance on employees' income potential or job security. This is a psychological and an economic phenomenon: psychologically, the company becomes part of an employee's self-image so that company performance is felt as if it were the individual's own performance. This is not too different from the avid sports fan's "living and dying" with the ups and downs of his team. This is my team; this is my company.

Individual employees usually come to mind when managers think of differences in enthusiasm. There are, of course, differences in proneness to enthusiasm among individuals (some people are by nature more "up" than others), and no company has policies, practices, and managers that suit everyone and evoke uniformly positive attitudes. But, as our data show, there are very marked organizational and unit differences in the enthusiasm felt and displayed by workforces as groups. Let's examine a few specific organizations that have enthusiastic workforces.

A Few Leading Organizations

For about 20 years, Intuit has led a burgeoning industry of software development and sales in the important area of business and financial management of small organizations, the accounting professions and consumers, through its wildly popular Quicken, QuickBooks, and TurboTax products. Intuit also surveys its workforce regularly, most recently through Sirota Consulting.

Take a look at their data. First, overall satisfaction measures at 83 percent. This, in and of itself, is a very high percentage—much higher than the Sirota norm of 64 percent. But, the Intuit data are yet more instructive and impressive. The Intuit survey includes questions that address the three factors. For example, the company asks its employees to rate management on its respectful and dignified treatment of workers (equity), the extent to which employees are encouraged to find innovative ways to do things (achievement), and their sense of belonging to a group that works well together (camaraderie).

Table 2-1 shows that the Intuit results on those questions are well above external norms.

Table 2-1 Intuit Survey Results Versus the Norms

	%Favorable	
	Intuit	**Norm**
Equity	88%	67%
Achievement	79%	61%
Camaraderie	83%	63%

Intuit gives its workers something to achieve: "Our goal is to create new ways to manage finances and small businesses that are so profound and simple that our customers cannot imagine going back to the old way." The company has an Employee Value Proposition that it takes seriously and tracks continuously. The proposition states that Intuit will create a great place to work by fulfilling the following employee expectations:

- Help me be productive, do great things, and be the best I can be.
- Let me know where I stand and how I'm doing.
- Invest in me to help me grow fast.
- Pay me based on performance.
- Make me an integral part of the team and create a positive work environment.

Intuit's dedication to fulfilling its promises to employees is exemplified by its tracking of how they are doing: "The measurement system [employee surveys] at Intuit provides an ongoing check on how the company is living up to its values, values that reflect what managers know to be related to the firm's ultimate financial success."[1] The fact that survey results are taken seriously by the company is indicated not only by the high scores it achieves, but by the 90%+ response rates to its surveys year after year. Employees clearly trust that the surveys—and the Employee Value Proposition—are more than public-relations exercises.

Employee enthusiasm is not just a feeling or an attitude: it is a motivated state, impelling people to action. And unlike sports fans, employees can do a lot to directly affect the success of their team; in fact, if all they do is cheer from the sidelines, the company gets into trouble. Everyone who has worked knows the potential that can be tapped when people really care about their companies and their jobs. That potential is an employee's discretionary effort, that is, the difference between the minimum an employee has to do on the job and what he is capable of doing.

Enthusiastic employees routinely produce significantly more than the job requires, often working all kinds of hours to get things done (and done right); search for ways to improve things rather than just react to management's requests; encourage co-workers to high levels of performance and find ways to help them; welcome, rather than resist, needed change; and conduct transactions with external constituencies—such as customers—in ways that bring great credit (and business) to the company.

A moderately satisfied workforce, on the other hand, is a generally willing workforce, doing what the company wants (and usually without complaint). However, it is more of a passive loyalty. Enthusiastic employees don't need to be asked. Consider this example from Herman Miller, an office-furniture company widely admired both for its business success and for its highly progressive employee relations practices:

> On learning that the American Airlines national office was about to become their neighbor, enterprising employees at a Dallas branch of Herman Miller, the office-furniture company, wrote a letter asking the airline to consider furnishing their new office with Herman Miller products.

> Their initiative paid off in a sizable order. But, the week before the airline office opened, the employees who went over to check that the order had been delivered properly found that the packing crates had crushed the plush on the fabric of hundreds of chairs. So, the employees formed teams to work around the clock and over the weekend to raise the plush with steam irons.[2]

The management literature is replete with anecdotes from companies such as Herman Miller that demonstrate the great lengths—sometimes, nothing short of heroic—to which highly motivated employees will go to serve their company and its customers. Frederick Smith, the founder of Federal Express, tells this story:

> ...a Rocky Mountain blizzard had knocked out a mountaintop radio relay, cutting off phone service at several Federal Express offices. The phone company would not be able to repair the connection for five days. So, Hal (a FedEx telecommunications

expert) chartered a helicopter (using his personal credit card). When the pilot couldn't land, Hal jumped out, slogged through waist-deep snow, and reconnected the cables. He didn't go through layers of approval. He just acted. He knew what he had to do was right.[3]

Enthusiasm is actually one of the stated "values" of Crescent Realty Trust, which is a well-known real-estate company. The company values include "integrity, leadership, people, teamwork, innovation, service, communication, relationships, discipline, and performance." Detailing its "people" values, Crescent declares, "We will hire, develop, retain, and reward exceptional and *enthusiastic* (emphasis added) people." CEO John Goff pointedly commented to us, "I'd rather have enthusiasm than smarts." So, the following comments by Crescent workers should not come as a surprise:

> *We never stop trying to outdo ourselves in regards to the services/ amenities that we provide. Our people bring pride, passion, and commitment to real estate. Everyone I talk to takes pride in their work, with a passion to see our company succeed.*

> *The people respect each other and believe there is value in the contribution they make individually and as a team to make the workplace environment "solution oriented."*

> *Coming to work does not feel like a chore but a joyful part of the day.*

> *No matter what the problem may be, they [the company] always seem to go the extra mile to try and solve the problem and make sure the person and/or persons are taken care of.*

> *Crescent really cares about its employees. That personalization, in my opinion, is what breeds loyalty by team members. (You feel like a real person—not just a number.)*

Enthusiasm is not a recipe for perpetual bliss or automatic success, and it has little in common with "contentment." Avid sports fans want their team to win all the time and so frustrations are inevitable. So, caring employees are often frustrated employees. After all, they care. Not only does their company—their team—sometimes lose, but in a changing and competitive business world, the status quo is rarely good enough, so the drive for success translates into a continual striving for improvement. It is no wonder that people who strongly identify with an organization can, in response to praise about the organization's performance, often say that they are still unhappy with where things are. It's the curse of caring.

As previously mentioned, there is a marked decrease in employee enthusiasm in most companies after the first year of employment. Our surveys show that the percentage of very satisfied workers drops after six months and continues to drop, while the unsatisfied group steadily increases. This shift would be even more marked if first-year attrition were taken into account, because most voluntary turnover occurs within the first year of employment (as people and their employers learn whether they've found the right "fit"). Those employees who leave are, on the average, much less satisfied than those who stay and, if they were not able to leave, would depress the later satisfaction scores.

Yet, although the overall results show marked declines, there are many companies where the decline is much less sharp. These companies are the "10 percent" that we referred to earlier—the companies that manage to maintain high levels of morale. It is from these companies that we draw examples of the policies and practices that harness, rather than depress, the initial enthusiasm and excitement that people bring to their work.

Before concluding the discussion on enthusiasm, we need to consider the other end of the morale continuum, namely, severe discontent. Approximately 16.4 percent of the units that Sirota surveys can be characterized as having highly discontented and, perhaps hostile, workforces. Hostility is obviously different from enthusiasm, but one major similarity exists between them: they are both highly motivated states that impel people into action. In that sense, they are different from both moderate satisfaction and neutrality. ("What the heck, it's a job," typifies the neutral employee's attitude.)

Anger is primarily a product of a sense of injustice. Although the motivation of an enthusiastic employee is to go beyond the job requirements, the motivation of an angry employee is to do less and often to influence others, formally or informally, to restrict their work. In other words, the goal is to somehow harm the organization because this, in the minds of the aggrieved, redresses the felt inequities: it brings their performance in line with what they feel they receive from the organization. This is not just an economic issue. People who feel unjustly treated also don't want to feel stupid by allowing themselves to be exploited. Other consequences of anger are poor treatment of the company's customers, poor treatment of "internal customers" (that is, a lack of cooperation with other units), absenteeism, tardiness, theft, and, in more extreme cases—when anger turns into rage, such as in explosive labor disputes—violence and acts of sabotage to the company's property.

A feeling of injustice, then, produces anger but, as we have shown, feeling equitably treated does not produce enthusiasm (for most people and by itself). It is a precondition for enthusiasm. That is, although it is nearly impossible to be enthusiastic about an organization that treats its employees poorly in terms of the basic conditions of employment (pay, for example), being treated well in those respects is just a part of the story. An assembly-line worker can be very well paid, have good benefits, and so on, but be terribly bored with the tedious routine. He is then likely to be "moderately satisfied." But, because the equity needs are being met, the employee doesn't feel much anger. Also, bored workers figuratively or literally go to sleep; they don't strike out at the company. However, add a sense of injustice to that and anger is the likely result (remember the speed-up at the Lordstown Plant that was discussed in Chapter 1).

Enthusiasm and Business Performance

Thus far, our evidence for the relationship between morale and performance has consisted of anecdotes. As interesting as anecdotes are, we don't rely only on them to make our point. After all, as we have said, any argument can be proven (or disproved) with a few stories. A very large and impressive body of evidence, which comes from solid, systematic research conducted over many companies, clearly demonstrates the strong statistical relationship between policies and practices that generate employee enthusiasm and business performance. Here is just some of the relevant research.

Jeffrey Pfeffer, in his comprehensive review of the research, concludes that gains of about 30 to 40 percent can be realized by companies implementing work practices that result in high employee commitment. The studies covered by his review are wide-ranging; they include investigations of the survival rates of initial public offerings of companies with different work practices and detailed research on the impact of these practices on profitability and stock price in many different industries. For example, a study of steel mini-mills reveals that mills "...using commitment-oriented management practices required 34 percent fewer labor hours to produce a ton of steel and showed a 63 percent better scrap rate." A study of nearly two hundred banks finds that differences in such practices are associated with an approximately 30 percent difference in financial performance.[4]

Fortune Magazine compiles and publishes many lists, including one called *America's Most Admired Corporations* (based on ratings of factors such as value as a long-term investment) and the *100 Best Companies to Work For in America* (based on a review of companies' policies pertaining to employees and employee attitude survey data). Year after year, the correlation between these two lists is strong. For example, in 2001, of the 15 companies rated as the "most admired," 9 are on the list of the best companies to work for. (Not all companies choose to compete to be placed on the "100 Best" list.) But none of the "100 Best" companies are in or anywhere near the list of the 50 *least* admired companies.

Our research on the relationship between employee morale and business performance is equally striking. To take one recent example, consider stock-market performance in 2002, which was a bad year for the market (the S&P Index declined 19 percent). We analyzed the performance of the publicly traded companies we surveyed in 2000–2001. Using overall satisfaction as our measure, we divided the companies into high morale (75+ percent favorable), moderate morale (between 74 and 60 percent favorable), and low morale (less than 60 percent favorable). The stock market performance in 2002 of each company was determined and the average performance for the three morale categories calculated. Since different industries perform differently on the stock market in the course of a year, and the companies in our morale categories differed considerably by industry, it was necessary to compare the performance of each our companies with the performance over the year *of its own industry*. Table 2-2 shows the average changes in stock market price of the companies in each morale category, the average changes in the industries of those companies, and the difference between the two.

The companies with high morale performed considerably better than their industry comparison group—about 20 percent—actually showing a slight increase in stock-market value in a bad year for the overall market. The moderate and lowest morale companies performed somewhat worse than their industry comparisons, about 5 percent. Similar findings are found for other standard measures of company performance, such as return on investment and return on assets.

Table 2-2 Employee Morale and Stock Performance

	Average 2002 Stock Market Performance		
	Of Companies in Each Category	Of Industry Comparision Companies	Difference
Morale Category			
High	+1.80%	−18.23%	+20.03%
Moderate	−14.41%	−9.19%	−5.22%
Low	−24.92%	−19.93%	−4.99%

The broad measures of business success are heavily influenced by how people perform day-to-day on the job. Our own research shows, for example, that enthusiastic workers often increase the quality of work by huge percentages—up to a 75 percent reduction in defect rates.[5] We and others find high positive correlations between employee satisfaction and customer satisfaction and sales.[6] In a fascinating study done for the National Oceanic and Atmospheric Administration, strong positive relationships were found between the "organization culture" index of their various national weather service offices (as measured by an employee satisfaction survey) and a "critical success index," which is an objective measure of tornado warning performance that takes into account positive forecasts followed by an occurrence, occurrences that were not predicted, and false alarms.[7]

In short, the evidence for the positive impact of very high levels of employee morale on their performance and on business success is strong.

Or is it? A statistician might object to the suggestion that we have provided "proof" that morale has a positive impact on performance. We know that our kind of research—as opposed to a pure experiment—never permits firm proof of causality or its direction. We can speak of a "statistically significant relationship," but the relationship may be from performance to morale rather than the reverse; that is, it is business success that breeds happiness, not happiness that breeds business success. As one executive commented to us regarding the rather mediocre survey results for his company, "Look, what we've got to do is get the profits up and the stock price up—that'll take care of morale. The morale problem is that our performance has been lousy." With this comment, the executive minimized the importance of both employee morale and the management practices that impact morale, such as treating employees respectfully. The only practices that matter, in his view, are those that he believes directly impact profits, such as the company's business strategy and economic and marketplace conditions.

There is no question that business performance has a major impact on employee morale, because an organization that performs well generates employee pride and optimism about job security and advancement opportunities. Furthermore, such organizations can afford to do concrete things, such as increase pay, that elevate morale.

But, does morale also have an independent effect on performance?

Building the People Performance Model

It is extremely difficult to statistically disentangle the various elements of the management-morale-performance equation. There are many variables to deal with and the statistical methods for determining causality provide rough approximations at best. In a laboratory experiment, you can hold constant all the variables except the one of interest, the one that is being manipulated. However, in addition to the fact that many of the factors with which we deal cannot easily be manipulated in a laboratory (such as job security), the applicability of the findings in such an artificial environment to the real world is often questionable.

However, a great deal of research has been done that bears, at least indirectly, on this matter. We integrated the best research and thinking in this area and developed a model called the People Performance Model, which encompasses all the key variables (leadership and management practice, morale, and performance) and the way these variables relate to each other. This section shows how the model was built piece-by-piece.

To start, the research we and others have done, plus simple logic, suggests that the relationship between morale and performance is *reciprocal:* each is both a cause and an effect of the other. Some research shows the causality mostly in one direction, some mostly in the other, but most indicate that it likely goes both ways.[8]

As we build the model, you will see that we deal with a *system* of relationships with numerous feedback loops. As regards employee morale and performance, the morale that business success generates enhances employee performance, which enhances and sustains business success, which enhances and sustains morale, and so on. It is a system of interlocking, mutually reinforcing factors—a virtuous circle or a vicious circle (if the direction is negative).

A good example of how this works is the relationship that's quite consistently found between customer satisfaction and the satisfaction of employees who deal with customers. What causes what? Logic and experience tell us that happy employees make for satisfied customers (that is, morale results in performance), but it goes both ways: having satisfied customers boosts employee morale because it is a key source of pride for them (and generates improved business performance, which we discuss later). Figure 2-1, then, is the first component of the People Performance Model.

Figure 2-1   The People Performance Model—employee morale and individual performance.

As we develop the model, we shall see that it includes a number of reciprocal relationships (or feedback loops). Because we said that employee performance positively affects business performance, Figure 2-2 adds business performance to the People Performance Model, taking into account that business performance also has a positive effect on employee morale.

Figure 2-2   The People Performance Model—adding business performance.

Now, bring management into the equation. Throughout this book, we discuss how management practices affect performance by their impact on employee morale. But, management's actions also directly affect performance. For example, consider teamwork. A management that encourages teamwork achieves higher performance because of the teamwork itself (for the great majority of tasks collaboration improves performance) and because teamwork elevates the "spirit"—the motivation, the enthusiasm— of employees (by satisfying the camaraderie need). This causes employees to perform at an even higher level. Because the morale-performance relationship is reciprocal, the higher level of performance raises morale further, which leads to even higher performance. Figure 2-3 adds the practices of management into the People Performance Model.

Figure 2-3   The People Performance Model—adding management practices.

The management practices that are of the most significance in this model—the ones that have the greatest effect on employee morale and performance—are those that relate to equity, achievement, and camaraderie needs.

Let's get more complicated. It is helpful to distinguish management (those whose practices directly impact employees on a daily basis) from leadership (senior management who sets the organization's overall direction and culture). This distinction is important to understand both how organizations function and to target leverage points for action. Little of lasting significance changes in an organization without the concurrence and involvement of the leadership.

Similar to management, leadership has both direct and indirect effects on performance. Leadership determines the business strategy. Although this book focuses on employee morale and performance, they are obviously not the only determinants to business success. Aside from non-controllable aspects of the business environment, the other major variable in business success is the sheer competence of senior management, especially the CEO, and the soundness of its business strategy. The soundness of the business strategy, as measured by business success, then loops back to affect employee morale and performance and so has a multiple effect on the performance of the business: directly and through the impact of success on employee morale.

The effect of leadership is further greatly magnified by the fact that it sets the organization's culture; therefore, to a large extent, leadership determines the daily management practices that impact employees. Although differences exist between managers in their practices (for example, some are more respectful of employees than others), there is a broad conformity to what senior management wants and stresses. The proportion of disrespectful managers is much greater in organizations where the leadership is either indifferent to, or disdainful of, the importance of treating employees respectfully. These broad cultural differences are true of all the management practices that affect employee morale and performance. Figure 2-4 adds the effect of leadership into the People Performance Model.

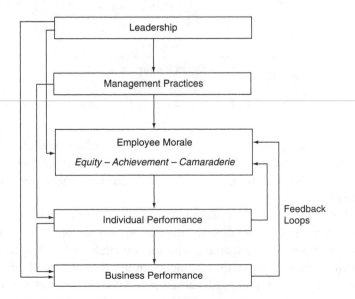

Figure 2-4 The People Performance Model—adding leadership.

No organization exists without customers, and numerous studies have been performed that link the satisfaction and purchasing behavior of customers to the attitudes and performance of employees. This link allows us to include customer satisfaction and behavior in the model (see Figure 2-5). Customer satisfaction with a company has quite consistently been found to relate to a company's profitability.[9] We find that customer satisfaction is a function of the products or services purchased from a company, the business processes with which the company interacts with its customers, and the way customers are treated by the company's employees. The treatment employees give customers, in turn, largely depends on how an organization treats and manages its employees (for example, how organizations pay, show respect for, and assign goals for its employees). As previously noted, customer satisfaction is also part of a feedback loop: it is both a cause and effect of employee morale.

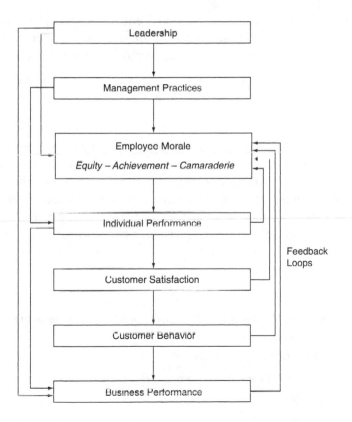

Figure 2-5   The People Performance Model.

Although it might seem complicated, in fact, the People Performance Model we show is actually a pared-down version of its full model. For example, we have omitted the other factors that obviously affect customer purchasing behavior, such as price and competitive alternatives and the differential effects various management practices have on morale. Also, we have not discussed a few arrows in the model, such as the way individual performance (especially employee efficiency) directly affects business performance. No matter. The key points are as follows:

1. People and their morale matter tremendously for business success, including customer satisfaction.

2. Employee morale is a function of the way an organization is led and the way that leadership is translated into daily management practices.

3. Success breeds success (the feedback loops). The better the individual and organization perform, the greater is employee morale, which, in turn, improves and sustains performance.

4. The management practices that matter most boost an employee's sense of equity, achievement, and camaraderie.

As we have said, what leadership does—the sheer competence of it, such as setting business strategy—obviously has major and direct effects on employee performance and business success. That is the focus of business scholars and journalists who endlessly write and lecture about the strategic effectiveness (or lack of it) of organizations: products, markets, pricing, mergers, acquisitions, and so on. But, as any true leader knows, having the correct strategy is just part of the story. To be fully realized, especially in the long term, the workforce at all levels needs to be mobilized in its execution.

> *"The first thing a young army officer must do is to fight a battle, and that battle is for the hearts of his men. If he wins that battle and subsequent similar ones, his men will follow him anywhere. If he loses it, he will never do any real good."*
>
> —Bernard Law Montgomery, British Field Marshal

"It is a terrible thing to look over your shoulder when you are try-ing to lead and find no one there."

—Franklin D. Roosevelt

The remainder of this book discusses the ways in which to win the battle for the hearts of workers. The next chapter begins with justice: basic fair-ness in the way workers feel their company treats them.

PART II

Enthusiastic Workforces, Motivated by *Fair Treatment*

CHAPTER 3

Job Security

Let's begin our exploration of the policies and practices that facilitate employee enthusiasm with the concept of equity (i.e., the degree to which people believe their employer treats them with fundamental fairness). This can be addressed either from the point of view of individual employees (perceptions of treatment relative to others in the company) or the treatment of large segments of a workforce. Our focus is on the treatment of large groups, potentially an entire organization. For these purposes, equity refers to the collective treatment of workers relative to fundamental and generally accepted societal standards. Examples of such societal standards are a "living wage," adequate non-wage benefits (such as medical insurance), sensitivity in handling layoffs, safe working conditions, a reasonable workload, and equality of employment opportunity.

These standards are usually seen as defining the fundamental relationship of employers and their workers, and the extent to which groups collectively conclude that they are decently treated. Traditionally, unions have been concerned about these issues, but the matter is somewhat more complex.

Perceptions of equity are not limited to the obvious physiological and economic factors that are normally the focus of collective bargaining. So, for example, a key psychological essential in most workers' concept of fairness or justice is the need to be treated with respect. In the workplace, respect means simply to be treated as responsible adults, rather than as children, criminals, or enemies. Respect might not feed families, but it is vital for employee self-esteem. The extent to which that need is satisfied has wide-ranging and profound implications. Chapter 5, "Respect," discusses respect in detail. The subject of this chapter is the most basic of most workers' economic needs, namely, job security.

Justice and Job Security

First, a caveat: the fact that we address job security and its importance for employee morale and performance does not mean that we advocate life-time employment guarantees. That's impossible for just about any organization. We do urge, however, that if an organization seeks to have enthusiastic workers, it must understand that those employees are not fungible objects.

How do workers, in general, view their job security? Our survey "norm" (or average) is 60 percent, which is not too bad, but the range across organizations is enormous: 90 percent to 6 percent.

To be sure, the lowest scores are, in part, explainable by reality. All the organizations with scores at the lower end of the range are, in fact, those that recently experienced employee layoffs, had announced plans to do so, or where rumors were rampant that a downsizing would soon occur. For example, in one company whose data are at the bottom of the range, a very large downsizing had just been completed. In another example, a company had sharply cyclical sales, more than most, so it was repeatedly laying-off and staffing up by large numbers. It, too, had a low score for this item.

Another company went through a series of layoffs (three waves in only three and a half years), even though the company had promised that there would be no more layoffs after the first wave. Surveyed employees expressed a belief that the layoffs were merely short-term measures to please the investment community and were driven by broad quotas, paying no attention to the critical skills the company lost, had destroyed morale, and had a devastating impact on one small community.

One conclusion might be simply that when workers express anxiety about their job security, it is because their jobs are insecure! Of course, that is only part of the answer. It does not, for example, explain why some companies report much higher scores on attitudes toward job security despite the fact that they, too, have experienced layoffs caused by economic downturns. Nor does it address the rather straightforward notion that if job loss is the result of financial necessity, why don't workers simply understand that and "suck it up" (emotionally speaking)? Why, in so many cases, is there anger? Why don't "these people" simply understand that job loss is one of the most commonly used and necessary organizational responses to the ups and downs of the economy and that business conditions are often unpredictable?

The fact is that workers often experience layoffs not as prudent business stewardship but rather as base inequitable treatment. Where does this attitude come from? The answer has two parts: the sense of substantive equity (whether the thing itself is fair), and the sense of procedural equity (whether what is done is done fairly). First, consider substantive equity.

Alan Sloan captured the spirit of a new era in a 1996 *Newsweek* article:

> *Firing people has gotten to be trendy in corporate America, in the same way that building new plants and being considered a good corporate citizen gave you bragging rights 25 years ago. Now you fire workers—especially white-collar workers—to make your corporate bones...Wall Street and Big Business have been in perfect harmony about how in-your-face capitalism is making America great.[1]*

This new management attitude includes ordering layoffs when a company is doing *well*. In the early 1990s, several large corporations downsized despite being profitable. In 1993, *The New York Times* reported that "...despite being consistently profitable, the Xerox Corporation... (stated)...that it would cut...nearly 10 percent of its workforce over...three years to improve productivity." In so doing, Xerox became another big company trying to improve the efficiency of its operations by dismissing large numbers of people. The day it announced these layoffs, its stock went up about 7 percent.

What message does management convey by these and similar actions? It might be an encouraging message to the investment community (although later we argue that it should not be) but to workers it is simply this: "Forget all that talk about you being an *asset* to the company; you are really a cost and a disposable commodity. And we will keep our costs down!"

How do workers react to the type of corporate conduct described by Sloan or displayed by Xerox? Consider these comments made to open-ended questions in our surveys:

> *...the greatest detriment to morale in this company...(is) the frequent layoffs. Layoffs have become a lifestyle. You may feel such action is necessary so that a real profit can be made even in bad years, but you are paying a huge cost in disloyalty of employees, stress-related illnesses, etc. I understand you feel you have no choice, but I can't help but wonder if there wasn't another way.*

> *There is no job security. Skills and training do not provide job security. Employees are commodities, not assets. No one gets credit for past performance, now it is passed performance.*

> *How can an employee feel any loyalty to a company whose top management keeps reaping benefits in the millions of dollars and keeps laying off employees to better their position? The golden umbrella is another example of upper-management benefits.*

People react strongly to loss of security and the lost sense of fair treatment that comes with it in circumstances such as these. We already noted that the need for people to feel that they are being treated fairly is basic, and nothing is more basic for most people than job security. The impact of people feeling that they are not treated equitably in this respect can be strongly negative on the organization. Again, look at a few more real-life comments:

> *How can people be expected to grow and better themselves when faced with constant layoffs? As a young person, I know there is little opportunity here for me. That is why I have recently accepted an offer with another company and will be leaving soon.*
> (The result: "brain drain.")

> *This company's plans for the future are easy to state—layoffs. Isn't that what they keep saying? I am a contributor...(but) now they say they may consider outsourcing! The moods and attitudes are worse than they have ever been, except for the execs!*
> (The result: polarization.)

> *There is absolutely no loyalty to people here—it's here today, gone tomorrow. What's the point of working hard? Whatever you do, you're just as likely as not to be out on the street tomorrow.*
> (The result: lessened effort and performance.)

> *These continual layoffs lead me to believe it's time we got union representation. We hear they'll be outsourcing jobs while they're laying off domestic employees. Unions have the power to protect against that. We need that power.*
> (The result: industrial conflict.)

We've seen that although companies can preach forever that "our people are our most important asset," that means little when dismissing workers in times of economic difficulty is the first thing a company does instead of the last. What's even worse is when people are laid off despite the business being successful. The impact is equally negative when standards of "procedural" justice are violated, such as when employees who are laid off are provided with minimal financial and other assistance or where the layoffs occur with little or no notice. No magic potion exists, and no one would rationally suggest that companies should not lay off workers when there is no other choice. However, even where workers understand the financial necessity, the manner and methods used by the company may be perceived as unfair.

Again, look at some real-life comments:

> *I feel the layoff policy is unfair. I am leaving the company soon and told my manager so because we know that layoffs are coming in our group.... He told me I would probably save someone's job by telling him and creating a vacancy. However, when I asked for the package, I was denied. He did not even try to see if it was possible. My feeling is this: if they are going to let a certain number of people go and my job will be considered as one of those, why should I not be entitled to the same treatment (the layoff package)? Management has consistently said it's not voluntary, but this case is different. They're counting my vacancy as one of their "numbers" to lay off.*

> *We are treated as stepchildren compared to other companies! I come to work, do my job, and go home at night wondering I really don't think the company realizes what its employees go through with all these layoffs. If you are going to lay off, "do it all at once." Get it over with and stop the phony promises that "this is the last one." These people who don't get laid off this time are not survivors because you'll do it again! Please do what you have to and get it over with.*

A major issue is the amount of notice that employees get before being laid off. Here are some horror stories from dot-com companies as they down-sized during the implosion of the industry in 2001:

- In one company, emails were sent to 20 percent of the workforce telling them to be at a meeting at a local hotel in 15 minutes. There, they were told that they were being laid off; they were locked out of the building and had to make appointments to clean out their desks.

- In another company, 60 employees met in a large conference room where the names of the 40 who were being laid off were announced.

- Employees in a company went to a meeting where they were told that some of them would be laid off; they were instructed to return to their desks and check their email. Forty of them received email that communicated their dismissal.

- An employee in a company returned from his vacation to find his work-team's desks occupied by an entirely new group of people. Half an hour later, management told him that he had also been laid off.

How companies deal with job security is one of the defining characteristics of a company in its employees' eyes. It is a defining characteristic because, in addition to its economic effects, a decision to lay off people sends a message of fundamental importance to the workforce about the way the company views its people: as assets or as costs (necessary evils).

We argue that the way many American companies now seem to operate, by essentially using downsizing as a strategic maneuver rather than as a last resort compelled by economic necessity, is largely misguided and self-defeating. It violates a fundamental need of workers and, in doing so, severely damages the sense of equity that's necessary for effective organizations.

Some people urge that this argument is old-fashioned and that today's workers have different attitudes about job security. Their view goes something like this: starting in the mid '90s, a "new generation" of workers entered the American workforce, young people who readily move from company to company and for whom job security is a low priority. These thinkers posit that the "new workers" want an environment where they feel "empowered" and "self-actualized" and, above all, in which they can develop the necessary skills to find a job in another company when they decide to leave.

Suppose, however, that employment elsewhere is difficult to find. How uninterested in job security are these young people then? It was not security in general that became unimportant for many young people in the '90s—instead, it was security *in one company*. The late 1990s were boom times with plentiful job choices; why be concerned about continued employment in any one company if employment elsewhere is so easy to obtain? But, times changed in late 2000. The high technology sector imploded and the country experienced its first economic downturn in a decade. Hundreds of thousands of workers were laid off and, once again, the media were filled with tales of high anxiety in the workplace. Surveys clearly showed that job security rose to its usual high position on the list of worker concerns. For example, workers in the telecom industry ranked job security as the number-one attribute they looked for in employers.[2]

Don't believe for a moment that stable employment—the predictability, not just the size, of a paycheck—is ever a trivial issue for most workers. An environment in which many jobs are available is, by definition, a secure environment. The late '90s-type boom is uncommon in the career experiences of the great majority of workers, so for most people most of the time, the employment stability that a company offers is critical. When a company downsizes, it's a major event and, for many employees, it is traumatic, even if they have not been laid off (at least not yet).

Equally momentous is a company's decision *not* to downsize when other companies in the industry take that path. Such companies exist. The in-your-face capitalism described by Sloan and others, while increasingly prevalent, is not a universally accepted model. The alternative philosophy is exemplified by these comments from two highly successful CEOs:

> *"Sure, we could take out a lot of our people. But we could give up our future. One, we'd demotivate the people who remained. Two, they surely wouldn't have the loyalty they have now. Three, if there were any good people left, they wouldn't be here long. They'd be looking around. And uncertainty reduces risk taking."*

—Wolfgang Schmitt, Rubbermaid CEO,
when growth of his company slowed

*"I had always figured out how to maintain full employment,
because I totally believe that when you bring people into your
workforce, they're taking on debt, they're building families.
They're trying to go forward in terms of their lives. To pull that
from under them is probably one of the biggest disgraces I could
ever imagine."*

—Jack Stack, CEO of Springfield Remanufacturing Corporation

The policies represented in these views are not just humanitarian—*they
are the best for the business*. How do we know that? Let's examine the
heart of the claim, which is that layoffs are good for a company in the
ordinary course (the implication being, of course, that the financial benefit
trumps the human issues). To some readers, Xerox's actions (described
earlier) will no doubt sound like good business. These are the kinds of
actions that, we are told, have finally dispensed with old-fashioned and
inefficient paternalistic management.

Sure, a layoff often results in a short-term spike in a company's stock
price. However, the impact on the long term can be quite different. *There
is now a mountain of evidence that casts doubt on the efficacy of downsizing for many companies as a cost-reduction strategy.* At the least, the
projected savings are greatly overestimated. Basically, the studies show
that only about one-third of companies that downsize gain increased productivity and profits over the subsequent 3- to 5-year period. Further,
these companies *underperform* the stock market over that time. Research
done in the mid 1990s found that downsizing companies outperformed the
S&P only slightly during the 6 months following news of a restructuring,
then lagged badly, netting a negative 24 percent by the end of 3 years.[3]

The theory of keeping a company "lean and mean," then, may really
be only "mean." One study found that, on average, a 10 percent reduction
in workers resulted in only a 1.5 percent reduction in costs.[4]

Why the surprisingly poor results for downsizing companies? Lester
Thurow of MIT writes, "Layoffs are painful and costly. There are innumerable reasons they should be avoided if possible: Severance payments
must be made. Higher training costs lie ahead. The skilled members of
the team whom a firm has laid off will not be there to be rehired when
times get better. Morale suffers among the remaining workers, and fewer
will be willing to make personal sacrifices to help the company while it
needs it most."[5]

Contrast the in-your-face-capitalism approach with the approach of *highly successful* enterprises that have made it company policy to avoid or minimize layoffs:

- Southwest Airlines has never laid off any workers, not even after September 11, 2001. CEO James F. Parker said at that time, "We are willing to suffer some damage, even to our stock price, to protect the jobs of our people."[6]

- Federal Express is dedicated to the principle that its people are its most important asset, as evidenced by its "People, Service, Profit" corporate philosophy. People are deliberately placed first because, in the company's view, putting people first makes good business sense. These are not just words: FedEx has an explicit commitment not to lay off employees except under the most extreme circumstances as determined by the CEO.

- Lincoln Electric is a Cleveland manufacturer famous in the management literature, both for its extraordinary business success over more than a century and for its innovative management practices. These practices include guaranteed job security for its employees. The former chairman, James F. Lincoln, wrote, "The greatest fear of the worker...is lack of income. The industrial manager is very conscious of his company's need of uninterrupted income. He is completely oblivious, evidently, of the fact that the worker has the same need."[7]

- Nucor, a successful steel company—by far the most profitable in its industry—has never had a single layoff. Ken Iverson, Nucor's former CEO and the creator of its culture, writes, "'Painsharing' has helped us get through the tough times without ever laying off a single employee or closing a single facility for lack of work, even when the industry overall was shedding thousands of jobs. But, our history of no layoffs is not noble, altruistic, or paternalistic. It's not even a company policy. We've told our employees time and again, 'Nothing's written in stone. We'll lay people off if it is a matter of survival.' The question is, when is laying people off the practical and sensible thing to do? To compete over the long term, a company needs loyal, motivated employees. Can management expect employees to be loyal and motivated if we lay them off at every dip of the economy, while we go on padding our own pockets?"[8]

Our point, obviously, is not that companies should never lay off employees. For some, that would be suicidal. For example, Continental Airlines, a company very similar to Southwest in its approach to employees and in its business success, laid off 12,000 workers in the aftermath of September 11.

The real issue is whether employees see the company's decisions as balancing its immediate business interests with a consideration of how those decisions affect employees. Or, is it all just this quarter's earnings and stock price, and everything else be damned?

Few people would expect employee well-being to be the sole, or even the paramount, consideration in business conduct. Certain actions had better be taken in the short term because, otherwise, there might not be a long term! However, things are rarely that black and white. Many factors affect a decision, and the problem, from the point of view of employees in so many companies, is that employees' interests are a distant last in top management's calculations (if they count at all).

As we have seen in most companies, downsizing the workforce is frequently a short-term solution with little or no long-term benefits.

A short-term orientation is decidedly not characteristic of companies such as Southwest Airlines. A significant part of its longer-term perspective is a respect for employees as assets that are not lightly disposed of. Another example: *Fortune*, in its 2002 report on the 100 Best Companies to Work For, describes the philosophy of Edward Jones, a stock brokerage that is now Number 1 on this list: "Edward Jones was hit particularly hard by the gloomy stock market, and it responded by cutting back bonuses. But none of its 25,000 employees got the ax. 'We want to build the kind of relationship with workers that makes them willing to go the extra mile,' says Jones' CEO, John Bachmann. 'You can't do that if you get rid of them whenever times are rocky.'"

The *Fortune* report continues, "Of course, sometimes…pay cuts, reduced workloads, hiring freezes, and so on aren't enough, and companies are forced to take the most drastic step: firing employees. So when layoffs did happen, we gave companies credit [for placement on the 100 Best list] for offering generous severance and compassion. Cisco, Number 15, for example, garnered goodwill by offering to pay terminated employees who chose to volunteer for a social service agency one-third of their Cisco salary for a full year. Cisco also threw in full benefits and a promise of priority if the company starts hiring anew."[9]

The report also contains a description of how Agilent Technologies responded to suddenly plummeting sales and a large workforce surplus.

Agilent is a Silicon Valley company whose major products are chips, electronic components, and testing and measurement devices mostly for telecommunications companies. The description of what Agilent did in this time of distress is titled "How to Cut Pay, Lay Off 8,000 People, and Still Have Workers Who Love You." The title is not facetious. Agilent management worked long and hard to, first, avoid layoffs and, then, when that was no longer possible, to cushion the blow. This company exemplifies the kinds of steps that demonstrate a genuine concern for people and their interests.

The Agilent story in *Fortune* begins by describing Cheryl Ways, an employee who was told she would be laid off:

> What is surprising is the manner in which Ways left: Not by
> spending her lame-duck days updating her resume on company
> time or prying the A's off office keyboards, but by working hard-
> er, longer, and with an intensity that rivaled the most productive
> periods of her five years at Agilent. The answer to why she did
> it—and how Agilent was able to wring such performance and
> devotion from tens of thousands of employees working beneath
> an ax—provides a lesson for all companies struggling to slim
> down in these post-boom years…. The Hail Mary steps the com-
> pany took to avoid downsizing; the barrage of emails and face-to-
> face meetings with top management; even the tired sound in the
> CEO's voice as he delivered news of mass layoffs. Together, these
> created an atmosphere in which people like Ways—three months
> after being axed—could say of her bosses, "I felt horrible they
> had to do this," and of her former co-workers, "This was my gift
> to them: To leave my job in the best way possible."

Can a better example be offered of employee dedication to a company? Can anyone doubt the enormous value to a company of such dedication—a value in both good times and bad? Cheryl Ways is not unusual as a personality—she is what many people are like under the right conditions. It is the policies and practices of companies such as Agilent that are unusual.

An implicit theme of our argument and the evidence we marshaled is that companies should unhesitatingly scrap the notions that "loyalty is dead" and that displaying a genuine concern for the interests of employees is a sign of inefficient, outmoded, paternalistic management. "You get what you give" should be emblazoned on the office walls of all executives wondering why their employees are indifferent to the goals of the company. Perhaps this motto should be placed on their mirrors because the problem stems from the executives themselves. For, ultimately workers will not reward the indifference of managers to their employees' basic interests with high levels of enthusiasm and performance. Practices relating to job security are central to employees' basic interests.

Best Policies and Practices

So far, we provided glimpses of how companies that are genuinely committed to providing their employees with stable employment treat those employees. This section gives a more systematic review of these practices, organized under the following five basic principles to which all these companies appear to adhere:

1. These companies are dedicated to exhausting all possible alternatives before laying off people.

2. When layoffs are impossible to avoid, these companies use voluntary methods if at all possible.

3. When layoffs are impossible to avoid and voluntary methods are not feasible, too costly, or do not achieve the required numbers, they handle involuntary layoffs with generosity and care.

4. They communicate honestly, fully, and regularly with their employees throughout the entire process.

5. They are cognizant of the impact of the layoff on the survivors and take steps to minimize the impact on them.

The specific practices are as follows.

Principle 1: Exhaust all possible alternatives before laying off people.
The alternatives to layoffs are most usefully thought of as "rings of defense;" that is, defenses against involuntary layoffs. They fall into three categories:

- Providing meaningful work for surplus employees through measures such as the following:

  - A hiring freeze that, because of normal attrition, opens up jobs that surplus employees might fill, or be trained to fill.

- The elimination or severe restriction in the use of temporary employees, which again results in jobs that surplus employees might fill.

- Bringing in work that had been subcontracted.

- Accepting lower-profit work the company would normally reject.

- Having people perform other useful tasks, such as deferred maintenance.

- Providing the training that had been postponed because of the prior heavy workload.

- Putting people into sales to increase demand.

- Building inventory.

The solutions for dealing with surplus employees are, of course, easier to implement when the surplus exists in only one segment of a company that has other growing segments that seek workers. In that case, the company's own people have preference over outside hires, assuming that they have the skills or can be trained.

- Reduction of non-labor expenses through measures such as the following:

  - More efficient purchasing and use of resources (materials, etc.).

  - Deferring capital expenditures.

  - Travel reduction.

  - Cutback in minor expenses, such as newspaper subscriptions and holiday parties.

  - Reduction in dividends to stockholders.

- Reduction of labor costs through measures such as the following:

  - Major work-process restructurings that enhance labor productivity.

  - Reduction or elimination of overtime.

  - Salary freezes.

  - Across-the-board pay cuts.

- Elimination of bonuses.

- Shortened workweeks.

- Unpaid vacations.

- Unpaid leaves of absence.

- Reduction in company contributions to employee benefits.

- Temporary loan of employees to other companies, such as customers and suppliers.

Taking these steps before considering layoffs has a major positive impact on employee morale, but there are significant ancillary benefits as well. For example, a policy that seeks to avoid layoffs imposes a planning discipline on the organization: Workload and staffing projections must be made carefully. When the organization is clearly committed to avoiding layoffs, recruiting and hiring is more likely to be more purposeful and far more carefully carried out. We are not aware of research on the matter, but it is our impression that, by and large, companies that engage in these policies are more selective in their hiring practices and wind up with significantly more capable workforces. Because these companies typically gain reputations as good places to work, the pool of prospective workers from which these companies can draw is larger than for an average company. Such organizations also do more training and retraining than the average because a premium is placed on workforce flexibility. They will also more likely promote from within the company. Thus, the set of mutually reinforcing policies and practices makes a company's orientation toward the workforce as a genuinely valued asset a reality.

A particularly impressive demonstration of the impact of a layoff-avoidance policy on planning can be found in Reflexite, which is a small U.S. manufacturer of reflective materials. As described in a publication of Business for Social Responsibility,

> [Reflexite] has a Business Decline Contingency Plan (BDCP), designed to take the uncertainty out of the situation when faced with a downturn or flat sales. The BDCP outlines four levels of severity, the symptoms of each situation, the actions to be taken at each level, and the expected results of that action. So, for example, at Stage I, with 'sales below budgeted sales but ahead of the same period in prior year,' the plan dictates that the company

'defer some budgeted hires,' 'defer some budgeted activities,' 'heighten awareness of current situation,' 'discuss at staff meetings,' and 'monitor overall economic conditions.' In the middle stages, the plan calls for, among other things, soliciting ideas to cut costs and improve productivity and efficiency; cutting overtime; accelerating new product introductions; voluntary leaves and furloughs; deferring lower-priority capital items; deferring raises; and reducing hours. At Stage IV, the most severe condition, where Reflexite 'generates losses for a period of two quarters or more,' the plan calls for 'salary deferments or reductions for balance of exempt employees,' 'trim benefits,' 'early retirements,' 'voluntary resignation offering,' and—finally—layoffs.[10]

Principle 2: When layoffs cannot be avoided, first ask for volunteers.
After all the options are exhausted, before resorting to involuntary layoffs, these companies seek volunteers to leave the company, through either voluntary separations or early retirement. This is accomplished by offering financial incentives (for example, cash bonuses coupled with an extension of health insurance coverage and other benefits). Invariably, outplacement assistance is provided. Such programs are typically very successful in producing the number of volunteers the company needs.

The major reason the programs succeed is that, for many employees, the offers are simply too good to refuse. They make it financially possible for people nearing retirement to retire early and for others to begin new careers that might not otherwise have been feasible. Also, employees who do not accept the packages leave themselves open to the possibility of involuntary layoffs if the company cannot achieve the sufficient numbers of volunteers from their efforts.

For many companies and employees, therefore, voluntary downsizing is, to a large extent, a win-win situation. To the company, the downsides of these programs are that, in the short term, they're more costly and time-consuming than involuntary layoffs. Also, by offering voluntary separation, a company might lose some employees with the most-needed skills because of opportunities that, prior to the offer, the employees could only dream of. Companies that have successfully downsized often make a special point of telling these employees how much they are valued and encouraging them to stay.

Principle 3: When layoffs cannot be avoided and there are no more volunteers, act generously and decently. From an organizational standpoint, you're not doing it just for those who are let go, but for those who will stay.

When a company must resort to involuntary layoffs, the best companies—best in our terms—do so in ways that are most supportive to the people being laid off and least damaging to the morale of those who remain. As we saw in the case of Agilent Technologies, doing it right may actually strengthen the bond between the company and its employees.

Doing it right has three components: financial assistance, outplacement assistance, and communications. With regard to financial and outplacement assistance, the best companies tend to be uncommonly generous and helpful in what they do for employees. Thus, while a fairly typical severance for lower-paid employees is one or two weeks for each year of service, these companies might offer a month's pay for every year of service, plus assistance with medical- and dental-insurance coverage. Although it's become the norm in the industry to provide outplacement assistance to help find a new position, these companies might provide supplements such as financial consultation (including preparation for the tax implications of their severance packages) and an allowance for retraining, education costs, or a small-business startup. They often actively help employees find other jobs. Also, they usually guarantee laid-off employees priority consideration for rehire when business conditions improve.

Whatever the specifics, the basic principle is simple: provide the assistance to employees that makes it clear that the company is doing a great deal to buffer the impact of the layoff. This is putting your money where your mouth is and, when preceded by visible and genuine attempts to do whatever possible to avoid layoffs, has a large positive impact on the morale of those laid off and those who remain with the company.

Principle 4: Communicate honestly, fully, and regularly throughout the entire process.

These companies do not adhere to the usual communications criterion, which is to communicate to employees only what they need to know. The "need-to-know" rule is precisely the wrong one at this time for this population. That rule says, basically, "Tell them as little as possible," and is appropriate for adversaries from whom a company wants to keep information. But, employees whose jobs are—or might be—in jeopardy are not adversaries. The criterion in this situation should instead be, *"Tell them everything they will find useful and that is not clearly confidential."* And give them that information as early as possible.

We previously showed how insensitively some dot-coms acted in laying off employees. Although those actions are not necessarily typical of American companies—they might not even be typical of dot-coms—most organizations are not particularly adept at communicating in ways that promote an appreciation on the employee's part that the company genuinely cares about their situations. We are referring to communications not just at the time of involuntary layoffs, but rather to communications from the time that it begins to appear that there is a reasonable possibility the company will have surplus employees. What have we learned from companies that do it well?

For one, these companies communicate to employees as early as possible—even when the need for downsizing is just a possibility. In addition to the "need to know" criterion that causes little information to be communicated, a common management assumption is that it is important to shield employees from upsetting information. Although it's ostensibly an attempt to be helpful to people, this attitude is profoundly unhelpful, of course. If a company were truly interested in assisting its people, it would supply as much information as possible as early as possible so that employees would make important decisions on a more informed basis, such as contemplated major expenditures.

Credible management is one of the factors that most affect employees' sense of being treated justly. This is nowhere truer than in relation to job security. Being seen as hiding known information in this respect—or providing it only when it is absolutely necessary to do so, such as at the last minute—is extraordinarily corrosive to employee morale and to the performance the company receives from its workers. The converse is equally true: leveling with employees, when combined with clearly genuine efforts to maintain security to the extent possible and to buffer the impact of job loss, is a precondition for workforce enthusiasm as we have defined it.

Are we serious? Can we speak of employee enthusiasm when there is a serious prospect of being laid off? Isn't that a contradiction? Of course, no one is enthusiastic about being laid off. Here, we refer to how employees—those who have been laid off and those who remain—view the company. People are realistic. They know about business cycles and the ups and downs of individual companies. As we mentioned, the basic question for them is, "Is the well being of employees given serious thought in management's decisions?" If so, employees can be enormously appreciative of their organizations, even in times of pain (as we saw in the case of Agilent). Consider Continental Airlines, which laid off about one-fifth of its workforce in the wake of September 11. In its story on the event, KPRC, a Houston radio station, reported the following:

> *Thousands of Houston-based Continental Airlines Inc. employees found out Friday that they were on the list to be furloughed and left their workplace carrying boxes filled with personal items. Hugs and tears were a common sight at Continental's head- quarters in downtown Houston.*
>
> *"My boss took me in. She's good people, and I felt sorry for her more than I did myself because that would probably be the hard- est part—letting other people go that, you know, you worked with for 15 years because they're like family," said Troy Curtis, who lost his job.*
>
> *"I'm being laid off, but I'll be back. It's the best company I ever worked for and I'll be back. They're going to rebuild and they're going to need people back," said a former employee....[11]*

Continental's problems, of course, came on suddenly. More typically, the problems emerge over a period of months. The following should be con- tinually communicated to employees from the time that labor surplus becomes a possibility:

- The company's business environment, both current conditions and, to the extent discernable, future prospects.

- The company's vision and strategy to deal with the business envi- ronment, such as new product development, sales initiatives, and the restructuring of work processes to make them more efficient.

- How the company seeks to enlist employees' help to deal with the business conditions, such as getting ideas for cost reduction.

- How the business environment can affect employees and what the company will do to buffer that impact.

- What, to the best of the company's knowledge, employees can expect—in general and as individuals.

Here are some additional communications guidelines:

- The communicators should include various levels of management, especially top management and the immediate supervisor. Employees much appreciate the involvement of the top person. Lower levels of management can handle more specific questions and concerns, and managers must receive training to learn how to conduct these meetings.

- Formal media, such as the house organ, should supplement—not be a substitute for—face-to-face meetings.

- The meetings should be designed to give employees the opportunity to register their concerns, ask questions, and make suggestions.

Principle 5: Recognize the impact of what you are doing on the survivors, and take steps to minimize negative impact.

A major purpose of everything we've suggested is to assure that those who are not laid off maintain their commitment to the company and their jobs. What we have described will, in fact, *enhance* that commitment because a company's basic attitudes toward its people are most convincingly displayed when times are tough, when being generous does not come easy.

Although business operational and strategic issues are beyond the scope of this book, note that an additional key variable in determining the impact on the survivors is the degree to which the downsizing process takes place in the context of a serious business improvement plan. That is, the impact is a consequence of the way people are treated and the way the company is, in effect, treating itself by effective business management.

We previously mentioned that layoffs often bear little in terms of long-term cost reduction and profitability. In addition to the harmful consequences of lower employee morale, a major factor in these failures is that these efforts are often undertaken as short-term fixes rather than as part of a plan that involves rethinking a company's culture, structures, systems and processes for lasting improvement. When not part of this broader plan, the likelihood is high that, over time, costs will again inflate as the company seeks to complete its work in the original inefficient ways.

Survivors' morale is both a cause and effect of business inefficiency. A downsizing that's handled poorly in terms of employee treatment has a negative impact on employee morale and, therefore, business performance, but morale is also markedly influenced by whether employees view the downsizing as just a short-term fix. In those times, it is especially important that the survivors have a vision of where the company is heading and their role in it. They want to know how the downsizing will serve to not only cope with the company's immediate business difficulties, but also provide it with competitive advantage and a more secure future. Laying off individuals without basic changes in the company's operations and strategies doesn't provide much ground for optimism. We previously noted that the company's approach to coping with current business difficulties and its vision for building a successful future are key elements of what needs to be communicated to the workforce.

In conclusion, a final caveat: do not confuse providing employment stability with tolerance for unsatisfactory employee performance. We must distinguish between conditions over which employees have no control—such as a market downturn or the introduction of labor-saving technology—from those where an individual simply chooses not to perform. The latter—whom we estimate to consist of about 5 percent of the average workforce—should, after appropriate counseling and warnings, be terminated. Let's face it: some people would rather not work, at least not work hard. This chapter is not about them.

CHAPTER 4

Compensation

Although job security is a critical concern of workers, it is also true that compensation is extraordinarily important for worker morale and performance. Don't believe anyone who tells you that money is "way down on the list" of worker goals—that what they really want is "appreciation" (or whatever) and they clamor for money only when those other things are lacking. That's psychobabble. As we said, they want a lot of things and money is way up there.

Money as Seen by Workers

Workers see money as:

- Providing for their basic material needs and, ideally, to live in a manner that satisfies them.

- Providing a sense of equity (that is, receiving a fair return for their labors).

- Providing a measure—one of the major measures—of their personal achievement.

- A potent symbol of the value that the organization places on the contribution of both the workforce as a whole and of the individual employee.

Money as Seen by Employers

Employers want money to:

- Attract and keep the number and kinds of employees they need.

- Define the organization's objectives, because what the organization pays for—not necessarily what it says—is what it truly wants.

- Motivate employees to perform at the highest possible level in the service of the organization's objectives.

- Avoid labor conflict.

Although executives generally (and incorrectly) assume that "employees will never be satisfied with their pay," they are aware that extreme dissatisfaction—a sense of great inequity—hampers the achievement of their attraction, retention, motivation, and industrial peace objectives. To avoid this, companies install pay systems that they hope prevent inordinate discontent and that can be held up as fair but ones that, at the same time, meet the organization's desire to obtain services at the lowest overall cost. What does our research (and the research of others) show about attitudes toward pay, its determinants, and its consequences? Here are the basic findings:

- The level of compensation, and the system by which it is determined and distributed, are generally equal in their importance to workers.

- People want to earn as much as they can, and it is rare for workers to express that they feel overpaid. In fact, because most employees (about 80 percent) rate their performance as "above average" in their organizations, it logically follows that people would not feel overpaid.

- However, although it is the rare employee who feels overpaid, only about 23 percent (which is our "norm") actually express *dissatisfaction* with their pay. Simply put, only 23 percent of our sample feel underpaid. Forty-six percent of workers express satisfaction with their pay.

- The higher the level of an employee in an organization, the greater the satisfaction with his pay. In our surveys, senior executives are usually ecstatic with their pay.

- The greater the satisfaction with pay, the higher is overall satisfaction with the organization, trust in management, and a sense that management treats the workforce as an important part of the company.

- We have shown that tremendous variability exists across companies in the percentages of employees satisfied and dissatisfied with their pay. The range is 69 percent to 16 percent satisfied and 8 percent to 64 percent dissatisfied.

- At the extremes—very low or very high actual pay—pay attitudes are determined primarily and simply by the amount of compensation. It's difficult to be satisfied at barely subsistence levels of pay; or for one's complaints to be taken seriously, even by one's self, about pay when earning millions. In between those extremes, the degree of satisfaction with pay is very much a result of *comparison*—with others, with one's history, with one's perceived performance, with the cost of living, and so on. In roughly the order of their importance, here are what we find to be the major determinants of pay satisfaction:

  - How well the organization pays relative to what employees believe other organizations pay for similar work.

  - Whether pay increases over time and how it increases in one year compared to increases in past years. Tenure, whether explicitly acknowledged or not, is therefore a major criterion people use to judge the fairness of their pay.

  - The extent to which pay increases are believed to reflect the employee's actual contribution (performance) and potential contribution (what the employee is able to do because of his training and skills and expanding experience over time).

  - The extent to which pay increases reflect increases in the cost of living. During times of high inflation, the cost of living becomes an all-consuming issue.

- The perceived generosity of non-wage benefits, especially medical insurance. As healthcare and medical insurance costs have skyrocketed, employees have increasingly come to see pay and benefits as one package: in the minds of many, the increase in medical costs and premiums offset pay increases and, therefore, they see the latter as little or no increase at all ("just barely breaking even, if that").

- How well the employee is paid compared to what other employees in the company, especially those at similar skill levels, are believed to earn.

- Company profitability (i.e., how much the company is believed to be able to pay).

- The discrepancy between the compensation of the general workforce and that of senior management. A large discrepancy is not an issue when the organization is doing well and the workers feel that they are also benefiting from that success: "Let him earn as much as he wants—he deserves it and it's been good for me."

- Almost invariably, in surveys, among the most negatively rated areas is the degree to which organizations that profess to pay for individual performance are seen as actually doing so. Our norm on perceived pay for performance is 40 percent favorable and 40 percent unfavorable. In other words, pay-for-performance systems, especially "merit pay," are not credible for a large numbers of workers.

We describe in this book the conditions that distinguish enthusiastic from unenthusiastic employees. Pay is vital in that respect, both substantively—it provides the material wherewithal for life—and symbolically—it is a measure of respect, achievement, and the equitable distribution of the financial returns of the enterprise. As shown in the last chapter, a sense of equity—of which pay is a key component—acts something like a "gate" to the functioning of achievement and camaraderie. Without a feeling of being treated fairly, the impact of the latter two is greatly diminished. The power of pay is further amplified by the fact that, in and of itself, it is a satisfier of both the equity and achievement needs.

Pay also affects the fundamental credibility of an organization in the eyes of its workers: is it putting its money where its mouth is? For example, is an organization that does well and that claims that its employees are "its most important asset" seen as nickel-and-diming the workforce when it comes to pay? Is a stated emphasis on product quality and customer service made real with rewards for those who produce high quality and provide good customer service? Our surveys frequently reveal large gaps between words and deeds, with employees often defining "deeds" in terms of how an organization pays.

Typically, management bases its evaluation of its pay-system effectiveness on "objective" data, such as labor cost percentages and trends, salary surveys, and formal job evaluations. Aside from the question of the validity of such data, they beg the fundamental question, *"How do workers see things?* For example, if they see no pay for performance, *there is no pay for performance.* To reward and motivate, pay for performance must be seen *by workers* to exist. As we now explore pay attitudes and their effects in detail, keep in mind the basic proposition that management's views of its policies—pay fairness, its relationship to performance, and so on—are irrelevant (except for management's views of *its own* pay).

In thinking about pay and formulating recommendations for effective compensation policies, it is useful to distinguish the level of pay from the way it is distributed, especially in relation to performance.

The Level of Pay

We previously mentioned that it is virtually impossible for companies to inspire loyalty and commitment in workers who are treated as disposable commodities. Similarly, it is difficult for a company to obtain loyalty and commitment from its workers when it's seen as one of the lower-paying companies (especially in relation to its competition or its profitability). Still, for many workers, job security comes first; when a choice has to be made, workers will usually moderate their pay demands to preserve their jobs. But, pay is a close second.

Contrary to popular belief, employees don't expect wildly generous pay for their labors. In fact, they would likely question the motives or competence of management if pay were astonishingly high. Therefore, we must differentiate between the wish for a lot of money and workers' views of what is reasonable and fair. They are capable of separating wishes and fantasies from realistic expectations. Most workers express satisfaction with pay that they consider to be "competitive" and *great* satisfaction with pay they consider to be even a few percentage points above the competition. A few percentage points can mean hundreds of dollars, and that's significant to the average employee.

A few examples of individual comments might help give meaning to our argument. These comments are responses to the question, "What do you like most about working here?"

> *The medical benefits are good and the pay is comparable to other companies.*
>
> *What I like most about the company is that the pay is decent.*
>
> *I like the pay that I receive here. It is the highest, although by a slim margin, among other companies in the same field. The company shows it values its employees.*
>
> *The opportunity to contribute to a high-class business such as this one and make a pretty decent paycheck in the process.*
>
> *The pay is above average for the type of work we do.*
>
> *I think that the benefits are outstanding and the pay is very reasonable in today's workplace. I also appreciate that the company reimburses my tuition costs.*

Unfortunately, the same principle of differentiation holds when pay is below that of the competition: just a few percentage points count significantly. This principle also comes into play in how workers react to pay increases. An increase that's even slightly below the rise in the cost of living is generally considered as a pay *decrease*. Most workers know the rate of inflation, especially in times of high inflation, down to the last decimal point.

Furthermore, workers are often upset if a pay increase they have just received is less than increases they previously received. This can also be viewed as a decrease or, at least, a disappointment.

To workers, it is critical that their standard of living not fall (as is the case when pay does not keep up with inflation), and it's important that the *rate* at which they move ahead does not decline. These might appear to be small, and even trivial, concerns to highly paid executives, but they are terribly important to the masses of workers who count every dollar. Of course, it is not just a material issue because pay has great symbolic value to workers—it signifies respect, achievement, and equity. Therefore, attitudes toward pay and pay increases have enormous consequences for pay-for-performance systems. For example, if a "merit" increase is not felt to be an increase because it does not keep up with inflation (in fact, if it is viewed as a decrease), how credible, satisfying, and motivating will the merit pay system be for that employee? We discuss merit pay later in this chapter.

The opinions workers have of their pay are also greatly affected by how they see their organization's financial condition. We have repeatedly asserted that the overwhelming majority of workers are realistic and reasonable. Therefore, they expect more generous pay and pay increases when times are good and less when times are bad. When times are truly bad, they often are willing to accept pay cuts, especially if it seems necessary to avoid or reduce layoffs.

But, acceptance of pay cuts—or reduced increases or no increases—as legitimate depends on whether employees trust their management. Trust, which is often lacking, is a function of the following:

- The overall views that workers have, based on the totality of their experiences in an organization, of management's credibility, and its interest in the well-being of the workforce.

- The openness with which relevant financial information is shared with the workforce.

- The degree to which sacrifice in bad times is seen as shared from top to bottom of the organization.

When trust is present, the kind of support an organization can receive from its workers is absolutely amazing.

Here are some additional open-ended comments that demonstrate the various points we have made about pay. They are responses to the question, "Now, what do you like *least* about working here?"

> *I have had difficulty over the past year with finding the ability to have respect or regard for the leaders of this company. In the face of many of my friends and colleagues being let go because of the economy, the leaders of this company accepted bonuses that were shocking and distasteful. At best, these bonuses were inappropriate, at worst, criminal. We get tiny increases.*

> *I have no trust at all in the brass and what they tell us. This company is doing well now. Why is so little trickling down?*

> *Additional work loads that are constantly placed on you and really no compensation in pay. We could be equal in pay to other companies but we do about 12 times the amount of work.*

I don't like the fact the pay in my area is not adjusted according to cost of living at all. We've fallen behind.

Other employers are offering somewhat higher pay. I can't continue to work here when I know there are better opportunities.

The worst thing is working and doing so many tasks at work and not getting compensated for it. The pay here really sucks in that regard. It's at least 5 percent below what other companies pay.

Medical and dental plans increase much more each year than the pay does. Therefore, we are not increasing our pay but decreasing it.

We work for a multibillion dollar company and still cannot pay for rent, utilities, and food. With overtime, I cannot support my family of three. Shame on you!

The pay scale and raises are also disgusting. I have been here for 4 years and barely get paid $9.00 an hour. New employees here are currently hired here at $10.00 (on the average) an hour.

Being able to make ends meet. Salary needs to be more competitive. I don't feel that we are paid enough to do the job that we do. Stop with the balloons and silly games and pay us instead. Most people today do not have the luxury of two incomes.

The pay rate for employees is below industry average. No wonder the turnover rate is so high here.

The fact that my benefits are going up, my co-pays are increasing and my prescriptions cost more yet we cannot get a decent percentage in our merit raises. A cost of living increase would be appropriate, even a couple percent.

This company does not even keep up with the cost of living index, thus any annual raise is no raise at all. In essence the longer you are at this company you are actually staying the same or going backwards pay wise. I feel this is one of the main reasons good, qualified people leave the company.

Our take-home pay should be much better. This company makes billions. Give us a bigger slice of the pie; there is no you without us.

Now, what is the impact of pay level on organization performance, such as profitability? One would think that, everything else being equal, the higher the pay, the greater the cost to a company and therefore the smaller the profits. We already commented on the relationship between pay and enthusiasm, so there is some reason to believe that the relationship between pay and cost would by no means be perfect—the positive effect on employee morale and performance should offset to some extent the impact of labor costs on profits. But, it goes further than that.

In economics, there is a body of theory, termed "efficiency wage theory," that deals with this issue. On the basis of observations such as the fact that higher pay rates are found in more profitable industries, the theory states that compensation above what a firm has to pay (that is, above the "competitive market-clearing wage") drives up labor costs, but also produces other benefits, such as greater work effort, and thus output and revenue for the firm. In his article, "Can Wage Increases Pay for Themselves?," David I. Levine concludes that "business units that increase their relative wages for workers of similar human capital [skill level, training, etc.] have productivity gains approximately large enough to pay for themselves." He found that, in units where wages declined over a three-year period (factoring in inflation), worker output increased 2 percent. Where wages increased, worker output grew by 12 percent.[1]

The research evidence points to four explanations for the relationship between wages and productivity:

- **Worker reciprocity and morale.**   The "gift" of higher wages from the employer is reciprocated by a "gift" from workers of higher productivity. This is in line with what we have said about the impact of morale on performance. Employee performance over the long term, of course, is not just a matter of productivity, but also the cost savings and profits generated by higher quality, better customer service, and so on.

- **Lower turnover.**   Higher paying companies lose fewer people and, therefore, have lower turnover-related costs, especially for recruitment and training.

- **Decrease in "shirking."**   For those employees not inclined to work hard, higher pay means that dismissal is a greater penalty than if the job paid less.

- **A superior pool of job applicants.**   Higher pay attracts a larger number of better job applicants from which to choose.

All four factors appear to play a role.

Obviously, there's a limit to the relationship between high wages and productivity. Levine found that the relationship holds less strongly in firms with large percentages of unionized workers. In those companies, he suggests, wages have gone beyond what could be made up by increased productivity.

An important practical lesson of the research on wages is the error of confusing labor *rates* with labor *costs*. Labor costs are a function not just of how much is paid to workers—that's the rate—but also how much workers produce. The correct measure of the labor cost to organizations is the ratio of wages to productivity, what economists call unit labor costs (ULCs). Low wages and low productivity can offset each other in terms of their effects on ULCs, potentially making labor "expensive" when wages are "low." In this connection, it has long been observed that the nations with the highest wage rates tend to be the most productive. Although low-wage countries still have a competitive advantage, that advantage is cut in half, on the average, when comparing ULCs.

The analysis also applies to individual companies within a country where there are large differences in productivity. For example, Japanese automobile manufacturers in the United States have long had a huge labor-cost advantage over their American-owned counterparts, despite similar wage rates, because they are much more productive. Table 4-1 shows the historic difference, which was measured in 1996, between the labor hours that North American automobile manufacturers require to produce a vehicle.[2]

Table 4-1   Labor Hours per Vehicle Produced by Manufacturer

Automobile Manufacturer	Average Labor Hours
Nissan	27.36
Toyota	29.44
Honda	30.96
Ford	37.92
Chrysler	43.04
General Motors	46.00

Differences in labor cost say little about quality and other key aspects of company success. Few systematic studies specifically correlate wage rates with product quality, but the research available suggests a positive correlation.[3] High wage rates should affect quality in much the same way they affect productivity (for example, by allowing the organization to attract and retain more highly skilled workers that will do higher quality work). That was the reasoning of the president of Wendy's, who was confronted with soaring costs and declining sales in 1986:

> "[I] found we had lost our focus—on people. We had such fear in
> our hearts about numbers, about the power of computer printouts
> and going by the book, we'd managed to lose sight of our cus-
> tomers and employees both. There's a special purgatory for serv-
> ice businesses that forget their business starts with people...Ours
> is an industry once defined by high employee turnover. It was
> viewed as normal...We questioned that view, and decided the
> best way to become the customer's restaurant of choice was to
> become the employer of choice. A number of basic changes were
> made, including significant improvements in compensation—both
> base and variable pay—and benefits. It worked. Our turnover rate
> for general managers fell to 20 percent in 1991 from 39 percent
> in 1989, although turnover among co- and assistant managers
> dropped to 37 percent from 60 percent—among the lowest in the
> business. With a stable—and able—workforce, sales began to
> pick up as well."[4]

What is our conclusion about pay level? To coin a phrase, "You get what you pay for." The evidence suggests that the normal inclination of many executives to pay as little as possible is often misguided. Organizations need to strive to compensate their workers *well*—even *above* the competition to the extent affordable. The advantage over the competition, how-ever, does not have to be in base pay—in fact, we suggest it usually not be. We discuss variable pay later in this chapter, such as profit sharing and gainsharing. Our suggestion is that it is variable pay that is best used to differentiate an organization from its competition. This has great advan-tages, including providing an organization with a mechanism that adjusts compensation to the performance of the workforce and the fortunes of the business.

Pay for Performance

Now, we come to the system by which pay is distributed, especially how it relates to performance.

In our preceding discussion, employee performance was treated as a "dependent variable;" that is, as an effect of the level of pay. Let's turn that around and think of it in a more customary way; that is, as an "independent variable": the way employees' performance affects their pay.

Most organizations have a pay-for-performance system of one kind or the other. The organizations that don't—or have it for just a segment of the workforce—tend to be in unionized environments or government agencies. In those cases, pay increases are negotiated or are simply the consequence of tenure and *in-grade* promotions (promotions where compensation increases, but job responsibilities basically do not.)

First, let's consider systems meant to pay employees for their individual performance. The two most common such systems are piecework and merit pay. Both sound terrific—they certainly fit the American ideology of individualism—but they have been found to leave much to be desired in practice.

Piecework

As the name says, employees working under this system are paid by the piece. The occupations to which it is most typically applied are production workers and salespersons. For the latter, the "piece" is the amount of the sale and the system is a commission plan. We first discuss piecework as applied to production workers.

Piecework in a production environment appears to be eminently sensible and fair because it aims to tie compensation directly to performance, and the measure of performance is objective (pieces produced that can be counted). The reality, however, is that disputes about these systems are extremely common. In many unionized environments using piecework, the system is the largest single source of employee grievances. For this and other reasons, the percentage of organizations that employ piecework has been declining.[5]

What are the issues? In factories, the key problems concern the way productivity standards are developed on which the piece pay rates are based. The standards define what is expected of the workers, the number of pieces per unit of time (hour, day, and so on). Typically, industrial engineers who rely on time study or some form of predetermined (synthetic) data develop the standards. The organization decides—or, in negotiation with the union agrees—on what a fair wage would be for a job if the employee meets the standards. The piece rate, then, is the standard number of pieces per time period divided into the agreed-upon fair pay for that time period. For example, if the standard is 100 pieces per day and the fair pay is $100 per day, the piece rate would be $1. Workers could earn more than $100 per day if they produced more than 100 pieces.

The measurement approach generates two serious problems. First, there is the question of the fairness or accuracy of the standards. Typically, workers complain that they are unreasonably high. In union shops, these often become the subject of an endless stream of grievances and negotiations. The "objectivity" of the standards—a key assumption of the system—is, obviously, a matter of considerable dispute.

The second issue is equally important although it's less commented on. The standard is production expected *using a particular method.* If a worker were to think of a better way of doing the job—increasing her production, say, by 25 percent—the standard would almost invariably be changed to take this improvement into account (that is, it would be "tightened"). The term "piecework," therefore, is in part a misnomer. The employee is not being paid for pieces produced per se; she is paid for pieces produced *within the context of a given method.* This has two consequences:

1. There is little or no motivation for employees to make method improvements that increase the overall output of their jobs. It is true that employees, after some time on the job, usually discover how to improve methods, but these improvements are typically kept to themselves because to reveal them brings no reward; in fact, it is seen as punishing. This represents an enormous waste of an extremely important resource—the talent, the initiative, and the creativity of the workforce—and is antithetical to improvement goals. Although the system is designed to get workers *up to* the standards, it discourages them from *beating* the standards. The losses in productivity that are engendered are large.

2. By treating workers as if the only thing that matters is their physical exertion, we remove from them a major source of achievement and self-esteem—namely, the opportunity to demonstrate their ability to think. We set up systems in which we have specialists in thinking: the method engineers. Their job is to develop "best methods" by which the workers should get their jobs done.

All we ask of workers is that they follow orders and work hard. But anyone familiar with such factories knows that workers can be mighty creative as they go about making life difficult for line management and its staff representatives: fooling the time-study man when being studied, submitting formal grievances whenever possible, and hiding new methods.

The theory of piecework—that a straight-line relationship exists between the wages a worker can earn and the effort he is willing to expend on the job—is therefore seriously flawed. An additional important problem for such systems is the effect that they have on group cohesiveness. It has often been observed that individual incentives discourage teamwork because each employee is out for himself. Although this is true in many white-collar occupations, the opposite is often the case on the factory floor. The systems often *increase* cohesiveness among workers, but in *opposition to management*. Workgroups set their own production norms and expect their members to adhere to them. The worker exceeding the norm is the *rate buster* (that's one of the more polite terms), and he does not have an easy life on the factory floor.

Most production workers are not like most salespeople for whom individual competition on the job is normal and a pathway to a sense of achievement. We elaborate on that difference later in this chapter.

In factories, the piecework system results in a continual tug-of-war between labor and management: workers and workgroups pressuring to hold down production, and management pressuring to increase it. This seems to contradict our earlier optimistic view of workers and worker motivation, but keep in mind that workers' attitudes and behavior are a function of not just who they are, but how they are treated. In the situations we described, workers see deceiving management, submitting grievances, and restricting production as a means to survive in the face of a management that's bent on turning their workplace into a sweatshop and limiting their pay opportunities. That's usually not the way management sees it, but that's the way *workers* see it.

We focused on the employee relations and productivity consequences of piecework. There is another issue, one that afflicts many pay-for-performance systems. A company that seeks to pay for performance must define what performance means. Part of the attractiveness of piecework (whether on the production floor or in sales) is that it relies on objective measures (things get counted). So, the definition of performance is often narrowly limited to what is countable. Because people focus on what is measured and rewarded, we often find workers cutting corners to produce what is expected. Workers might run machines at higher speeds than instructed, the quality of the output might be sacrificed, and so on. This is not only an attempt to reach the expected production levels, it is also part of the game, the tug-of-war between workforce and management. "Okay, you want x number of pieces, we'll give it to you and wait until the junk comes back!" Management has to then introduce additional controls and penalties to help assure quality and protect the equipment. It's all expensive and, as we will show, needless.

Is piecework ever appropriate? Yes, if it's applied in the right conditions and to the right people. The problems and costs of piecework tend to be least when the tasks are simple, repetitive, and can be done independently, and when management genuinely responds to workers' concerns about wages and the accuracy of the standards. Complex, non-repetitive jobs generate the most disputes about standards, and the impact of individual incentives on teamwork is largely irrelevant if teamwork is rarely needed. Coupling those conditions with a management that has a genuine concern for their employees' well being can make individual piecework the most effective system. A good example of this is Levi Strauss, a progressive management that switched from individual piecework to group-based incentives and suffered a decline in production.

Some workers *prefer* an individual piecework system. Research done in the 1950s by William F. Whyte[6] found that these workers tend to be socially isolated from their co-workers, owners of their own homes, and Republicans. Making money has a moral dimension for them, providing proof that they work hard. They are the rate busters, disliked, but uninfluenced, by their fellow workers—and beloved by management.

Salespeople are similar to the rate busters in their compensation preferences. Differences exist between the two groups in their personality traits and abilities—on the average, salespeople have much stronger social and communications needs and skills—but great similarity on traits such as independence, assertiveness, confidence in their ability to achieve high earnings, and high earnings serving as a major source of self-esteem. The salesperson personality profile fits the sales job perfectly and is, of course, why those people gravitate to that type of work. It is also why a compensation plan that is oriented to individual rewards attracts them (the sales commission plan). For most of them, it would be frustrating to work in any other environment and, with few exceptions—such as when teamwork is absolutely essential for high performance—that is the incentive plan that is recommended for them.

This is not to say that individual incentives in sales do not present problems, some of them similar to what we find in factories. Sharp disagreements can occur about the fairness of quotas and commissions, the amount of differential payment for different products, and how chargebacks should be handled. A frequent and major concern is the way high productivity and earnings are dealt with. As with factory workers, salespeople are often faced with disincentives to high performance because, if they produce and earn a lot, their quota is raised or their territory reduced. Therefore, salespeople seem to continually negotiate with management about the terms of their commission plans.

Despite the problems, our survey data show that professional salespeople are significantly more positive toward their compensation than non-management employees in general. This is so because, for one, an incentive compensation system fits their personalities and objectives. Second, they tend to be among the more highly paid employee populations. They arc paid well because their performance is seen as among the most essential to the success of business: they bring in the money! Finally, because they are so vital, they have a lot of bargaining power—especially the more successful salespeople—and management usually makes the arrangements that keeps them at least reasonably happy.

Besides matters of equity, sales-compensation plans can generate *organizational* issues, such as the deleterious effect individual commissions might have on needed teamwork and the tenuousness of the ties of salespeople to their organizations when a large proportion of their compensation is commission (rather than salary). Over the years, these problems have been recognized and, increasingly, when teamwork is essential, group incentives have become the norm. Today, most salespeople are paid a base salary with commission averaging about 10–35 percent of their total compensation.

Merit Pay

The great majority of salaried (as opposed to hourly) workers in the United States work under some form of "merit pay" plan. One of the major differences between merit pay and piecework is that in the former, pay adjustments are made not directly and immediately on the basis of production; instead, they are made on the basis of the boss's subjective evaluation of the employee's performance over a period of time (usually a year). The survey data that show significant percentages of employees unhappy with the relationship between their pay increases and their performance were collected almost entirely in organizations that use merit pay systems.

Part of the problem stems from the boss's evaluation of the employee's performance. It is not that employees disagree with the evaluations; in fact, our research shows that there is considerable agreement.[7] Instead, it is that the evaluations are biased upward. That's why so many employees agree with them! It is only slightly facetious to say that, in effect, merit increases determine the performance evaluations rather than the other way around. That is, to avoid unpleasantness in their performance-evaluation sessions, many managers tend to rate just about everyone highly (at least "satisfactory" or its equivalent). The tendency would be less pronounced if pay increases were not tied to the evaluations but, because the latter means money, the positive bias is strong indeed.

The problem of biased evaluations is magnified by the systems through which pay increases are supposed to be related to performance. A common approach is to use a "grid." Figure 4-1 shows an example of this grid.

Figure 4-1   Example of a performance-based salary grid.

The vertical axis of the grid defines the pay range of the job (from minimum to maximum). The line graphs represent employees at different levels of evaluated performance. The major objectives of the grid are to differentiate the increases of employees with different levels of performance while containing salary increase costs. These objectives are, in practice, somewhat contradictory. For example, newer employees are typically at the low end of the range *no matter what their performance*. Also, the salary increases of employees at the upper end of the range level off *no matter what their performance*. Both outcomes help contain costs, but greatly dilute the relationship between salary increases and performance. Technically, the organization *is* paying for performance with this system, but *controlling for position in range*. Unfortunately, employees don't perform the mental gymnastics required to allow them to feel that they have indeed been rewarded for their performance. An employee doesn't say, "It's okay that I received a smaller increase this year than last year, even though my performance was the same. After all, my pay is now higher in the range." It would take a saint to accept that reasoning—and a clairvoyant one because, in many companies, employees are told little about what's going on concerning ranges, grids, and so on.

The following further compounds the problem:

- **Budgets.**   In recent years, organizations' salary increase budgets have been approximately 4 percent. These budgets are especially important to control because they are not one-time costs: a salary increase becomes part of an employee's base salary and is therefore an expenditure as long as the employee stays with the company. But, managers with a 4 percent budget cannot make a lot of differentiation among employees without angering those who are not outstanding, but still satisfactory performers.

- **Change.**   Salary increase budgets change year-to-year depending on how much the organization believes it can afford to pay. The amount of increase for a given level of performance will therefore change with the budget, adding to the ambiguity and perceived arbitrariness of the relationship between an employee's performance and the size of her salary increase.

- **Inflation.**   We have said that if an increase does not exceed the rate of inflation, it is usually not viewed as an increase; if it is less than inflation, it can be felt as a decrease. If, then, inflation is 4 percent and managers with a 4-percent increase budget are asked to differentiate increases on the basis of performance, some—maybe half—of their employees will feel that their pay has been cut. Most of these employees are likely to be wholly satisfactory performers. Furthermore, companies almost never distinguish for employees the amount of the increase that is due to the rise in the cost of living, which makes the performance-pay relationship even more ambiguous. Market-based increases to meet the competition—again, rarely distinguished from merit increases—add to the problem.

We can now understand why it is so difficult for many employees to see a relationship between their pay and their performance. It comes down to this: most managers very much want to pay for performance, but to get their day-to-day management jobs done, they tend to be more concerned with minimizing employee discontent. The merit pay system, coupled with their own discomfort at delivering unpleasant news, makes it difficult to reward as they truly believe they should. Therefore, managers focus on figuring out the size of the increase for each employee that results in the fewest problems for them. They know, for example, who is likely to complain and who is likely to accept their word that, "This is really a tough year for the company, I don't have much money to spread around; I'm doing the best I can." They try to make sure that all—or almost all—of their employees receive as much of an increase as their budgets allow and then give some more to those who are likely to give them a particularly hard time. This minimizes differentiation among employees, with the exception of the "squeaky wheels" and, sometimes, those whose performance is truly and visibly inadequate.

Managers also seek ways around the system: for employees who are likely to leave the organization (and whose leaving would be a loss), or who might raise hell, or who are, indeed, truly outstanding performers, they might seek "exceptions" (a larger increase than the grid suggests), or in-grade promotions, or position re-evaluations to move the jobs to higher levels. It depends on what is possible and what will least frustrate other employees and those in a position of power.

The result is a half-baked version of pay for performance with which not many are satisfied, but one that normally doesn't have serious repercussions: people "live with it." Our statistical studies of organizations' merit pay systems show that *tenure*, not performance, is by far the highest correlate of employee pay within a job grade. That is, the net effect of the system, and the machinations that surround it, is not that much different from approaches that base pay exclusively on seniority. Only, it is less clear.

Strategies for Effective Compensation

We have been hard on individual pay-for-performance systems. It is difficult to argue with approaches that are designed to pay individuals for their performance—it's almost un-American to do so—but the fact is that they tend to have numerous and severe problems. For many companies, they become bureaucratic and administrative nightmares without doing much to further their basic goal: rewarding people for their performance.

Is there anything better? Yes.

The better alternative is not to junk pay for performance and simply pay all employees in a particular job grade the same or pay by seniority. Those should be avoided because, when implemented properly, pay for performance can indeed be very positive and powerful in that it does the following:

- Gives financial reward to employees for reasons of both equity (sharing in the organization's financial returns) and recognition.

- Gives direction to employees by aligning rewards with the organization's goals and objectives. Pay is probably the most salient communicator of organizational goals.

- Can provide a mechanism for adjusting compensation costs to the ability of the organization to pay.

Therefore, it should be clear that we are in no way opposed to rewards based on performance. The question is, *how*? We know that organizations—and segments of organizations—differ, so no one approach will be appropriate for all. Here are the basic principles we believe should guide the design of pay-for-performance plans and concrete illustrations of how these have been put into practice. The principles are as follows:

- Employee compensation should include both base pay and variable pay.

- Base pay should be competitive and should keep up with inflation.

- Variable pay is on top of base pay and should, for the large majority of employees, be based on the performance of *groups* rather than individuals.

- Variable pay should be distributed as a percentage of the employee's base salary.

- Individual performance should be rewarded by "honors."

Let's elaborate on these:

- **Variable pay versus merit salary increases.** The basic structure we recommend is one in which employees receive base salary
  or wages *plus* variable pay that is geared to performance. This is
  similar to piecework systems where employees receive base pay
  plus an amount per piece; the difference, as we shall see, resides
  in the way we recommend performance be measured (as a group
  rather than on an individual basis).

  Using a base-plus-variable-pay approach is different from merit
  pay. A merit pay increase becomes part of the salary—it is, in
  effect, an annuity cost for the organization. Variable compensation, on the other hand, is tied to the organization's ability to pay,
  such as to its profitability or to cost savings that have been
  achieved. This is an enormous advantage because it makes payroll
  costs much easier to control. It might not seem like a plus for
  employees because the extra compensation does not become part
  of their salaries. But employees' base pay will increase anyway to
  compensate for inflation, and most people are pleased to know
  that. *And the recognition and reward portion of their pay is clear*,
  which eliminates the ambiguity of the merit pay system where
  performance, cost-of-living, and market-based increases are
  confounded.

- **Group versus individual performance.** For the great majority
  of the workforce, we recommend that variable pay be based on
  group, rather than individual, performance. We have two reasons
  for this preference. First, performance of a group is usually easier
  to measure; it's more objective and credible than that of an individual. At the total company level, for example, contrast the relatively objective measurement of company profit with the highly
  subjective judgments about the contributions of individual senior
  executives to that profit. In a cost center, such as a manufacturing
  plant, contrast measuring the cost performance of a plant as a
  whole with measuring the efficiency of individual workers. We
  saw how individual production standards can generate a flood of
  grievances about their accuracy. If the goal is to distribute financial rewards among workers according to their individual performance, workers must be *compared* to each other. How is the
  performance of a maintenance person to be compared with a production worker? Not easily.

The second reason for preferring group measurement is that performance almost always depends not just on individual capabilities and effort but also on teamwork. The profound power of pay should be used to encourage, not discourage, teamwork. Individually based plans do little, at best, or nothing to stimulate cooperation; at worst, it can produce dysfunctional competition and conflict. The teamwork that group pay plans encourage has two positive effects: it boosts performance in and of itself, and it satisfies workers' camaraderie needs, which adds to their enthusiasm and performance.

How about the "shirkers," those who prefer not to work hard? Doesn't a group approach give them an out, a way to be rewarded for not much effort? Research shows exactly the opposite: under a group pay plan, the responsibility for dealing with workers who won't work is shouldered in part by the work group. Shirkers hurt group performance and, therefore, workers' pay, and a group norm develops that puts pressure on low producers to produce. This is almost invariably more effective than management dealing with the problem alone.

How about the truly outstanding performers? Isn't a group payment approach unfair to them? Our experience with employees working under these plans reveals few problems in this respect. The reason is that these outstanding performers are contributing significantly to the well-being of the entire group and receive a great deal of recognition from their co-workers. This contrasts starkly with the reactions of workers to "rate busters" working under piecework. In those cases, high performance is seen as detrimental to the group's interests. However, later we suggest that the informal recognition that high performers receive under group plans be supplemented with individual formal awards.

What are the group compensation plans that are available to organizations? Countless plans exist, but almost all can be grouped into three major categories: stock ownership, profit sharing, and gainsharing. Which one(s) to choose? Here are the criteria that should govern the selection of a plan. A plan is more effective to the extent that:

• It steers employee performance to the achievement of important organizational goals.

- It allows employees to see the impact of their performance and to see that impact in a timely way.

- The optimal achievement of the goals requires teamwork as well as individual effort.

- The performance measures are clear and credible.

- The financial return to employees is, in their eyes, substantial.

- The plan serves to satisfy employees' equity, achievement, and camaraderie needs.

- The plan enhances employees' identification with the organization.

Of all the plans, gainsharing meets the above goals to the greatest extent by far. But it, too, has gaps and so for most organizations a combination of the plans is preferable. The following are descriptions of the plans and the key research findings on their effects.

Employee Stock Ownership

The ownership by employees of stock takes three basic forms: employee stock ownership plans (ESOPs), pension assets invested in employer stock, and stock owned directly in the company through stock option and stock purchase plans. Combining the three forms of owning stock, it is estimated that about one-fifth of American workers hold stock in the company in which they work.

Employee stock ownership has strong proponents, some almost evangelical in their advocacy. Their arguments are based on both financial and motivational considerations. Stock ownership is touted as a good way for employees to increase their assets through participation in the growth of the American economy. This certainly was a credible theme in the late 1990s, but the recent severe decline of so much of the stock market has made that argument somewhat shaky, at least for the time being. On the motivational side, two claims are made. First, by creating a "capitalist working class," stock ownership increases the identification of workers with the free-enterprise system. Second, and of particular relevance to this book, is the argument that ownership of an employer's stock increases employees' identification with their companies and their motivation to perform.

What is the research evidence concerning the impact of stock ownership on employee attitudes, behavior, and on company performance?

Overall, the findings are modestly positive, the largest impact tending to be on employees' identification with the company. A smaller percentage of studies—but still most—show a positive effect on more specific employee attitudes, such as job satisfaction; on employee behavior, such as absenteeism; and on company performance, such as overall labor productivity. Regarding labor productivity, the average productivity improvement that appears to result from employee stock ownership is on the order of 2–6 percent. To our knowledge, there has been no instance (at least none published) where the effect on performance has been demonstrably negative. (The studies in which the results were not positive simply showed no significant impact one way or the other.)

Why is the impact on firm performance not greater, especially because stock ownership seems to increase employees' overall identification with the company? Part of the answer lies in the indirect relationship between how employees perform on the job and the performance of their company's stock. Numerous market forces affect stock price well beyond employees' control (and even a company's control). Even if these broad market forces did not exist, in most corporations there are few individual employees (or groups of employees) whose performance realistically can be said to have an impact on stock price. Workers can feel proud of their company's stock performance and feel good about the financial benefits to them—those are important—but what is almost entirely missing is the personal sense and pride of *direct impact and achievement*. Recall that one of our criteria for the selection of a variable pay plan is that it should allow employees to see the impact of their performance. Theorists in the field refer to this as "line of sight," which is the extent to which employees can see the impact of their work. Of all the variable group pay plans, stock ownership is the weakest on this criterion.

Employee identification with the company in relation to stock ownership needs some elaboration. Although systematic research is lacking on this, anecdotal and indirect evidence point to the company culture—especially employee participation in decision making—as affecting the impact of stock ownership on performance. Think about it: suppose a company has a broad-based stock ownership plan, but has a top-down management style (a "do as you're told" style). The problems of line of sight are then compounded because employees have no mechanism—other than sheer physical effort—to influence even their own performance, much less the firm's overall performance. For most employees, ownership is both a psychological and a financial matter. To obtain the full power of ownership, owning shares and "owning" psychologically the product of one's job (because of involvement in decisions about it) should reinforce, not negate, each other. The strength of gainsharing, which is discussed later in this chapter, comes in significant measure from this reinforcement.

With regard to financial and psychological ownership, consider the condition opposite to that we have described; namely, employees have much decision-making involvement, but no financial return that is a direct result of that involvement. The theory behind many participative approaches (such as "quality circles") seems to be that virtue—such as employee ideas that cut costs—is its own reward. Not quite. In the U.S., the history of these techniques suggests that, when successful, employees at some point begin to question why they are not sharing directly in the financial gains. This is more than employees seeing an opportunity for additional income. At least equal in importance is their sense of equity: the desire not to feel manipulated and exploited. Also, the impact of money on an employee's sense of achievement is lost when participation is not accompanied by financial return.

Another important issue regarding stock ownership is, of course, the impact on employees of a drop in stock value. Things are terrific when the stock appreciates but a decline can be not only disappointing but can threaten to severely decimate an employee's life's savings This can hap pen when the stock price drops simply due to economic or market conditions but, as we have seen, sadly, in recent years, can be the result of unethical or blatantly illegal financial manipulations by corporate executives, The risk inherent in stock ownership can therefore militate against this vehicle being selected as the primary—not to speak of the sole—means of variable compensation for a workforce.

Profit Sharing

About one-fifth of U.S. firms have some form of profit sharing, with the percentage among publicly held firms being close to two-fifths. The bulk of profit sharing is deferred, where the share is put into an employee retirement account.The plans are cash-only in one-fifth of the cases and, in one-tenth of the cases, employees can choose whether to defer or receive their share as cash. There is great variability in the profit-sharing formulas that are used—both in the amount distributed and in the threshold before distribution—and, in many firms, the formula is discretionary and can change each year.

As with employee stock ownership, profit sharing has its strong advocates. The argument is that it is not only a way of sharing with employees the financial fruits of their labors, but a mechanism to increase employees' understanding of the financial condition of their firms and their identification with their firms.

What does the research show about the effects of profit sharing on employee attitudes, behavior, and on firm performance? Surprisingly, there is little research evidence concerning employee attitudes and behavior. About the most that can be said reliably on the basis of the research is that employees generally like the plans, which should come as no surprise. The exceptions, of course, are the times when there is little or no profit to share, especially after years of significant profit sharing when it has become an "expected" part of one's earnings or retirement savings.

Although research is lacking on the impact of profit-sharing on attitudes such as identification with the firm, we would be surprised if they were much different from stock ownership. Profit sharing should promote a feeling that "we're all in this together," especially if there are not large discrepancies between the profit-sharing bonuses of top management and those of the rest of the workforce.

Quite a bit of work has been done on the effect of profit sharing on firm performance. The findings are similar to employee stock ownership (that is, the results range from positive to neutral, with the average improvement in labor productivity also in the 2–6 percent range). The proportion of studies with positive results is actually somewhat greater than is the case with stock ownership.

Profit sharing is similar to employee stock ownership in its relatively weak "line of sight" between employee performance and the end result. The flaw might be less severe than with stock ownership, because profitability is not as affected by uncontrollable events as is stock price. Nevertheless, the contribution that most employees and employee groups can make to overall firm profitability is indistinct, so there is little impact on one's personal sense of achievement. Some companies have sought to deal with this issue by instituting unit—such as divisional—profit-sharing plans. But, these units have also tended to be rather large entities, and it is doubtful that much improvement in line of sight was realized. In truly small organizations, such as small business units or independent businesses, the problem should be much less severe.

In both stock ownership and profit sharing, the lack of timeliness of the reward magnifies the line-of-sight problem. It is well established that a reward has more impact if it is given close in time to the behavior being rewarded. (It better reinforces the desired behavior.) This is a major problem in merit increase programs (where the employee's performance is typically appraised and the salary increase is given annually) and is also a problem in stock ownership and profit-sharing plans.

As with employee stock ownership, some evidence shows that profit sharing has a greater impact when it's part of a generally compatible culture, such as a high level of employee involvement in decision making.

Gainsharing

Although it's not as well known to the general public as stock ownership and profit sharing, research shows that gainsharing has the largest positive impact on employee attitudes and performance. As the name says, it is a method for sharing gains with employees (the gains that employees themselves, as a group, achieve for the organization). Although a number of gainsharing plans exist, the most common being the Scanlon Plan, the Rucker Plan, and Improshare, they share the following characteristics:

- They are used in relatively small organizations (most successfully when the number of employees is less than 500).

- The performance is an operational measure, such as productivity or costs, rather than a financial measure such as profitability; only employee-controllable performance is used.

- The organization establishes a historical base period of performance for a group.

- Performance improvement over the base creates a bonus pool, which is the savings that the improvement has generated. Typically, about one-half of the pool is paid to employees, usually as a percentage of their base pay, with all participating employees receiving the same percentage. If there has been no gain, there is no pool; the bonuses are usually paid on a monthly or quarterly basis—the idea being that they should be paid as closely as possible to the performance that is being rewarded.

- Almost all gainsharing plans include employees' heavy involvement in developing and implementing ideas for improving performance.

Although gainsharing was employed mostly in small manufacturing organizations, recently it has spread to service organizations, such as hotels, restaurants, insurance companies, hospitals, and banks. Estimates vary, but a good guess is that about 20 percent of American companies have gainsharing plans. In most cases, however, it is applied to just a minority of the workforce, such as those in a corporation's manufacturing facility. The popularity of this approach appears to have substantially increased over the last two decades.

A review of the research on gainsharing shows significant improvement in productivity in the large majority of organizations using the plan. The range of improvement, however, varies widely, it's as low as 5 percent and as high as 78 percent (the average being about 25 percent). Therefore, the results can be substantial. "The most important thing we know about gainsharing plans is that they work," says Edward Lawler, probably the most prominent organization psychologist studying compensation systems and their effects.[8]

Here is an example of how a simple gainsharing plan might work:

- The average monthly sales in a base period, usually the previous year or 18 months, are calculated; say this is $1 million.

- The average monthly wage costs over the same base period are calculated; say this is $200,000.

- The ratio of wage costs to sales in the base period is therefore 20 percent.

- If sales in the first month of the gainsharing period is $1.2 million, the application of the ratio produces wage costs of $240,000.

- If the actual wage costs are $210,000, there is a $30,000 savings, which is split 50/50 between the employees and the company.

This is a "simple" plan because it focuses on just one performance measure: the ratio of wage costs to sales. Other plans include a number of factors, such as quality and delivery performance, with each factor given a weight in the calculation of the "gain."

The reasons gainsharing usually works so well should be clear from our previous discussion. Of all the plans but individual piecework, it provides the clearest linkage between what employees do and the performance measure that determines the payment. It has advantages in this respect even in comparison to individual piecework. In the latter, the "standard" developed by an engineer is often disputed and is likely to be increased if exceeded by the worker (through greater effort or a change in work method). Therefore, doing more (especially by being smarter) is usually the path to a heavier workload, not greater earnings. In gainsharing, the "standard" is the past—workers know it can be met because it *has* been met, and rewards are distributed based on improvement over the past. The linkage is clear—do more to get more—and the system encourages, rather than discourages, improvement.

It is fallacious to think that gainsharing, despite its obvious advantages, can be introduced simply as a formula mechanically relating productivity improvement to compensation. Its organizational context is critical: by far, the most successful applications are paralleled by a highly participative and team-enhancing process because the primary way gains are realized is by employees working collaboratively and innovatively to improve performance. We made this same point about "ownership" in our discussions of employee stock ownership and profit sharing, but it is even more obvious and important here. Gainsharing ties the bonuses of a group of employees to their ability to improve performance—the performance that they control—over the last year. Because gainsharing focuses on a specific group, it would be self-defeating—even ludicrous—if the organization were not to encourage the group members to work together to generate and try out improvement ideas. The very structure of gainsharing calls for a process that achieves results greater than the sum of the efforts of individual employees. This is not nearly so much the case with employee stock ownership and profit sharing where, because of the broad compass of the measure (usually an entire company), the emphasis can still be on individuals' performances.

Given its proven effectiveness, why is gainsharing not more widespread? Among the most important of the conditions that make gainsharing difficult to implement are the following:

- When it is difficult to quantitatively measure the output of the organization, such as that of a research laboratory.

- When performance measures fluctuate widely because of factors beyond the employees' control, and the employees' impact can't be reliably assessed.

- When it is difficult to differentiate relatively autonomous, properly sized entities in an organization to which the plan can be applied.

- When little or no interdependence exists among the members of the group, or the group members are strongly disposed to working on an individual incentive basis.

- When the organization is not culturally ready for gainsharing (for example, when management fundamentally does not believe in the value of employee participation, or when there is great distrust and conflict between management and workers).

A few words about trust: although gainsharing can reinforce and strengthen trust, it should not be expected to turn a hostile environment into one of sweetness and light. To be successful, gainsharing *depends* on mutual trust and confidence. Especially important, obviously, is that workers trust that higher performance leads to better pay. Even though a performance formula—such as the ratio of labor costs to sales—looks simple, it can be subject to considerable dispute and will be disputed if fundamental trust is lacking. Therefore, when there is a history of conflict and distrust, it is important to make significant progress on those issues before introducing gainsharing.

Employees must also feel they won't be punished for higher performance. How can a reward program be punishing? Ask workers what "higher productivity" means to them, and you often discover that it means "fewer workers needed." Rate busters, in fact, are often called "job killers." Workers won't voluntarily participate in the arrangements for their own funerals, so guarantees need to be given to them that any gains from gainsharing won't result in job losses for them. The most successful gainsharing programs do that.

Even when all the conditions we have described have been met, gainsharing still has two major gaps. For one, because it lacks a total organization focus, it does little to enhance organization-wide identification or increase employees' understanding of the broad financial condition of a business. Lawler suggests that "the ideal combination for many large corporations would seem to be corporate-wide profit sharing and stock ownership plans, with gainsharing plans in major operating plants or units."[9] In other words, the three types of variable group pay plans we have discussed should be viewed as having somewhat different objectives and are often best used in combination.

The second gap is the lack of individual financial reward. We believe that in most situations—covering the great majority of workers—this should be handled not by differentiating bonuses by individual perform-ance, but by giving special awards to group members who make particu-larly outstanding contributions. Although these awards should have a monetary value, their basic function is to *honor* individuals. Chapter 9, "Feedback, Recognition, and Reward," discusses such outstanding contri-bution awards. Suffice it to say for now that they should be truly special—given infrequently, given publicly, and signify appreciation from both management and peers.

CHAPTER 5

Respect

"The best index to a person's character is (a) how he treats people who can't do him any good, and (b) how he treats people who can't fight back."

—Abigail Van Buren, Advice Columnist

"The real judges of your character aren't your neighbors, your relatives, or even the people you play bridge with. The folks who really know you are waiters, waitresses, and clerks."

—Katherine Piper, Author

"Nearly all men can stand adversity, but if you want to test a man's character, give him power."

—Abraham Lincoln

It's not particularly noteworthy that people in organizations are "respectful" of their bosses and that the higher in the hierarchy a person is, the more deference he receives. Whether or not appreciation is genuinely felt by their subordinates, bosses receive lots of thank-yous, and they rarely receive any verbal abuse or even sharp disagreement. We put this type of respect in quotes because this is not the kind of respect we address in this chapter.

The kind of respect that we have in mind—and that has such profound implications for worker morale—does not come from deference to power or the expectation of reward, but from a sense of the intrinsic worth of human beings—*all* human beings. We define the equity need as the desire to be treated justly in relation to the basic conditions of employment. These conditions are expected simply by virtue of being employed and derive from generally accepted ethical and community standards. The two major financial components of equity are job security and pay. The major non-financial component is respect.

A few "write-ins" from our surveys vividly illustrate what we mean by respectful and disrespectful treatment of workers.

First, here are some comments from workers who obviously struggle with a sense of disrespect:

> *My boss acts like a prison guard...and we're the chain gang! The way he barks orders feels like a threat. And he expects obedience. I've never felt this lack of basic human respect before.*

> *The most frustrating aspect of this company is the low degree of respect our management portrays toward employees here. I believe that all employees on my team are responsible adults who constantly make decisions based on what is needed for the client. Our team leader...has no respect for us. She is always passing nasty, sarcastic comments on to me and everyone in my team. She herself doesn't have respect for our so-called corporate values.*

> *Working with...leaders who...are mean spirited and tear individuals down instead of building them up. Senior leaders do not get after them for their behavior.*

> *The same commitment and respect given to customers is not given to employees who are the building blocks of the company.*

> *The total lack of respect and general condescending attitude of our management and supervisors' attitudes, shows as a daily and constant reminder of incompetence and the lack of direction in which this establishment is headed. What is preached is blatantly not practiced, there is discrimination and favoritism, so many undesirable traits which our leaders all possess. I challenge top management to do a thorough clean up, or can they!*

> *[The manager] is the most unprofessional "manager" I have ever met. He intimidates and humiliates many of my peers. He seems*

to lack respect for anyone. He is extremely controlling and hot headed. I feel this could be a great place to work if he would not treat people so poorly.

The hourly workers here are like peons. If you're not one of the suits, you're nothing, a moron. It's from the union that we get self-respect.

We're always being watched like children who can't be trusted. The supervisor sneaks around to make sure we are not playing games on the computer or making personal phone calls or talking to each other. It's amazing we don't have to ask her for permission to go to the bathroom. That's probably next.

Now, here are some write-ins from workers who are more positive on this point:

The people I work with are the best thing about this company. From my senior director and immediate supervisor and all of my fellow reps, I feel everyone respects each other, and work very hard for one another.

My leader shows integrity and supports me when it may not be the popular thing to do. I have a lot of respect for her, and value her input.

It is also wonderful to know that my leader treats me individually and considers whatever challenges I face with respect and consideration.

My supervisor…is honest and forthright and has had to make and deliver difficult decisions, but has done so with sensitivity and respect.

My immediate supervisor has terrific people skills and for that he is well respected and highly regarded as a role model. His open door policy is the best I have experienced at work.

I enjoy working here because of what my leader has created. He…understands people's needs and pays attention to every employee request. He is well respected for his honesty, dedication, and people skills that is a God-given talent. He is caring about employees and spends the time to solve employee issues. Every employee that reports to him enjoys working for him and the job. He is the best.

Treating people with respect and dignity and providing the generous severance packages during the reduction in force was extremely positive. During 9/11/01 and beyond, every level of the company demonstrated great care for our employees and customers which is a positive reflection on the people that make up the leadership.

The best thing about working for [company] is the environment that surrounds you. You have the right to give ideas and improve work procedures that concern the front lines with our clients. Our leaders are open to new ideas and feedback at all times, and are always there when you need them. You receive the respect expected in a work environment and even more.

This company has made a deliberate attempt to treat all employees as human beings. Their policies are wonderful like being able to take time off when there's an emergency at home without being questioned to death. They trust the workers and the workers want to give their all for the company.

The Heart of Respect

Equality is at the heart of respect—the treatment of each individual as important and unique without regard to any other characteristics, such as gender, race, income, or even perceived performance or contribution to the organization. Does equality mean that it is inherently disrespectful for some people to earn more than others, or for some to have more power than others? That is the view only in extreme forms of egalitarian ideology, such as communism. The rest of us *expect* differentiation in income according to responsibilities and would find an organization with no differentiation in power as ludicrous and dysfunctional.

The core issue is how people at legitimately higher income or power levels *treat* those at lower levels (that is, how they use their power).

To take a simple-minded example, do passengers on a plane see it as illegitimate for a pilot and crew to be in command and give orders? Of course not. But, in manner and attitude, how are passengers treated by the crew? Do they feel themselves treated as welcome guests of the airline, or rudely, as necessary evils, or, perhaps most commonly, indifferently, as "seats?"

How customers are treated has a large impact on their willingness to continue doing business with a company; the impact is no smaller on employees and their willingness to perform at high levels. Here, we are dealing with a fundamental human need that, although it might sound trivial and corny—such as wanting to work for a boss with a friendly manner—has enormous consequences for human behavior and the effectiveness of organizations.

Lest we be misunderstood, we reiterate here that respectful treatment is terribly important to people, but it is not a substitute for money. Both needs are *independently* important. In fact, respectful treatment and other aspects of good "human relations" are viewed as a sham if employees feel that they are at the same time being economically exploited. "Human relations" should not be treated as "public relations" in the sense of a friendly facade masking basic inequities.

What do our data show with regard to respectful treatment of employees? The question we generally use to measure respect is, "Rate the extent to which management treats you with respect and dignity, that is, as a responsible adult."

On the whole, the answers to this question are not negative. On average, 67 percent respond positively, but the range is large: the most positive organization has 91 percent of workers responding favorably while the lowest has only 32 percent of workers answering this way.

Three broad levels of respectful treatment in organizations can be distinguished: positive, indifferent, and humiliating. Let's begin at the negative end of the scale.

Humiliating Treatment

According to our survey results, humiliation is a relatively rare condition, at least in most organizations and at least at the present time. But when it does occur—and it can occur in the treatment an employee gets from a particular boss in an otherwise respectful organization—it devastatingly impacts people and their performance.

Humiliation means to be treated blatantly as a lesser being: as incompetent, untrustworthy, or as a member of what is, in effect, a servant class. It comes in two forms: interpersonal, such as an employee's work being ridiculed by his immediate boss; and structural, such as formal organization controls that allow workers absolutely no decision-making authority in the performance of their jobs. Also on the structural side are practices that sharply differentiate status in a way that is particularly demeaning to those at lower levels (for example, separate entrances for hourly workers, separate and thoroughly unappetizing eating facilities, and separate parking areas that are long distances from the plant).

The major point of these managerial behaviors and status distinctions is to clearly delineate higher from lower orders of humanity in the workplace. They have no other goal because they have little to do with actual function—that is, with getting the job done. In more traditional societies, they are a way of saying (both on and off the job), "I was born right and you weren't." In America, their meaning usually is, "I've achieved and you haven't."

The civil rights, women's rights, and gay rights movements demonstrate the degree to which American society can be "traditional": being born with the "wrong" race, sex, ethnicity, or sexual orientation causes people to be classified as "less than" those in the more favored strata of American society. These social movements are all about equity, certainly economic equity, but also psychological equity in terms of respectful treatment. We don't need to repeat the innumerable humiliations that various disfavored groups have been subjected to. Suffice it to say that they have not been just petty annoyances and frustrations, but often sources of rage and powerful drivers for change.

In organizations, the consequences of humiliation show up most dramatically in labor conflict. The humiliation felt by workers has been significantly present in *all* the serious industrial disputes we have studied. These disputes have also been about economic issues—we make no claim that economic demands are less important than, or somehow a displacement for, psychological deprivation. But, we have not seen genuine *rage* by large numbers of workers unless they have also felt seriously demeaned by management in their daily jobs. Labor and management can disagree about money but, despite their angry public rhetoric, can still respect each other and work toward a settlement in a business-like way. That's collective bargaining. But, how does one bargain about assaults on workers' dignity?

The incidence of the more severe forms of humiliation—both interpersonal and structural—has almost certainly lessened over the years in the American workplace. There are numerous reasons for the change, including the reduction in manufacturing employment as a proportion of the U.S. workforce (by and large, factory workers are treated less respectfully than office workers), the influence of modern management theories being taught in U.S. business schools, the demonstrated effectiveness of "softer" management styles as antidotes to unionization, and the influence that Japanese industry has had on American management practices. The last reason has been especially profound because Japanese companies have been remarkably successful in competition with American businesses, so what they have espoused cannot easily be relegated to "egghead" or "soft-headed" theory.

The Japanese approach to workforce management emphasizes employee participation in decision-making, teamwork, the minimization of status distinctions within a firm, and job security. Although few U.S. companies have embraced the Japanese philosophy fully (especially the importance of job security), its influence has nevertheless been significant.

Indifferent Treatment

More common than blatant humiliation is simple indifference. Indifference covers a wide range of management practices. Sometimes, it appears to overlap with outright disrespect, but is often better termed benign neglect. As an example of the former, consider American Airlines, which is a company with a long history of contentious labor relations. In 1993, P.T. Kilborn wrote in *The New York Times* about the causes of strikes at the airline:

> *It is not so much the pay or benefits or sometimes grinding four-and five-city, one-day trips or the interminable, unpaid delays between some flights. It is the little things that striking flight attendants at American Airlines say grate on them and amount to a lack of respect. "They treat us like we're disposable, a number," said Helen Neuhoff, a 33-year-old flight attendant. Another attendant said, "I'd rather be on the planes. But I've got to stand up for what I believe. My self-respect is more important than my job." Nor did the issue go away. Four years later, when troubles at American Airlines brewed again, the theme remained the same. A disgruntled pilot complained, "As long as you treat your employees as merely 'unit costs,' like the Styrofoam coffee cups we throw out after every flight, morale will remain at rock bottom."[1]*

The felt indifference of the company to its workers was aggravated over the years by the in-your-face style of the then-chairman, Robert Crandall. He was seen as being only interested in the bottom line and as being extraordinarily aggressive in his methods—with competitors, the community, the industry's regulators, and with the workers and their unions. Crandall was labeled with nicknames such as "Darth Vader" by his employees who feared his wrath.[2] In other words, he was an extremely tough and outspoken businessman who did not suffer fools (as he saw them) gladly or silently. However, employees believed him to be smart and, although insensitive to employees and their needs (as they defined them), dedicated 100 percent to the airline and its success. But, his adversarial and extremely brusque style greatly magnified otherwise manageable problems into frequent and serious labor conflicts.[3]

Crandall's style puts him at one end of the indifference continuum. Most managements that are seen as indifferent to workers don't experience the labor conflict that he suffered. Here are some typical comments from that other environment, the one we term benign neglect:

> *Here, you're pretty much a number. They don't care whether you stay or leave. I stay because the pay is pretty good and I like the people I work with. And I think most companies are pretty much the same.*

> *What can I say, it's a job. Management doesn't bother you too much—just do your work and follow the rules and they pretty much leave you alone. You will hardly ever see them. Most important for me, it's a very convenient location.*

> *I've seen better and worse. The wages are OK and the medical benefit is good. Medical insurance is very important to me because of my son's medical problems. On the other hand, I don't get much feeling here that your work is really valued, I almost never hear from my boss—just see him from a distance except when he has to appraise me.*

> *Employee comments, suggestions, and concerns get ignored. Management lets me know that I am just a number and the company does not really care about my ideas.*

> *Management does not seem to care about you or your ideas. Their attitude is you are replaceable.*

*I don't feel management cares what or how the lower-level
employees think or feel about their jobs. Some employees have
more knowledge and know-how than management gives them
credit for. They should start listening instead of always telling. If
you don't have a college education it doesn't mean you are stupid.*

*They're businessmen—they're not mean, but when it comes down
to it, all they care about is profits.*

*I have a negative feeling about the lack of leader presence. He
does not make his presence known to staff and if in the work area,
he is on a cell phone. It would be nice if the leader of the department could take a few moments to extend common courtesies, i.e.,
hello, good morning.*

*My supervisor arrives at work several hours after I start, and
never ever comes over to say hello or even let you know that she
has arrived. Some days, you never even see her, even though you
hear her.*

Why do we say that an indifferent management, even one that's relatively
benign, is inherently disrespectful? It is disrespectful in its implication
that workers are not worthy of management's time and attention; therefore,
workers feel insignificant. Indifference is a sin of omission—involving
what management does *not* do—rather than a sin of commission, such
as humiliation. Indifferent managers are not cruel or abusive, they are
simply unconcerned with workers other than as replaceable economic
entities. It is the essence of the previously described "transactional"
worker-management relationship, epitomized by the view that, "We paid
you, now we're even."

We defined respect as the treatment of workers as important and
unique. Indifference conveys the message to people that they don't matter,
at least not much. Being made to feel insignificant by being ignored is
more difficult to deal with than being humiliated. Is the worker expected
to shout, "Pay attention to me!"? In fact, other than in opinion surveys and
among themselves, workers are unlikely to voice their need for attention.
The desire for attention might be a profound human need, but in the business environment, it is not thought of as acceptable to come out and say it.

Unless aggravated by the behavior of someone such as Robert
Crandall at American Airlines, the workers' response to indifference is
less anger than disappointment and withdrawal. It is usually accompanied

by a sort of free-floating anxiety because workers get little feedback from management on their performance and often assume the worst. Although they might receive annual performance reviews, the reviews are usually formalities and not too informative. On a daily basis, they hear about their performance mostly when management is unhappy with it:

> *I feel like the most challenging aspect of the job for me is always having to pat myself on the back for the things that I do over and above for the client. You always hear the things you do wrong and the consequences for those, but people tend to grow when they are praised. I feel like my work ethic alone should speak for itself.*

A situation largely devoid of positive feedback gives rise to a feeling that management doesn't care whether an employee stays or leaves. In fact, management will probably fire the employee at the first sign of a business downturn or if he can be replaced with someone less expensive or who is judged to be a better performer or who is otherwise more favored (such as being a friend of a manager). Therefore, job insecurity can be pervasive in an indifferent environment:

> *It seems like we are easily replaced if we make a mistake or two.*

> *We are all tired of hearing about outsourcing. At every meeting, my team leader threatens us that we are going to be replaced because outsourcing would be cheaper for the company.*

> *They seem to make some of the metrics unattainable and harder to meet. It really doesn't motivate me into coming to work or making it a happy place to be when you feel you are being weeded out because there is always someone to replace you, or at least that is what they tell you if you're not happy.*

> *I see people around me being let go without good reasons, which makes me feel like we are not worth much to the company and are easily replaceable.*

> *I feel as though I am not truly valued by the company. That at any given moment, I could be replaced and no one [in management] would care.*

Of course, the reality is that rarely is any one person indispensable. But, that's irrelevant to the point we make. Feeling indispensable to an organization is usually an immature wish. But, a worker wants to believe that she *counts*, that she is not invisible, and this is not a childish wish at all. It is an important need throughout life. When workers have that feeling, it pays off in incalculable ways for the organization.

Indifferent managements are usually exclusively focused on the bottom line; for them, it's all business, and usually short-term business results at that. Because of this, one group of employees does receive much favorable attention: those who, at any point in time, are clearly the top producers. This small fraction of a workforce—perhaps 10 percent—often receives lavish praise and rewards. But, we don't categorize that type of attention as respectful treatment because what those employees receive is strictly a function of their performance, and it can quickly evaporate.

Although they overlap to some extent, it is important to distinguish between respect and recognition for performance. The key difference is that respect is unconditional; it does not derive from what the employee *does* but what he *is*—a human being. Recognition, on the other hand, is given to workers who have earned it by virtue of their contribution to the organization. Both are important, and Chapter 9, "Feedback, Recognition, and Reward," explores recognition.

Is unconditional respect—is unconditional anything—realistic in an organization? It sounds more like advice for a sound parent-child relationship (the admonition for unconditional love) than one between management and workers.

Whether it's financial or non-financial, the point of basic equity is that *everyone* is entitled to it. Not everyone is entitled to the same degree and kind of recognition. The distinction is seen most clearly in the way recognition and respect might conflict with each other. For example, not everyone can be promoted, and not everyone will be a boss. Promotion is an important form of recognition for most people, and no organization can function without bosses. Is not being promoted to a managerial position disrespectful? Only when it serves not just to get the right person in the right job, but in addition comes to signify, by the way the promotion is handled, the essential inferiority of those who didn't get the promotion. In other words, although it is rarely possible to promote someone without disappointing others, it is possible to do so without demeaning others. Demeaning others does not have to be consciously humiliating; it can simply be the result of indifference to the needs of those others (for example, to understand why they were not selected for the promotion, and what they might do to increase their chances for future promotions).

In a similar vein, we know that people don't want to be laid off, of course. But, as Chapter 3, "Job Security," showed, there are respectful, indifferent, and downright disrespectful ways to handle layoffs.

The Specifics of Respectful Treatment

Having discussed humiliation and indifference, let's now be more systematic and specific about just what respectful treatment is. We define respect as the treatment of people as unique and important. An important sign that a worker feels treated respectfully is her belief, simply, that *management is pleased that she's there.* She is not just being tolerated (as in a "necessary cost"), but she is made to feel welcome and genuinely included. In that sense, it is the opposite not just of being humiliated, but also of being ignored. *Feeling welcome is a tremendous morale booster for every person.* We know that from our lives outside of work, and it is no less true at work.

What causes a worker to feel welcome, or not welcome, in an organization? Let's begin with what is one of the first introductions many new workers get to an organization: the employee handbook. Most handbooks are a lengthy recitation of rules, regulations, and warnings. The inherent message, then, is that employees are necessary evils: true, the company has to have somebody to do the work, but workers are troublesome and must be controlled through monitoring and discipline.

The focus on rules and their enforcement is the essence of the bureaucratic mentality that is so aggravating to those who deal with it. As customers, we have all encountered service personnel who seem set not on helping us, but, rather, enforcing a company policy that blocks or makes it difficult to resolve a complaint. In these interchanges, we're frequently made to feel that we are a source of problems for the company instead of the source of its livelihood. The story comes to mind of the librarian so intent on having books returned that, when she finally gets them all, she locks the doors to the library so that no one will ever be able to take out a book again! No customers, no problems.

The bureaucrat might be defined as one so obsessed with his organization's rules that he forgets its purpose.

Now, consider this one-page employee handbook for Nordstrom, which is the hugely successful Seattle-based retailer:

WELCOME TO NORDSTROM

We're glad to have you with our company.

Our number-one goal is to provide outstanding customer service.

Set both your personal and professional goals high.
We have great confidence in your ability to achieve them.

Nordstrom Rules:
Rule #1: Use your good judgment in all situations.
There will be no additional rules.

Please feel free to ask your department manager, store manager,
or division general manager any question at any time.

This one-page handbook speaks volumes about the company. It highlights Nordstrom's focus on customer satisfaction, its deliberately non-bureaucratic culture, and the trust it places in the capabilities and character of its employees. The statement is the epitome, in words, of a welcoming and respectful organization.[4]

Of course, words must be translated into deeds. The following is a categorization of the specific deeds that cause employees to feel welcome and respected by their organizations. Much of it is neither surprising nor complicated; with some exceptions, it comes down to matters of common courtesy and decency that are familiar to us all. As we previously mentioned, it is not particularly noteworthy to see someone showing courtesy and decency to someone in a position of power. *The major criterion here, therefore, is whether people of less power and importance are treated similarly.*

Physical Working Conditions

We begin with the basics: physical working conditions:

> *If the washroom isn't good enough for the people in charge [of the corporation], then it's not good enough for the people in the store.*

> —From a speech by Marcus Sieff, former chairman of Marks & Spencer, describing why the washroom is his first stop whenever he visits a Marks & Spencer store[5]

It is impossible to feel welcome in an organization whose work environment is unnecessarily dirty, congested, poorly lit, poorly ventilated, or ugly. Not taking care of oneself physically—in dress, cleanliness, and so on—is usually a sign of self-disrespect. Not taking care of the environment in which employees work is a sign of disrespect for them. Workers don't expect lush surroundings; they would consider that a waste of money. However, they do expect an environment that, as the saying goes, is "fit for a human being."

Here are some comments from our surveys:

Physical office conditions are cramped and shabby compared to most companies. Getting away with least possible expense on employees in this area is clearly the priority. The company generally does a good job in many ways but working conditions is not one of them.

Deteriorating working conditions reflect how little the "leaders of the company" value us. We walk past rows of vacant full-sized cubicles on our way to the shoeboxes we share for 8 to 10 hours a day. And remember casual Fridays? The morale-boosting tool which didn't cost a red penny? Gone. I guess that's progress.

The physical working conditions are horrible. We have shared cubes and it is very difficult to get daily work done. No one has any room to spread out their paperwork. I'm very disappointed that we were not asked for any input. Everyone now knows exactly what grade you are by what kind of desk you have.

The restrooms are horrible. It's an insult to us.

One of the great things about this factory is the working conditions. You could eat your lunch off the floor! John [the plant manager] insists that we keep our work areas orderly and clean and that the clean-up crew doesn't slack off. What a difference from [company] where I used to work. It was dirty, greasy, messy, no air conditioning. They treated us like pigs. And because of it, tools and materials were always getting lost.

Good physical working conditions not only make getting the work done easier; it boosts worker morale and productivity because of the respect for workers that it conveys.

Status Distinctions

The discussion of physical working conditions brings us to consider status distinctions within organizations. A reader unfamiliar with organizations can be certain that few senior managers have filthy rest rooms or offices. Even when these conditions for the bulk of workers are decent, they are likely to be significantly better for those in senior management. When the food in the employees' cafeteria is quite acceptable, there is likely to be an executive dining room with superb food and probably waiter service. The list goes on.

Here is the question: if conditions for the masses of workers are decent, isn't it acceptable—indeed, appropriate—for those of higher rank to be treated still better, to have privileges not accorded to ordinary workers? After all, in addition to pay and power, isn't that what "rank" means?

Yes, that is what higher rank normally means—but no, these distinctions are mostly unwise.

It's not that employees who are generally well treated complain much about status distinctions. These differences are criticized in focus groups primarily when employees feel truly badly treated (not just comparatively so) or when senior management is viewed as incompetent (so why the perks for them?). Otherwise, employees tend to see the status distinctions as normal—the way things are.

This book is not interested "normality." In the last chapter, you saw that it is normal for most workers to believe that management has little loyalty to them, so their jobs can be cut with barely a second thought in the service of short-term profits. But, we also saw that certain organizations stand out as exceptions to the rule: they have a genuine commitment to their employees' well being, including job security, and that builds a foundation for high levels of employee commitment and outstanding performance over the long term.

Similarly, numerous companies deliberately and successfully sought to remove needless boundaries and distinctions among the levels of an organization. The operative word is "needless." Almost everyone concurs that an organization needs differential power, and compensation should be correlated with responsibility. But, what is the function of distinctions based purely on status? *Their major function is to feed the vanity of those at higher echelons.*

Don't get us wrong: nearly everyone, ourselves included, gets a kick out of being treated royally. It feels good. The issue, however, is whether it is good *for the organization* that only certain individuals and strata receive that treatment.

Status symbols are decidedly not good for organizations because, at the most obvious level, they can act to physically limit interaction among the organization's members. Executive floors, separate eating facilities, separate entrances, and so on isolate higher from lower echelons and severely reduce the exchange of information and ideas among employees.

Status symbols also inhibit interaction by reinforcing differentiations in importance and authority. In organizations, the problem with "respect for authority" is that there is generally too much, not too little, of it: most people feel a lot of inhibition about communicating candidly with those of greater power. The free exchange of information and views is critical for performance, and organizations should encourage this exchange by making people less, not more, deferential to power in the way decisions are arrived at. Eliminating or minimizing overt symbols of power helps greatly in achieving this because it makes power and position less "awesome."

For the sake of open communication and to demonstrate an egalitarian philosophy, an increasing number of companies have removed many of the status symbols. For example, author Shari Caudron writes that "…the new Alcoa Inc. corporate headquarters in Pittsburgh was designed so that workspaces, all of which share the same dimensions, are nonhierarchical." As Agus Rusli, architect for the project explains, "Cloistered spaces for the privileged few are replaced by open, flexible arrangements of workstations."[6]

A good rule to determine the distinctions among strata that should be eliminated is this: *consider eliminating all distinctions that serve no clear business purpose.* A business purpose refers to what is needed for effective on-the-job performance. What is the business purpose served by separate dining rooms, parking spaces, rest rooms, and entrances, or differentiations by colors of badges, uniforms, hard hats, type of coffee service, and quality of office decoration? Most often, none!

While he was on the Board of General Motors, Ross Perot observed, "In Pontiac [Michigan], GM executive parking garages are heated, while the poor guys who work in the plant freeze their tails off walking to work in the snow. It costs $140,000 a year to heat one parking garage. I'd shut that thing down. It has nothing to do with cars."[7]

Should executives have private offices? That sounds like a heretical question, but a number of organizations have entirely eliminated private offices. Meeting rooms are set aside for the times when privacy is needed for whoever needs it.

In the 1970s, one of the authors had an appointment with the CEO of Tektronix, which is located in Beaverton, Oregon, to discuss their state-of-the-art personnel practices.

At the time, the firm employed 20,000 people and was noted world-wide for the development and manufacturing of test, measurement, and monitoring technology. Today, Tektronix is said to be the pivotal influence in the development of Oregon's Silicon Forest (home of Intel and hundreds of other high-tech firms).

He entered the building and asked to be directed to the CEO's office. Eventually, he found himself sitting next to the desk of a young man finishing some paperwork. After a few minutes, he inquired where the CEO's office was located and when he would be available. The young man said he was the CEO and he would be free in a few moments.

Marveling at this arrangement, the author asked what he did when he required complete privacy. He pointed to a small, fully enclosed, but glass-windowed office in the corner. He said that everyone had access to that office when they needed it.

New York City's Mayor Michael Bloomberg had an open-office arrangement at the company he founded and led, Bloomberg LP, and has brought this idea to City Hall. Top officials of his administration, including the mayor, work in cubicles within a giant, open bullpen. Deputy Mayor Patty Harris says that the style extends to a first-floor conference room that is visible through glass doors from the City Hall rotunda. "The emphasis," Ms. Harris said, "is on keeping things open and transparent."

Compensation Status Is a Fundamental Distinction

One of the most fundamental status distinctions in industry is that between hourly and salaried workers; the former are paid for the number of hours worked while the latter's compensation is based on a longer time period, be it a week, a month, or a year. In practical terms, it comes down to this: hourly workers lose pay if they are absent from, or late to, work, and they are required to be compensated for overtime work; typically, salaried workers receive the same amount each pay day, regardless of the number of hours worked during the period.[8]

The distinction between the two categories of workers is based on the different kinds of work performed. Hourly people typically perform physical tasks with physical outputs, such as assembling widgets or processing papers. When they are absent or late to work, things don't get produced and an organization is not obligated to pay for work not done. On the other hand, the jobs of salaried employees more typically involve complex mental activities, such as managing, administering, and planning—in a phrase, using judgment. These non-manual activities are much less bound by time, so their effective performance is only roughly correlated with hours spent at work. For example, being an hour late to work rarely means an hour's less output from a salaried employee and, as managerial and professional people, they are not expected to "turn off the job" immediately upon leaving work or to be paid for the time they spend on evenings or weekends thinking about and actually doing work.

In workers' minds, however, this is what the distinction *really* comes down to: there are two classes (almost castes) of workers: those who are "part of the company" and can be trusted, and those who come to work simply for the wages to be made and have no particular loyalty to the company. In many unionized companies, in fact, hourly workers are considered almost as employees of the union, which is similar to the way temporary workers are considered as employees of their agency rather than the company.

Another way of putting the distinction is that salaried employees are seen to be "professionals," and that means more than having an advanced education. A professional cares about the quality of her work and the organization for which she does it. Close supervision of her work is not needed because, well, she's a "professional." The others—the "workers" or "hands"—are simply there to earn a living and, with a few exceptions, are believed to perform well only when carefully monitored.

Time clocks are usually used to monitor the time that hourly employees spend at work; they are rarely used for professionals, and time clocks are greatly resented by them when required. The president of the New York union of professional employees, the Public Employees Federation, put it this way in response to a contract proposal by the state:

> *The state wants to remove our contract's prohibition against punching a time clock, to allow the use of ID "swipe cards" for time keeping.*
>
> *We will not let the state erode our professionalism and attack our dignity by using ID swipe cards as a means to track our time and location at the worksite.*
>
> *The governor and his staff don't punch time clocks. And doctors, lawyers, computer programmers, engineers, and other professionals in the private sector do not punch time clocks. To ask us to do so is insulting and demeaning....*[9]

Isn't it "insulting and demeaning" for hourly workers to use time clocks? Interestingly, although hourly workers sometimes complain about the way time recording is administered (especially the often draconian punishments for falsifying time records), they rarely express resentment at having to use time clocks. More basically, hourly workers almost never complain about the system that differentiates employees into hourly and salaried. As with the status distinctions previously discussed, these systems are so deeply engrained in organizations and in the psyches of the workforce that they are almost like laws of nature.

As we previously mentioned, for many workers, frequent layoffs represent another "law of nature," except in those organizations that do everything possible to avoid layoffs and do so only as a last resort. Many of those organizations have abolished, or never have had, a distinction between hourly and salaried employees.

An all-salaried workforce strongly bolsters management's efforts to create a respectful work environment. It is a way of saying that the organization hires and compensates workers at *all* levels for the use of their minds, not just their hands. It is a way to express trust in their integrity and commitment. For example, an all-salaried workforce results, in effect, in a "no-fault" approach to absenteeism. The motivation to come to work every day is left in the hands of the employees. We don't know of systematic research on the matter, but the anecdotal evidence is that companies changing to an all-salaried approach initially experience an increase in absenteeism that then declines to levels at or below industry averages. Of course, those few employees who take unfair advantage of the system—and it becomes quickly obvious who those employees are—need to be warned and, if they don't change, dismissed. Those are the 5 percent—at *all* levels of the workforce, not just hourly employees—for whom the assumption of trust is not warranted.

Job Autonomy

The discussion of trust brings us to the matter of job autonomy for workers. The issue is covered in detail later when we show that giving trained workers latitude in the way they do their jobs has a major positive impact on their performance. This is because workers usually best know how to do their jobs most efficiently and because, whether their ideas are objectively good or not, they are motivated to make ideas work that are *theirs*.

Providing job autonomy to workers obviously has profound implications for the respect in which they believe they are held by management. An organization mandating every step to be taken by trained and experienced workers in the performance of a job, and then closely supervising them to make sure that the steps are followed exactly, is treating workers as untrustworthy or incompetent.

The following comments illustrate this point:

> *My manager is a nitpicker. He doesn't seem to make sound business decisions. He tends to challenge when unnecessary and challenge less relevant things. He has yet to think/act strategically. He doesn't respect us, isn't a leader, and he isn't respected.*

> *Currently, the biggest challenge I am facing is working for a leader that micromanages to a point where we all have a tough time doing our jobs to the best of our abilities.*

> *I feel excessive micromanagement by our leadership group. It is one thing to monitor day-to-day activity but yet another when someone has to sit with you and watch over your shoulder, audit your work, and listen in to phone calls that you are making to advisors and clients.*

> *The most frustrating aspect here is the low degree of respect or sense of competency our management portrays toward employees. I believe that all employees on my team are responsible adults who constantly make decisions based on what is needed for the client, but they are not treated that way.*

> *The bureaucracy is stifling. Upward feedback can get you fired. People aren't treated with respect. They are treated like children.*

The view that people at work can't be trusted to carry out their jobs without close supervision is one of the hallmarks of bureaucracy. As we previously said, a primary focus of bureaucracies is rules, especially what employees at all levels are not permitted to do or can do only if others approve. These rules affect a wide range of positions: from the plant manager who, even though he might be leading an organization that annually produces millions of dollars' worth of goods, can't purchase anything on his own that costs over $10,000 to the office worker who has to fill out a 15-line form and get it approved to buy postage stamps.

The rules, especially for employees at the factory and shop-floor levels, extend beyond the performance of the work itself to issues of "behavior" or "conduct." We refer to edicts about dress, tardiness and absenteeism, length of rest breaks, personal use of company equipment, freedom to leave work stations, conversing with co-workers, and, as one rulebook we saw put it, "loafing during working hours." Violating these rules is almost invariably accompanied by disciplinary procedures, up to and including dismissal.

In the discussion of employee manuals, we saw how in both substance and tone, the rules as typically written send a message to employees that they cannot be trusted. We contrasted that with Nordstrom's startlingly simple and respectful message to its employees—rule #1: use your good judgment in all situations. There will be no additional rules.

Unlike their reactions to time clocks, most employees resent the myriad, detailed rules organizations write to govern their conduct; they see these as appropriate for children, not adults:

> *I hate being micromanaged (time off, phone breaks, lunches) and being watched like children.*

> *This job is demeaning. Having every moment micromanaged, being accountable for going to the restroom, being reprimanded for 2 to 3 minute variances is degrading. It's easy to dread coming here.*

> *Dealing with my leader everyday is a challenge. He treats everyone here like grade-school children and has no respect for what you think. What we do at work is less important to him than that we get here on time and don't leave a minute early.*

> *We are on the front line taking care of people, problems, messups, questions, concerns, and we are the lowest paid and treated the worst. We are treated like we are in grade school, not adults. God forbid if we have to take a trip to the restroom, everybody knows about it and supervisors make a big issue out of it.*

> *You are always being watched. It's very Big Brother here. They are always listening to your calls, always monitoring, always coming around your desk, don't want you to talk to each other on the job. Treat us like responsible adults!*

Does an organization need standards of conduct? Of course it does. Even Nordstrom, through its training and daily communications makes its standards clear. But, such organizations are different from others in two respects. First, they would never even consider rules such as prohibiting employees from conversing on the job. What could be more demeaning or ludicrous when applied to adults? Enormous costs result from trying to enforce this kind of restriction (in supervisory time and employee resentment). Second, when rules are needed, they are expressed in a positive tone and mostly as general guidelines or expectations rather than as rigid requirements. For example, consider the following "paid time off" guideline:

> [Company] is a dynamic organization of skilled professionals. Our clients often retain our services in no small part because of our ability to perform complicated and large projects on a timely basis. The scheduling of these services is often done by our clients on the senior management level and affects thousands of people throughout the clients' organization. Our ability to meet deadlines and delivery goals is of paramount import.

> This high level of responsiveness requires that we all, in turn, be as flexible as possible in scheduling time off, whether for vacation, personal days, sick days, family emergencies, or religious observance. As fellow employees, we acknowledge that we need to support and contribute to the company's efforts; as individuals, we know that each of our personal needs for time off work will be unique and changing.

> Please note that paid time off does not normally carry over into the next calendar if unused. However, we recognize that there may be unusual circumstances related to workload or other intervening factors and your department head is authorized to make special arrangements to carry over some or all of the paid time off days for a period of time that they will determine, not to exceed one additional year.

> We recognize that there may be times when emergencies or other unanticipated occurrences will cause someone to be unavoidably absent or late. Please notify your department head as early as possible if this occurs and, if at all possible, in advance. However, please note that simply notifying your supervisor that you will be

absent or late does not mean that it is appropriate. In fact, absences and lateness are elements that will be taken into consideration during performance reviews. Your supervisor is expected to monitor excessive absences or lateness and take the appropriate remedial steps.[10]

The moral is that most employees are responsible and reasonable adults who understand reasonable rules and don't have to be threatened into compliance. The few employees who are, indeed, irresponsible need to be handled individually and firmly.

Constrained Communication

In discussing status symbols, we put forward a basic proposition: if a distinction between employees is simply puffery for those in higher echelons—not being made on the basis of a business need—consider junking it. The same holds for rules about communications (for example, who is told what when). Knowledge might be power, as the saying goes, but it is also *status*: "I know something you don't, so I must be more important."

In business, one of the most counter-productive guidelines is to distribute information on the basis of "need to know." It sounds right—we, too, stress business need as a criterion for designing policies—but as interpreted in practice, it is usually a way of severely, unnecessarily, and destructively restricting the flow of information in an organization. The spirit of the guideline is rarely inclusiveness: "communicate this to *all* who have a need to know," but rather exclusiveness: "communicate this *only* to those who have a need to know."

The constraint is meant to keep confidential information confidential. Every organization, of course, has information that needs restricted distribution. But, three problems undercut management's intentions. First, much less information needs to be confidential than management typically believes; second, plenty of information that management thinks is confidential is widely communicated anyway through the grapevine or other means; finally, employees fill in information gaps with surmises and, in these, they usually assume the worst.

Constraints on communication are often irrational and counterproductive, and they act to reinforce many employees' sense of second-class citizenship. Employees' frustration with a lack of communication is one of the most frequent comments we encounter in focus groups and in write-in comments. These comments are responses to the question asking what employees like least in their organization:

> *My three biggest concerns: communication, communication, communication. When new policies are implemented, not all associates are informed. Don't we need to know?*

> *The extreme lack of communication between the various offices as well as within each office.*

> *Everything here is held so close to the vest. It's ridiculous, we are not the CIA.*

> *I find it difficult to do my job when I am not informed of changes that affect me or have an easy way of getting the information.*

> *No communication between departments and what the function of our department is and what we handle. A lot of misdirected calls, causing frustration for the customer who has been bounced around. If the communication was clear, there would be less frustration for the customer and myself.*

> *The lack of communication has been a big challenge. We're given information on a "need to know" basis only and several times, the information has been too little, too late. Why do they hold back information we must have? It makes no sense.*

> *Lack of communication from management [about our] business practices. Overall, there is a high level of confusion, uncertainty, and fear of being displaced within the organization.*

> *The challenge in my department is keeping up with changes due to the lack of communication when changes are made.*

Organizations need to hold back very little information from employees. Consider financial information. Perhaps the most well-known proponent of sharing such information with all workers is Jack Stack, the CEO of SRC Holdings Corp. (formerly Springfield Remanufacturing Company). He has formalized his approach and termed it "open-book management." His view that financial information should be open for everyone to know, talk about, and focus on, is a marked changed from the "status" use of information:

> Do you want to know what I consider to be the biggest and most dangerous lie in business? Information is power. This wrong-headed cliche leads to much of the deceit that you see in companies today. It encourages people to hoard information—to use it as a weapon against colleagues rather than as a way to solve problems....
>
> That's why SRC embraces open-book management. We are building a company in which everyone tells the truth every day—not because everyone is honest, but because everyone has access to the same information: operating metrics, financial data, valuation estimates. The more people understand what's really going in their company, the more eager they are to help solve its problems. Information isn't power. It's a burden. Share information, and you share the burdens of leadership as well.[11]

Stack's open-book management approach is part of his broader management philosophy that includes sharing the financial gains of improvement with employees, and the company doing its utmost to preserve employee job security. His business results, which are largely attributed to this integrated philosophy, have been impressive.[12]

Both function (what employees need to do their jobs) and psychology (what makes employees feel respected, included, and confident in the honesty of management) dictate that few restrictions be placed on the flow of information to the workforce. Providing assurance that the company is run honestly is a particularly important matter for all of a company's key stakeholders who rely on accurate business information for their own decisions. This has come to be referred to as "transparency," and as recent events have shown has become a major issue of our times in corporate America.

There are only two limitations to our admonition to be fully communicative to employees. First, obviously, a few items are indeed confidential or need to remain confidential for a specific period of time. Second, the injunction to communicate fully does not mean flooding the workforce with unorganized, un-prioritized, and irrelevant information; that is another way of *not* communicating.

Day-to-Day Courtesies

In thinking about business and respect for people, it is easy to overlook the critical role of basic civility and courtesy. How a boss talks to employees is enormously important. It might sound trivial and even corny, but common courtesy reflects an egalitarianism at the most basic human level; it is the boss saying, "My authority and power in no way diminish your worth to me as a human being." This is illustrated vividly in the way workers react to an informal visit by the head of their company to their work area, especially if he refers to them by name. They are pleased, even ecstatic; they might talk about it for days and tell family and friends about it.

Interestingly, workers might feel that the friendliness is somewhat staged, that the boss has probably been briefed on their names and perhaps something about them individually. But, it doesn't seem to bother them; they'll say, "He's a smart businessman, he knows how to win over people." That is, they admire his understanding that winning over the *workers* is important to the effective functioning of a business. To them, that is a sign of respect and how different it is from the way they see managers who don't even make the effort to stage it and who, therefore, come across as indifferent to, or even contemptuous of, workers. The boss's friendliness boomerangs only when it is inconsistent with other practices. It's difficult to take a cheerful "good morning" seriously when it's given by someone who refuses to spend the money needed to correct bad working conditions.

One of Tom Peters' and Bob Waterman's major contributions in their popular and influential book, *In Search of Excellence*, is their emphasis on "management by wandering around," which is best known by its acronym MBWA. They suggest that supervisors should be out of their offices 75 percent of the time. Doing what? Mostly "wandering" to provide an opportunity for informal two-way communication with their people. The major functions of MBWA are "listening, teaching, and facilitating" and through this method—in contrast to the traditional and formal bureaucratic channels—managers can learn the most and help their employees the most.[13]

However, MBWA can backfire if it is a method for micromanaging employees. It needs to be a *conversation* through which the parties can exchange information and learn from each other. It can backfire as well if it is only a "state visit," with retinues, a rigid time schedule, and predetermined "canned" questions (and, likely, the company photographer to record the executive's visit with "the folks"). To be successful, the visit must be genuinely person-to-person. This brings us to a critical, usually unspoken, purpose of MBWA: to express respect for the value of workers as human beings. Status differences are reinforced when an executive sits in his office and "receives" his subordinates. An executive that comes out on the shop or office floor—informally, without the trappings of position—provides the opposite kind of symbol: people as colleagues working toward the achievement of common goals. A workforce enormously appreciates an executive who lacks pretense and pomposity.

Of the executives with whom we have worked, few exemplify our point more fully than Don Graham, who is the CEO of The Washington Post Company. The son of the late Katherine Graham, the former CEO of the company, Don Graham moved into a high-level management position at *The Washington Post* newspaper following a bitter strike by the pressmen in 1975. He played a key role in bringing peace to the pressroom after the strike, in large measure because of his unassuming personality, informal manner, and continual visits and conversations with the workers. It is not, of course, just blue-collar workers who are appreciative of that kind of treatment. Here are Roger Wilkins' observation of what happened when he went to work for *The Post* in 1972:

> *[Wilkins] was the first black editorial writer on the staff, and he would go on to write most of the Post's editorials on Watergate. "One day," Wilkins said recently, "this guy shows up at my door. He's a big friendly guy with a big smile and he says,—Wilkins's voice rises to a perfect imitation of Graham's all-American cadence—'Hi, I'm Don Graham and I just want to welcome you to the paper and I just hope that you just have the best time here.' Later, I figured out who he was. But, that was really nice, you know? Nice things like that do not normally happen in newspapers."[14]*

Hard-boiled, cynical newspaper employees are not supposed to care about "niceness." That's part of the mythology that they have created and try to foist on others (and perhaps themselves), but it's baloney.

Here's another example of the importance of courtesy and decency at all levels. In 1985, we worked with a railroad that needed help to establish a more positive relationship with its unions. The project was successful: among its achievements were highly productive joint efforts to improve performance and the quality of work life for the company's workers. Cooperative undertakings of that kind between labor and management would have been unthinkable on that railroad a year earlier. To a person, both company and union officials were pleased and a dinner was arranged to celebrate the project's success. At the beginning of the evening, while awaiting the arrival of the company's CEO, one of the authors was chatting with the president of the railroad's largest union. The union official commented on how amazed he was at the success of the undertaking, considering how rancorous relationships had been until then. He was happy with that, but then the company president arrived and the official commented to the author: "Watch now, you'll see how he won't even say 'Hello' to me. That hurts."

The company president didn't say "Hello" until he was reminded by the consultant to do so. The union official is a tough guy—known over the years as being particularly belligerent toward management—for whom small gestures of common courtesy would seem to be irrelevant. They're not. Underscored once again is the danger of oversimplifying human needs, trying to figure out what *one* thing matters to an individual. Many things are important to this union official, some are obvious, such as achieving results for his members, and some are not so obvious, such as being treated with basic respect by people in positions of authority.

PART III

Enthusiastic Workforces, Motivated by *Achievement*

CHAPTER 6

Organization Purpose and Principles

"Make no small plans...for they have not the power to stir men's blood."

—Niccolo Machiavelli, 1514

"The way I see it, leadership does not begin with power but rather with a compelling vision or goal of excellence."

Frederick W. Smith, CEO, Federal Express

A critical condition for employee enthusiasm is a clear, credible, and inspiring organizational *purpose*; in effect, it's a "reason for being" that translates for workers into a "reason for being there." This might seem odd when talking about for-profit enterprises—isn't the idea simply to make a buck and don't employees, in turn, understand that and simply want to be paid well? Well, in fact, no. We humans are not that simple. Not in what we want and not in what we expect from the organizations to which we belong and to which we are asked to give our talent and loyalty.

In this and the next few chapters, we address the conditions that provide workers with a sense of achievement and pride in their employment. We begin with the broadest level—the very purpose of the organization—and go on to what happens to employees day-to-day.

Elements of Company Pride

It is difficult to exaggerate the importance to most people of being part of something they can be proud of and care about. We clearly see this in the way people identify with a nation, an ethnic or racial or religious group, a city, a school, and even a sports team. Workers start their employment caring a lot about the company. When their caring diminishes, it is largely because of the characteristics of management and the company, not those of the individual. For example, people find it difficult to be loyal to, or feel pride in, organizations that treat employees as little more than costs to be tolerated or reduced, rather than as genuine assets to the business.

It is also difficult to be loyal to an organization that stands for nothing but making money. Obviously, making money is far from trivial; in fact, the financial achievements of a company can be an important source of pride for its employees. But, just as an individual employee derives pride from more than his income (from doing high-quality work, for example), so does pride in an organization depend on more than the amount of its profit.

Our research reveals a strong correlation between pride in the organization and the overall satisfaction of workers with that organization.[1] We find that there are four main sources of pride, all of which reflect different facets of a single attribute—*excellence*:

- Excellence in the organization's financial performance.

- Excellence in the efficiency with which the work of the organization gets done.

- Excellence in the characteristics of the organization's products, such as their usefulness, distinctiveness, and quality.

- Excellence in the organization's moral character.

People want to work for an organization that does well but also does good. Roughly speaking, the first two of the factors listed relate to doing well (working for a business that is profitable and well run), and the latter two relate to doing good (providing something of real value to its customers and conducting its business ethically). These four aspects of excellence are, of course, interrelated. It is difficult to produce excellent long-term financial results without providing value to customers, or to succeed for long with unethical business practices. But, as determinants of pride, each of the four is distinct and important. Thus, the desires of employees that their company act ethically and produce high-quality products are important in and of themselves, not just because ethical behavior and quality are good for business.

You might be surprised by our assertions about the importance to most people of working for a "good" organization. Our evidence comes from both the statistical analysis of our survey data and from our qualitative material (the write-in questions and the focus groups, where both doing well and doing good receive significant mention). Indeed, employees want their companies to do *very* well and *a lot* of good. Here are a few typical write-in comments from employees in a number of companies. First, positive comments (these are responses to the question, "What do you like best about working here?"):

> *The commitment to be the best. The folks who run [company] have the money to be the best, and they spend it.*

> *Keep up the good work of making [company] successful. I enjoy working for [company] and want to continue working for the company long term.*

> *Great product, great strategy, great leadership, great concern for employees, great care for customers, great honesty. Senior management is terrific. We are very lucky.*

> *It is a pleasure working with an executive leadership team that is willing to put actions to their words...gets it done for customers and shareholders. Thanks. It is great to part of the [company].*

> *I am insanely proud of my work as a [job] for [company] and insanely proud to be here. It is universally recognized as a great company with very high standards and integrity. Most importantly, I grow and learn every day, have a chance to show what I can do and feel I'm contributing to a common good...In fact, I still feel, after several years here, that I would almost pay for the privilege of working for [company]. I couldn't afford that, really, but you get the idea.*

> *It's the top of the game, like being on the roster of an organization like the New York Yankees.*

Now, some negative comments (these are responses to the question, "What do you like least about working here?"):

> As a company, we are not "leaders" in any areas anymore. We no longer strive for innovation or excellence. We do…what "everyone else is doing" yet we say we wish to be "best in class." You can't have it that way. The man who leads must break the wind…we sure are becoming mediocre.

> We seem to be going out of business with a knee-jerk approach to everything. We talk growth but that's all it is, talk and no growth. We are throwing out everything that's not tied down and that includes loyal workers. What happened to the great company that we were?

> Top performance is desired and is needed, but top management has done almost everything possible to make it a non-performer. The smallest detail must go to the top for approvals. Having the president determine the transfers within the lower levels of a technical function is incredibly inefficient and it takes forever to get a decision made. Where is the leadership?!

> They put up Quality posters all over the walls but the foreman tells you just get the pieces out the door. Nobody believes anything the company says; it's all baloney. They lie to customers.

> All they want to do is cut costs and people and the work today is sloppier than it has ever been. It's getting embarrassing to tell people where I work.

The desire for highly competent management—a real "winner"—will not come as a surprise to most readers, and most agree that employees don't want to work for clearly unethical management. But, *outstanding* regarding ethical standards? *Outstanding* regarding product quality? You bet! Again, read the positive comments to sense the worker pride that comes from corporate excellence and ethics. Keep in mind that, here, we discuss the determinants of employee *enthusiasm*, not "contentment" and certainly not just the absence of anger. It is difficult to be enthusiastic about a company whose financial performance is mediocre, but of comparable importance are the questions: how is the business being conducted and to what ends? Without good answers to these questions, one's job and organization tend to become mere means to the achievement of other goals, especially financial. They have no value in themselves and won't arouse or sustain enthusiasm except in those few people who are motivated by nothing but financial gain.

If you doubt what we say about workers, ask what, in addition to your pay and benefits, *you* want from your employment. For example, what does it mean to say, "I have done a good day's work"? Is it not a feeling that you did quality work that day, that your work showed skill, that your work was having a significant, positive impact on the organization or a customer? Furthermore, except for gangsters and other sociopaths, people usually don't feel good about a day's work that requires lying, cheating, or stealing.

And, people don't want to work for *companies* that act that way. People don't want to produce products of mediocre quality. In early survey work for U.S. automobile companies, in the late 1970s, workers complained bitterly about the poor quality of the cars produced by their factories. In that period, the workers and their union were often blamed for shoddy U.S. products. However, most *workers* felt terrible about what they said they were being forced to produce.

Enthusiasm about one's company requires a company with purpose, especially in relation to its customers, and principles.

Company Ethics and Business Results

> *I want to…express the principles which we in our company have endeavored to live up to…Here is how it sums up: we try to remember that medicine is for the patient. We try never to forget that medicine is for the people. It is not for the profits. The profits follow, and if we have remembered that, they have never failed to appear. The better we have remembered that, the larger they have been.*

—George Merck II, Former CEO, Merck and Company[2]

Why isn't it enough for an organization to focus just on doing well (as if that weren't difficult enough to achieve)? After all, pride in one's organization is certainly fostered by operational success in the sense of financial performance and excellence of process. Aside from purely moral considerations, is there truly that much more to be gained *as a business* by pursuing a higher good? Moreover, can most companies find a higher good to seek?

In fact, considerable evidence shows that organizations that "do good" show superior long-term performance. One of the most impressive studies in this area is the research of Collins and Porras, summarized in their highly regarded 1994 book *Built to Last*.[3] They compared companies that were the "best of the best" in their industries (and, importantly, had been considered so for decades) with companies that were just satisfactory. This was a comparison, as they put it, between the "gold medalists" and the "silver or bronze medalists." For example, General Electric ("gold") was compared to Westinghouse, Johnson & Johnson to Bristol-Myers Squibb, Procter & Gamble to Colgate, IBM to Burroughs, and so on. In 18 such paired comparisons, the best companies, on average, far outperformed the comparison companies, as well as the market as a whole, over the long term. For example, $1 invested in the best companies on January 1, 1926 would have been worth $6,356 on December 31, 1990. The worth of the stock of comparison companies would have been $955 and that of the general market $415.[4]

The Collins and Porras researchers sought to determine the factors that distinguished the best companies from the merely satisfactory. They referred to the former as "visionary" because among the key distinguishing features of those companies was emphasis on a vision that was "more than profits":

> *Contrary to business school doctrine, we did not find "maximizing shareholder wealth" or "profit maximization" as the dominant driving force or primary objective through the history of most of the visionary companies. They have tended to pursue a cluster of objectives, of which making money is only one—and not necessarily the primary one. Indeed, for many of the visionary companies, business has historically been more than an economic activity, more than just a way to make money.[5]*

Many examples are cited of the "more than profits" visions, such as the earlier quote from George Merck II and this one from an interview with John Young, who was the Hewlett-Packard CEO from 1976 to 1992:

> *Maximizing shareholder wealth has always been way down on the list. Yes, profit is a cornerstone of what we do—it is a measure of our contribution and a means of self-financed growth—but it has never been the point in and of itself. The point, in fact, is to win, and winning is judged in the eyes of the customer and by doing*

something you can be proud of. There is a symmetry of logic in this. If we provide real satisfaction to real customers—we will be profitable.[6]

That view is contrasted by Collins and Porras with HP's comparison company, Texas Instruments:

> *...we reviewed over 40 historical articles and case studies and could find not one single statement that TI exists for reasons beyond making money...TI appeared to define itself almost exclusively in terms of size, growth, and profitability. For TI, bigger was better, period—even if the products were low-quality or made no technical contribution. For HP, bigger was better only within the context of making a contribution.*[7]

Such contrasts in vision are found in pair after pair. The authors speak of the "core ideology" of a company, and they are at pains to stress that there is no "right" ideology—the key is that it consist of a vision that is "more than profits" and that it inspire and guide the company's employees. For the authors, Citicorp's value, "autonomy and entrepreneurship," is as expressive of a core ideology as Johnson & Johnson's, "the company exists to alleviate pain and disease."

Nevertheless, as we review each of the visionary companies' ideologies, a strong moral component is found in almost all of them. Here are some examples of moral components in the corporate ideologies of Collins and Porras' visionaries:

- **3M.**   Absolute integrity.

- **General Electric.**   Improving the quality of life through technology and innovation.

- **Hewlett-Packard.**   Technical contribution to the fields in which we participate ("we exist as a corporation to make a contribution"); respect and opportunity for HP people, including the opportunity to share in the success of the enterprise; contribution and responsibility to the community; profit and growth as a means of achieving all the other values and objectives.

- **IBM.**   Give full consideration to the individual employee; spend a lot of time making customers happy; go the last mile to make things right; seek superiority in all we undertake.

- **Johnson & Johnson.** The company exists to alleviate pain and disease; we have a hierarchy of responsibilities: customers first, employees second, society at large third, and shareholders fourth.

- **Motorola.** The company exists to honorably serve the community by providing products and services of superior quality at a fair price; continual improvement in all that the company does, in ideas, in quality, in customer satisfaction; treat each employee with dignity and as an individual; honesty, integrity, and ethics in all aspects of business.

- **Nordstrom.** Excellence in reputation, being part of something special.

- **Sony.** To experience the sheer joy that comes from the advancement, application, and innovation of technology that benefits the general public; to elevate the Japanese culture and national status; respecting and encouraging each individual's ability and creativity.

- **Walt Disney.** No cynicism allowed; fanatical attention to consistency and detail; to bring happiness to millions; to celebrate, nurture, and promulgate "wholesome American values."

Collins and Porras' data clearly support the proposition that, on the whole, a strong moral component in corporate behavior is certainly not inconsistent with long-term business success and, in fact, appears to significantly contribute to it. Other studies supporting the positive relationship between corporate citizenship and business success abound, and we cite a few here. In 1996, Waddock and Graves found positive correlations between the social performance of corporations and measures such as return on assets, return on sales, and return on equity. Social performance was defined by them as the way corporations treat not just shareholders, but other key stakeholders as well (such as customers, employees, and the community).[8] A recent longitudinal Harvard University study found that "stakeholder-balanced" companies showed four times the growth rate and eight times the employment growth of companies that focus only on shareholders.[9]

Besides the enthusiasm and pride that employees feel for an organization with "purpose," the research suggests a number of other reasons for the positive relationship between doing good and long-term corporate performance. One reason is the impact of broad corporate reputation, and the trust that it inspires, on purchasing decisions by consumers. Surveys consistently show that a large majority of consumers say they are likely to switch brands or retailers to ones associated with a good cause. This is not just because the consumer agrees with the cause. It is also that being "good" in one sphere—say, respecting the environment—generalizes, absent contradictory information, to other spheres, such as the quality of the organization's products. At the least, in modern marketing terms, doing good helps an organization favorably differentiate its brand from the competition.

In addition, the specific components of doing good yield tangible financial gains. High-quality products and services attract and keep customers. Beneficent personnel policies attract and keep employees. There are many instances of progressive community-relations policies generating community support for company business initiatives and protecting the company from activities that are unfriendly to it and its interests.

A particularly vivid example of the benefits of positive community relations was observed in 1987 when the Dart Group sought to acquire the Dayton Hudson Corporation of Minneapolis. A charitable giver of five percent of its pre-tax profit, Dayton Hudson had become an icon of good corporate citizenship. On the other hand, Dart was widely perceived as a predatory corporate raider. In defense against the hostile bid from Dart, the company enlisted the community goodwill that it had built up for more than 100 years and received overwhelming support. A special meeting of the Minnesota state legislature was convened to change the law relating to the timing and organization of company takeovers in the state. That helped defeat the hostile bid for Dayton Hudson.

At the negative end of the corporate citizenship continuum are companies that engage in clearly unethical behavior. A wealth of evidence shows that behaving in egregiously socially irresponsible and illegal ways is detrimental to shareholder value. In 1997, one study investigated 27 incidents of unethical or illegal corporate behavior and concluded that such behavior resulted in significant losses of shareholder wealth.[10] Recent corporate scandals have done nothing to alter that fact. Business leaders losing their moral compass of late have resulted in the destruction of hundreds of millions of dollars in shareholder value, not to mention the loss of "worker value" (such as jobs lost, pension accounts reduced to little or no value, and so on).

To summarize, the research appears to show that business profitability is not simply about making money in the short term, but it is also about building positive and trusting relationships with all major constituencies that promote and sustain long-term profitability. A company should want customers who are willing to go the extra mile to purchase its services, employees who give their all for the organization, suppliers who feel themselves as genuine "partners" with the organization and therefore seek to deliver their best work to the company and in a timely manner, and a community that vigorously supports the company's legitimate business interests. The importance of these relationships might not be obvious in the short run, and they won't appear to be needed in flush times, but they are critical to sustain good performance over the long haul and especially when business conditions turn tough. A major mistake that companies make is to take their key constituencies—their stakeholders—for granted.

More About Purpose

We have described doing good as consisting of purpose and principles. *Purpose* relates primarily to how an organization serves its customers, *principles* to its moral character—its behavior against legal and ethical norms in its dealings with all its constituencies.

Now, the fact is that most organizations produce some product or service about which their employees can be proud, at least potentially. We say "potentially" because workers might feel embarrassed by the quality with which a product or service is provided. Not just astronauts, emergency-room personnel, or special-forces soldiers feel pride in the type of work they do. We survey all kinds of organizations and occupations—from cleaning services to research laboratories, sanitation workers to investment bankers—and an overwhelming majority of employees feel that they provide a valuable service.

A sanitation worker in a focus group tells us, "There's no job in the city more important." A packer of cookies says, "I'm doing something that makes people happy." A cleaning lady asks, "Do you know what this place would be like without us?"

We must put ourselves into other people's shoes when we think about the meaning, dignity, and purpose of work. The fact that some people might not feel particularly proud of packing cookies is irrelevant. We want to know what *the cookie packer* feels and, for her, this is not demeaning work. Is collecting garbage demeaning? All of us might do well to consider whether our own jobs are indeed more important.

The strong desire to be proud of our jobs is the reason that the pride scores are as high as they are: the norm is 74 percent, with the least favorable company still being 48 percent. Despite this restricted range, our research shows that enormous gains in morale and performance can be reaped when management behaves in a way that moves the scores toward the high end of the range.

More About Principles

Some companies view business ethics only in terms of compliance with the law and contributions to charity. This chapter focuses on the impact that business ethics has on the morale of employees, and our research indicates that, in this respect, the definition of ethics needs to include much more. Employees are interested in the quality of the relationships the company enjoys with all its key constituencies, and genuine pride comes from more than simply obeying the law. It comes from going beyond that, and treating the company's constituencies with a genuine concern for their needs by having *outstanding* relationships with customers, employees, suppliers, investors, and the community.

Our discussion of purpose centered on customers and, therefore, overlaps with this discussion of principles. Customers are key stakeholders, and providing them with high-quality and useful products and services is not only the organization's purpose, but also an ethical consideration. Employees certainly see it that way. At a minimum, they expect their company not to cheat or deceive customers, whether or not some action is technically illegal. Ideally, they want the products and services customers buy to be exceptional. Questions relating to quality and customers show among the highest correlations with employee morale.

When asked what they like most about their jobs, many people talk about the customers:

> *There is a great sense of satisfaction when you help someone, customer or peer, who is really in need. That person thanking you for "stepping outside of the box" and helping them is what makes my day.*

> *I love working with customers, knowing that I impact people's lives. Without them, I would not come to work either.*

> *What I like best about this company is that it stands by its word to customers, and believes in doing the right thing.*

> *We never stop trying to out-do ourselves in regards to the services/amenities that we provide to customers. It is little wonder that we do a great job of retaining our customers.*

We strive to exceed our customers' expectations everyday and we love doing our job.

I see a real win-win atmosphere and attitude concerning the way we deal with our customers. As employees, we establish lasting relationships and partnerships with our customers and the benefits multiply as time passes.

I feel that we do put the customers first and that if the customer has a problem, we will always do the best to have the problem fixed as soon as possible.

Ethics in the Treatment of Employees

Not surprisingly, among the most strongly held employee views about the ethical treatment of stakeholders is the way *employees themselves* are treated. Previously, we noted that a major goal of workers is fair treatment in the basic conditions of employment, such as pay, benefits, job security, and physical safety. In those areas, too, we have a continuum that ranges from practices that are clearly illegal, to those that are borderline, to those entirely within legal and ethical norms, to those that exceed what's required and expected. Job security is an example. At one extreme are companies that violate the law by, for example, providing insufficient notice to employees before a layoff or using difficult economic times as an excuse to dismiss various protected groups, such as older employees, or to dismiss employees with union sympathies. At the other end of the continuum are companies that not only operate within the law, but do their utmost first to avoid layoffs and, when layoffs are necessary, treating those being laid off with care and generosity.

Another area basic to workforce treatment is safety, especially in traditional blue-collar industries. We did not discuss safety in detail in the equity section of this book; we purposely reserved it for this chapter.

A multitude of federal, state, and local statutes cover safety and some companies repeatedly violate them. At the other extreme are companies such as Alcoa that, under the leadership of former CEO Paul O'Neill (who later became the U.S. Treasury Secretary), compiled an extraordinary safety record. When we discuss what determines the success of statements of purpose and principles, we will see that CEO leadership is critical. O'Neill's role in Alcoa's safety achievements is highly instructive.

When he took over at Alcoa, O'Neill announced that he wanted a marked improvement in the company's safety record as a chief objective:

I said the first day that no one who works for Alcoa should ever be hurt at work...The world is so full of cynicism and disbelief about really caring about each other that the first response was predictable. The senior people came to explain to me that we were already in the top one third of all companies in the world in our safety performance as measured by the absence of lost work-day cases. At that time the lost workday average... was five per 100 employees per year. The 1987 number at Alcoa was 1.87, so they were very proud of themselves. They didn't say it to my face, but the hallway conversation was, "When the next tough econom-ic time comes, he'll shut up about this. He doesn't know anything about making aluminum; how can he be here telling us what we're going to do about safety?"

And so I set out to make it reality by traveling around to Alcoa manufacturing sites. The first place I went to was a plant in Tennessee and after lunch with 45 people that included top man-agement and top union representatives...I said...that people should not be hurt who work for Alcoa. I told them it's not a pri-ority, but it's a pre-condition. Important things are not priorities, they're pre-conditions. So I said to the management "From this day forward, we will not budget things that need to be done to improve safety conditions. If you have identified something that needs to be done, you should go and do it and you should not have an excuse list that says we'll put it into next year's budget and in the meantime hope that no one gets hurt." And then I said to the hourly workers, "If the management doesn't follow up what I just said to them, here's my home phone number." A lot of the management was really horrified I would give the hourly workers my home phone number, but I did. It's interesting that I got a few phone calls. Not too many because when people called me and they could demonstrate that the ideas were being violated, I took some action to clean up the situation.

From a speech at the University of Minnesota's Carlson School of Management, June 2002.

By 2000, when O'Neill retired, the injury rate at Alcoa was one-tenth of what it was when he arrived in 1987. George Becker, the union's president, describes O'Neill as "a man you can trust and believe what he says."

In O'Neill's approach to safety, we see that obeying the law and adhering to commonly accepted practices and ethical standards were not sufficient for him. The companies that generate employee enthusiasm are those that go beyond that and, in effect, act as true advocates for their stakeholders' interests. Their ethical commitments are not ancillary to the conduct of the business or a constraint on it, but rather an integral part of their operational and strategic decision-making. For O'Neill, safety was important in and of itself, but he also saw it as smart business. As Leslie Wayne of *The New York Times* put it, "...he figured out how to make money—not by cutting costs or slashing the payroll, but by improving productivity and making worker safety his top goal. His relentless push on safety had bottom-line benefits—he argued that a production process that was so flawed that workers got hurt was one that could not turn out high-quality products efficiently and cost effectively.[11]

More broadly, in O'Neill's own words:

> *For me, [it] is not about safety, per se; it's about leadership. And it's about a conviction I have that a truly great orgainzation requires that people be aligned around important values and they understand what they are. And no matter where you are in the world, they're the same.*

Remarks at the National Safety Summit, 2001

During O'Neill's tunure at Alcoa, the company nearly tripled in size, with shareholder value increasing from $4 billion to $32 billion.

Of course, we recognize that what a company says and does about its ethical commitments and social responsibility can sometimes be deceptive and hypocritical. Most frequently, this happens when a company is particularly and visibly generous in its relationship with the community but is diametrically opposite in its treatment of other constituencies such as employees, customers, and investors. As David Vogel pointed out in an article in *The Wall Street Journal*:

> Enron was long regarded as an exemplary corporate citizen. The firm and its senior executives were generous supporters of community institutions in Houston, and it captured international attention by building a power plant in India without resorting to

bribing government officials...And the company pleased many environmentalists with its investments in alternative energy.[12]

The moral of the story, obviously, is that any judgment about a firm's principles must be based on its behavior in relation to *all* its key constituencies. A company doesn't need to be outstanding in all these relationships, but it gets no credit—quite the opposite—from being outstanding in one or two spheres while clearly immoral in others.

Of course, as is usually the case, workers know exactly what is really happening. Consider these examples of comments:

> *What I am very unhappy about is the...hypocrisy under which the company is run. For instance, [specific example deleted]. The company says it values its employees but acts differently. Talk is cheap!*

> *I think outsourcing jobs to other countries is un-American and hypocritical. We jumped on the 9/11 bandwagon and sent U.S. jobs overseas.*

> *There seems to be a hypocrisy that exists in our company. We need to learn lessons from other companies' mistakes. Let's not be the next Enron or WorldCom and get back to our core values and remember the greatest asset we have, our people.*

> *The company is very hypocritical in its practices...Treating employees with dignity and respect is a core value, yet if the company can save money by firing people (while still reporting a profit) it will do so. Loyalty should be a two-way street.*

> *We must work to overcome the systematic maneuvers and the hypocrisy (true insincerity) of certain "leaders" who worry about showing "fake competence" to their superiors. They underreported the numbers this month so they can look better next month.*

> *Hypocritical leadership. We hear from our leaders that they want honest feedback from us. However, if that feedback happens to be negative, we are viewed as disgruntled employees who need to go elsewhere if we aren't happy at the company. We have been TOLD by our leadership how we should give feedback. So much for honesty.*

> *Trying to smile at the leadership when they preach loyalty to the company and they are only looking to make the most money*

themselves with our jobs, only to eventually outsource to other countries. This appears to be what employees will get for their loyalty to this company.

The management preaches that quality service is what they want you to give to customers. However...the...[employees] who have bad quality but good quantity get number one ratings.

They talk ethics but their advertising is totally misleading. They advertise items we don't even have in stock.

Getting Practical: Translating Words into Deeds

Many mission statements are unintentionally ridiculous. We've all seen them, companies that rhapsodize about customer service when customers are routinely disdained and disregarded, enthuse about employee empowerment when employees are treated with even less respect than the customers...In each case, thoughtful insiders might assess the date of achieving these goals as about the same as "when pigs fly."

Eileen C. Shapiro, *Fad Surfing in the Boardroom*

The overwhelming majority of companies with which we are familiar have formal statements of "purpose" or "mission" or "vision" or "values." However, in our surveys, we often uncover great employee skepticism about whether these statements are ever translated into practice. This is a shame; such statements can be enormously helpful to guide and inspire a workforce. They provide employees with both an overarching purpose for their individual efforts and basic decision-making criteria. But when they are seen as empty rhetoric, they do more harm than good.

Failure to make statements credible is rarely a result of insufficient effort spent on their wording. A lot of time is usually devoted to that, with no small involvement by senior management (often at two- to three-day retreats). Indeed, employees often wonder why such high-powered, high-paid time is devoted to a matter that turns out to have little consequence for the organization.

Here are three reasons why these statements are only sporadically implemented:

1. The most important reason is that, despite the resources devoted to their composition, the avowals by senior management that "this is really serious," and their widespread and repeated communication to everyone in the workforce, the statements are in truth felt by senior management as largely peripheral to the business. It is as if the executives attended church at the retreat, but it's back to business on Monday.

2. The statements' phrasing can be so general that they seem meaningless or so concrete and detailed that they become un-inspirational.

3. Other than telling everyone about the statement, the company lacks an effective method to translate it into a daily reality that endures over time.

What is decidedly not an issue is semantics. The meetings in which these statements are formulated are often filled with endless debates about the meanings of terms such as "vision," "mission," and "purpose," and whether all or just some of these should be incorporated into the company's statement. Who cares? Any one of a variety of combinations of these categories can be used to good effect. Our preference is to limit the statement to two categories: purpose (what the organization tries to accomplish) and principles (the values that guide it). Probably the most time-consuming and unnecessary semantic debate concerns the difference between "vision" and "mission." Despite having sat through innumerable lectures and discussions on the topic, we still don't understand the difference.

Let's look in detail at each of the real reasons "mission" (or whatever) statements often have little effect.

1. Lack of Senior Management Commitment

For "doing good" to be more than just subject matter for a retreat, two things are required on the part of top management, one emotional and the other a matter of business judgment.

At the emotional level, the requirement is a top management (especially the CEO) that is as passionate about products and people as it is about profits. These kinds of executives simply would not want to be associated with an enterprise that produced shoddy products or treated its employees and other constituencies badly (whatever the short-term business benefits). The first issue, then, comes down to the personal makeup of executives, what makes them, at their gut level, feel good or bad about the way their organization functions. They can be highly moral people and do all kinds of good outside of work, but unless an important source of personal pride for them is their *companies'* "doing good" (not just well), it is best to forget the purpose and principles exercise. It will be just that—an exercise.

The second aspect, business judgment, concerns the relationship between doing good and doing well in the long term. Personal values, passion, and pride are strongly reinforced if executives also believe that, over time, the impact of pursuing a higher purpose will significantly benefit the business. The ethical criteria that define a business purpose are rarely black and white; this allows for considerable flexibility before executives feel that a significant breech has occurred in their moral obligations to a constituency. Immediate business pressures, such as the desire to cut costs, therefore often override the doing-good considerations. A company that prides itself on customer service, for example, might respond to cost pressures by reducing expenditures in that area, or at least, no longer striving to improve service because doing so would cost money.

However, suppose that doing good is believed to be a *business* imperative, albeit long-term, not just a moral imperative or a matter of pride. Then, the argument on cutting corners with customer service becomes a *business* discussion, and the response to the question, "Can we afford to maintain this high a level of customer service?" might well be, "Can we afford *not* to?" This doesn't necessarily make the decision easier, but it certainly evenly balances the sides of the argument. Most frequently and beneficially, what it does is cause management to seek ways to meet *both* objectives to the extent possible: reducing costs in a way that minimizes damage to customer satisfaction with service. In fact, the total quality management movement offers many examples where the reduction of costs (such as by eliminating bureaucratic obstacles in responding to customers) leads to *higher* customer satisfaction.

How about *workers'* views about integrating doing good with business objectives? Although workers feel positive about an organization that does good, they understand that they are not working for a charity. Samuel Gompers, the first president of the American Federation of Labor, knew that. "The worst crime against working people," he declared in 1923, "is a company which fails to operate at a profit."

The second-worst crime, Gompers would no doubt add, is a company that operates at a profit through exploiting its workforce, or, we would add, through exploiting any of its key constituencies. Workers are especially appreciative of a management that sees doing well and good as not only compatible, but mutually reinforcing: doing good contributes to a company's long-term business success, and business success enables a company to do good things.

Doing good, then, should be treated as more than a collection of discrete practices or occasional gestures in parallel to the mainstream business and serving from time to time as the "conscience" of the business. Doing good should be viewed as a comprehensive set of policies, practices, and programs integrated by their connection with business objectives and by their reflection of an underlying system of values, that builds long-term, positive relationships with all major stakeholders of the corporation. In recent years, a particularly visible example of this has been Starbucks, the successful operator of coffee houses around the word. The moral purpose of Howard Schultz, the founder and CEO of Starbucks, includes worker protection (for example, being the first company to provide medical insurance for part-time workers), literacy, and environmental protection. Schultz' moral vision has not only earned him and the company much praise, but has resulted in tremendous worker pride.[13]

2. Poor Statement Phrasing

Given a genuine commitment to "doing good," how should the statement of purpose and principles be phrased? We suggest the following guidelines for the statement of purpose:

- It should be relevant to the business, not so general and filled with platitudes as to be virtually meaningless.

- It should be simple and clear, getting to the heart of what the company is without a lot of detail and qualifications. Too many words can obscure the central message.

- It should be inspirational in that it appeals to values that employees hold above and beyond profits (especially the usefulness and quality of the product or service), encourages excellence in the achievement of those values, and promotes a feeling of being special, an "elite" organization that is noticeably differentiated from others.

There are many particularly good statements of purpose. Here is one that we especially admire; it's taken from a three-person benefits department in a medium-size company:

> Benefits are about people. It's not whether you have the forms filled in or whether the checks are written. It's whether people are cared for when they're sick, helped when they're in trouble.

This statement is particularly impressive. After all, it was composed in a small organization devoid of the high-powered executive attention and professional "wordsmithing" such statements normally receive. It also was composed in the kind of department often known for its fixation on bureaucratic rules and procedures. It is a statement truly from the heart, with the focus in the right place: on caring for people, rather than having the right forms.

For the statement of principles (the values that guide the organization in the achievement of its purpose), the same three general guidelines described for the statement of purpose should be followed to the extent possible. A statement of principles will, of necessity, be more detailed than one of purpose, but brevity should still be a goal. Although certain ethical principles are indeed applicable to any organization (is honesty ever irrelevant?), the wording should reflect, as well as it can, the issues and conditions of the particular business for which the principles are being written.

In many companies, the statement of principles goes well beyond what might normally be considered "ethics" and depicts the major features of the company's desired internal culture. Thus, besides integrity, companies might stress the need for an internal environment that is open, empowering, collaborative, diverse, creative, and so on. These are perfectly appropriate and useful in the context of principles. In fact, these elements of internal culture often derive, in part, from ethical considerations—empowerment as an outgrowth of treating people with respect, and openness from the need for honesty and transparency.

Here are a few more particularly good examples of statements of principles from easily recognized companies:

Lands' End

1. *We do everything we can to make our products better. We improve material, and add back features and construction details that others have taken out over the years. We never reduce the quality of a product to make it cheaper.*

2. *We price our products fairly and honestly. We do not, have not, and will not participate in the common retailing practice of inflating mark-ups to set up a future phony "sale."*

3. *We accept any return for any reason, at any time. Our products are guaranteed. No fine print. No arguments. We mean exactly what we say: GUARANTEED. PERIOD.*

4. *We ship faster than anyone we know of. We ship items in stock the day after we receive the order. At the height of the last Christmas season, the longest time an order was in the house was 36 hours, excepting monograms, which took another 12 hours.*

5. *We believe that what is best for our customer is best for all of us. Everyone here understands that concept. Our sales and service people are trained to know our products, and to be friendly and helpful. They are urged to take all the time necessary to take care of you. We even pay for your call, for whatever reason you call.*

6. *We are able to sell at lower prices because we have eliminated middlemen; because we don't buy branded merchandise with high protected mark-ups; and because we have placed our contracts with manufacturers who have proven that they are cost conscious and efficient.*

7. *We are able to sell at lower prices because we operate efficiently. Our people are hard-working, intelligent, and share in the success of the company.*

8. *We are able to sell at lower prices because we support no fancy emporiums with their high overhead. Our main location is in the middle of a 40-acre cornfield in rural Wisconsin.*

Merck

1. *Our business is preserving and improving human life. All of our actions must be measured by our success in achieving this goal. We value above all our ability to serve everyone who can benefit from the appropriate use of our products and services, thereby providing lasting consumer satisfaction.*

2. *We are committed to the highest standards of ethics and integrity. We are responsible to our customers, to Merck employees and their families, to the environments we inhabit, and to the societies we serve worldwide. In discharging our responsibilities, we do not take professional or ethical shortcuts. Our interactions with all segments of society must reflect the high standards we profess.*

3. *We are dedicated to the highest level of scientific excellence and commit our research to improving human and animal health and the quality of life. We strive to identify the most critical needs of consumers and customers; we devote our resources to meeting those needs.*

4. *We expect profits, but only from work that satisfies customer needs and benefits humanity. Our ability to meet our responsibilities depends on maintaining a financial position that invites investment in leading-edge research and that makes possible effective delivery of research results.*

5. *We recognize that the ability to excel—to most competitively meet society's and customers' needs—depends on the integrity, knowledge, imagination, skill, diversity and teamwork of employees, and we value these qualities most highly. To this end, we strive to create an environment of mutual respect, encouragement, and teamwork—an environment that rewards commitment and performance and is responsive to the needs of employees and their families.*

Those statements from highly successful and respected companies were chosen to show that there are no rigid formulas for such things. They are all effective, yet differ from each other in significant respects. Don't be confused by the fact that these statements of principles often appear to overlap in content with statements of purpose. Merck's first principle, "Our business is preserving and improving human life..." certainly sounds like a purpose. Indeed, sometimes purpose and value statements are not distinguished from each other at all. Consider Johnson & Johnson's famous credo:

> *We believe our first responsibility is to the doctors, nurses and patients, to mothers and fathers and all others who use our products and services. In meeting their needs everything we do must be of high quality. We must constantly strive to reduce our costs in order to maintain reasonable prices. Customers' orders must be serviced promptly and accurately. Our suppliers and distributors must have an opportunity to make a fair profit.*

> *We are responsible to our employees, the men and women who work with us throughout the world. Everyone must be considered as an individual. We must respect their dignity and recognize their merit. They must have a sense of security in their jobs.*

> *Compensation must be fair and adequate, and working conditions clean, orderly and safe. We must be mindful of ways to help our employees fulfill their family responsibilities. Employees must feel free to make suggestions and complaints. There must be equal*

opportunity for employment, development, and advancement for those qualified. We must provide competent management, and their actions must be just and ethical.

We are responsible to the communities in which we live and work and to the world community as well. We must be good citizens— support good works and charities and bear our fair share of taxes. We must encourage civic improvements and better health and education. We must maintain in good order the property we are privileged to use, protecting the environment and natural resources.

Our final responsibility is to our stockholders. Business must make a sound profit. We must experiment with new ideas. Research must be carried on, innovative programs developed and mistakes paid for. New equipment must be purchased, new facilities provided and new products launched. Reserves must be created to provide for adverse times. When we operate according to these principles, the stockholders should realize a fair return.

The Credo's fame is well deserved: it is clear, relevant to the business, and inspirational. Since it was formulated in the mid 1940s by Robert Wood Johnson, then the CEO, it has had an enormous influence on the way Johnson & Johnson operates, and its employees conduct themselves. Most famously, perhaps, is the way the company responded during the 1982 Tylenol crisis, when seven people died after taking Tylenol that had been laced with cyanide. The company quickly stopped production and removed all Tylenol from the market. Jim Burke, chairman at the time, remarked, "After the crisis was over, we realized that no meeting had been called to make the first critical decision. Every one of us knew what we had to do. We had the Credo to guide us."[14]

Let's therefore not obsess over form. We have our own preferences, such as the distinction between purpose and principles, but other approaches serve just as well.

3. Lack of a Methodology

We come now to the third condition for assuring that purpose and principles statements are not seen as more executive bunkum: a lack of a methodology for translating the statement into a day-to-day reality that endures over time. Although much time and effort should be devoted to the formulation of the statement, this is but a small fraction of what will be required for it to be effectively implemented.

There is no great mystery about what is required to make noble-sounding words into a day-to-day reality:

- Strong and visible top-management support, especially the CEO's support.

- Clear, enforceable, and enforced policy.

- Internal processes that enable the policy to be carried out.

- Full communication to the workforce of the policy and its rationale.

- Training of the workforce in implementing the policy on their own jobs.

- Tools that the workforce needs to carry out the policy (including authority).

- The workforce's participation in developing the methods used to carry out the policy.

- Measurement of the results.

- A reward system geared to the results.

Two of those requirements—top-management support and workforce participation—deserve some elaboration. Much has been written about how important it is to get the workforce involved in defining organization purpose and principles. Our view is that, in certain key respects, this cannot be a participative process because its essence—especially of an organization's purpose—*must come from the top*. The exact wording and elaboration of the statements, and certainly their methods of implementation, will profit greatly from the involvement of others, but it is a little ludicrous for a CEO to expect others to give her a purpose for the organization. As we argued earlier, the CEO must be the type of person who, at a gut level, takes pride in achievements in addition to those reflected in financial statements and believes that such achievements are important for long-term business performance. The CEO then *demands* that the organization behave in conformity with these values; there can be no room for debate about this. The only question is *how* they will be achieved, including how their meaning can be best captured in words; for this, broad workforce participation is extremely beneficial.

We can provide many examples of effective implementation of purposes and principles. Throughout this book, we deal with such implementation in the employee realm. As the primary example in this chapter, let's use the implementation of statements of purposes and principles that relate to the customer constituency.

The great majority of purposes and principles statements by America's corporations contain commitments to excellence in the products and services provided to customers. However, in many companies, surveys of both customers and employees reveal large gaps between what companies say they aim to do, what employees say they actually do, and what customers say they experience.

The companies where those gaps are smallest—in fact, where customers often say that they receive *more* than they expect—are predominantly those in which total quality management (TQM), or some version of it such as "Six Sigma," has been effectively introduced. TQM originated in Japanese industry in the 1950s and has become steadily more popular in the West since the early 1980s. Although TQM was originally seen by many as another management fad, in our view, it has been an extraordinarily successful initiative for those companies that have taken it seriously. It is responsible in significant measure, for example, for the transformation of much automobile manufacturing in this country and that industry's ability to compete on quality with Japanese imports.

TQM is an outstanding example   when taken seriously—of how purpose can be successfully translated into action.

Many definitions of TQM exist, but we define it as a culture and methods that aim to provide customers with products and services that fully satisfy their needs. TQM requires continual improvement in the quality of all aspects of the company's processes so that things are done right the first time, and defects and waste are eradicated from operations. Included is a focus not just on "things"—processes, products—but on people as well, such as the need to obtain workforce involvement in ideas for quality improvement and getting people to work collaboratively within and across departmental boundaries.

TQM is not a one-time "event," as are so many management fads. It encompasses a detailed methodology that takes considerable effort, time, and culture change to carry out well. The systematic use of TQM has been greatly enhanced in the U.S.—and its definition sharpened—by the federal government's Malcolm Baldrige National Quality Award. Created in 1987 by congressional mandate, this program seeks "to create an awareness of quality as an important part of organizational performance and excellence, encourage the sharing of performance excellence strategies, and recognize those organizations with particularly effective practices."[15] The Baldrige awards are given to organizations on the basis of evaluations by trained examiners on a series of criteria that include both external and internal quality performance. The criteria provide a well-reasoned, well-accepted roadmap for companies that seek to significantly improve their performance, whether or not they apply for the award.

Many organizations have "quality" programs of one kind or another, but relatively few take them seriously enough to be strong candidates for the award, even if they were to apply. Sadly, professionals in the field estimate that only about 20 to 30 percent of TQM efforts have been implemented in a truly effective way in American companies, with significant and lasting quality results. For the majority, it is a fad or an isolated and staged event in one part of the business for public relations purposes.

What does taking a program such as TQM "seriously" mean? Earlier, we listed the actions that we see as necessary for turning noble objectives into reality (such as strong and visible top management support). Consider a specific case: Federal Express was a Baldrige award winner in 1990 and, Baldrige or not, is a company with an outstanding and widespread reputation for the excellence of its service to customers.

FedEx's quality policy calls for "100 percent customer satisfaction 100 percent of the time." That charge comes directly from the company's founder and CEO, Frederick Smith. How has this clear-as-a-bell policy been followed?[16] Here are some of the ways:

- Two customer guarantees: if FedEx is more than 60 seconds late in delivering a package, the customer does not have to pay for it. If the customer asks to trace a package and FedEx can't do it within 30 minutes, the customer doesn't have to pay for it.

- Many millions of dollars invested in the company's tracking system ("customers want the security that comes from knowing we can track their packages every step of the way").

- An executive quality board oversees the quality process; quality administrators and employee facilitators are assigned throughout the corporation.

- A Service Quality Index (SQI) measures service *failures* in 12 categories, such as delivery late on the right day, delivery on the wrong day, missed pick up, damaged package, and calls to the company abandoned by customers. (The focus is on failures because the company says that 99 percent is not good enough; 99 percent success in FedEx translates into millions of failures.)

- Twelve root-cause teams, one for each SQI category, seek reasons for failures in each category and act to assure they do not recur. Each team is led by a senior executive.

- Cross-functional teams in every geographic market that meet regularly to figure out what needs to happen in their market to get those airplanes and trucks out on time every night.

- Quality action teams work on specific projects.

- Regular surveys of customers (2,400 calls per quarter) to determine their needs, satisfactions, and dissatisfactions.

- Regular surveys of employees with disciplined follow-up on the issues uncovered. ("To achieve the greatest level of customer satisfaction you need to keep your employees happy. Customers can sense if employees do not have tremendous pride in their company….")

- Empowerment of employees to do whatever it takes to satisfy customers. (Frederick Smith says of FedEx employees, "Daily, they go above and beyond to serve our customers. They are the ones who trek through all kinds of weather; deliver every package, each one critical; they persist in solving every customer's problem; they ferret out the root cause of every problem to prevent it from ever happening again. Their talent, ingenuity, and commitment drive our quality standards closer to our goal of 100 percent customer satisfaction.")

- Intensive six-week training for couriers and service representatives in customer interaction.

- Employee satisfaction, service quality, and profitability goals.

- Bonuses are tied to the achievement of the goals.

FedEx's devotion to quality is a superb example of what we mean by turning an organization's purpose into a day-to-day reality.

Does serious attention to quality pay off in financial performance? Innumerable studies demonstrate unequivocally that it does. One such study involves the "Baldrige Index," which is a fictitious stock fund made up of the publicly traded U.S. companies that received the Baldrige award between 1991 and 2000. The Baldrige Index has consistently beaten the S&P 500 by ratios of three and four to one. "Even after a tough year for the stock market [2001]," said Commerce Secretary Don Evans, "especially for technology stocks, the Baldrige Index continues to make a terrific showing, outperforming the Standard & Poor's 500 for the eighth year. While performance in the stock market is only one indicator of success, this study and others show that businesses that seek excellence in everything they do can achieve success in many areas, including the bottom line."[17]

Of course, customers are an extremely important constituency of any organization, but they are just one. Detailed examples of effective implementation like FedEx's could be given for other stakeholder groups, such as suppliers, investors, and the community. In all these cases, the basic points are the same:

- Purposes and principles must emanate from strongly held convictions of senior management.

- Statements of purposes and principles will be exercises in futility unless they are accompanied by a serious implementation plan.

This chapter focused on one of the most important components of leadership, namely, providing an organization with purpose and principles of which employees can be proud and to which they will willingly and enthusiastically devote their skill and energy. You've learned in earlier chapters that we in no way minimize the importance to workers of equitable treatment in matters such as pay, benefits, and job security. In fact, having noble purposes—for customers, community, and so on…rings hollow if employees are treated shabbily. But, conceiving of employees as working "just for a living" and the corporation as strictly an economic entity misses a vital element of human nature: the need to do something that matters and to do it well. Ironically, seeing employees strictly in economic terms is a long-term economic disadvantage for a company because it loses out on the extra performance that people who are enthusiastic about a purpose will give.

CHAPTER 7

Job Enablement

"Most of what we call management consists of making it difficult for people to get their work done."

—Peter F. Drucker

People have a strong need to do something that matters and to do it well. Chapter 6, "Organization Purpose and Principles," discusses the purpose of work (doing something that matters). This chapter focuses on the business practices that enable people to get their jobs done well. Chapter 8, "Job Challenge," deals with the more inclusive concept of job satisfaction: what people feel about the nature of work itself.

At the end of a day's work, people want to feel that something was accomplished by virtue of their efforts. A factory employee becomes disheartened when he produces little during the day because of time spent struggling with faulty equipment and waiting for the maintenance person to arrive. An executive feels equally frustrated when she spends her day in endless departmental meetings with little discernable accomplishment. Those wasted days are depressing for most workers at all levels.

An enormous body of data supports these common-sense observations, but, as always, the qualitative data is compelling. There are so many complaints about obstacles; we highlight the various types just to make it easier to get through them. Here is a sampling of comments to our open-ended questions about what employees like least about their jobs and what can be done to improve effectiveness:

Our operations are <u>needlessly complex</u> which result in too many customer service and client-satisfaction issues.

I hate the <u>bureaucracy</u>—we need approvals for just about every-thing and the number of sign-offs is ridiculous.

I am constantly challenged by teams and individuals that <u>resist change</u> and have <u>silo mentalities.</u> <u>Cost control and management for technology spending is not well controlled or understood</u>. This restricts my business' ability to effectively understand costs and reengineer.

We must put an end to <u>obsolete practices</u>, with people who are <u>afraid of change</u> and who are an obstacle for the company. There's also the <u>lack of communication</u> about processes and poli-cies within the company, which results in redone work and failure.

We don't talk much to each other across department lines and so there's a lot of <u>duplication of effort</u> and continual "<u>reinventing the wheel</u>." It is extraordinarily wasteful.

We spend too much time <u>chasing numbers</u>. We are not looking at the product; we just make sure it moves fast. It can be dirty and ugly but let's make sure it moves.

A lot of time is spent satisfying some <u>ambiguous policies</u> that everybody has a different interpretation of.

Simplification of the work processes so employees can get their work done without <u>unnecessary delays</u>.

We need to <u>slow down with all the major changes</u> we make, as an agency. We have been inundated in the field and have to endure so many changes both systematically and programmatically, it has been entirely too much to absorb. The staff believes quality must come first but they also cannot afford to <u>spend hours search-ing for an answer to a question</u>.

The largest obstacle here is <u>too much work</u>...which hurts quality and creates a tremendous amount of stress due to...lack of bal-ance between work and family life.

One obstacle is the <u>lack of cooperation</u> with other departments in the organization. Everyone has an emphasis on satisfying "their" customer, which means that if you need their cooperation in serving your customer, your customer is not their customer so you are a low priority.

The <u>red tape</u> is an obstacle I face in getting my job done.

One obstacle is <u>company politics</u>.

There has been <u>little or no communication</u> from our management staff as to the direction, roles, and responsibilities that we will have.

We have been <u>fire-fighting</u> instead of...planning.

The <u>lack of training</u> to extend my areas of expertise is one obstacle I face in getting my job done.

There are constant <u>organizational restructuring</u> changes...I'm not even sure who my supervisor is at this point.

<u>Preventative maintenance</u> is a myth here.

Maybe I would feel better about <u>all the reports</u> we're required to fill out if I knew what they were for! They fall into a big pit never to be seen again.

However, when things go well, when workers genuinely feel accomplishment, their spirits are buoyed. Again, we highlight the key sense of the employees' comments:

The huge advantage this company enjoys in its industry is that employees like me are <u>empowered to make decisions</u> and there is very little to no red tape, unnecessary delays, no wasted time, no wasteful projects, and no unnecessary reporting. Management, keep up the good work.

The group I work with is led by a manager with a unique leadership style. <u>She allows individuals...to fully utilize their creativity, business knowledge, and talents</u>, in a <u>teamwork environment</u> to meet the challenges of our business. With each project, there is always a great sense of pride and accomplishment. My <u>leader is not the one in the spotlight</u>, she is the one leading the applause. Thanks to her for making the company the best place to work.

My immediate leaders both allow me to perform my daily duties at a high level. They have <u>confidence and trust in the decisions I make</u>. This trust and <u>their being available</u> allow for self-confidence and performance levels to be above expectations. I want to thank them for listening to and resolving our concerns when presented.

I have the <u>freedom to go above and beyond for the customer</u> and to put them first. That gives me a feeling of accomplishment.

I enjoy the <u>flexibility</u> offered by working from a <u>virtual office</u>. I like to create my own schedule in order to accomplish what I need to on a day to day basis.

The opportunity to <u>act independently</u> of my team when accomplishing the necessary work of my job, while at the same time knowing whenever I need my team's assistance, <u>they're always right there</u>.

I feel one of the main strengths of this company is its <u>willingness to work with their customers</u> on a one-to-one basis. This makes the customer feel more confident in the place they chose to do business and makes my job that much enjoyable.

You <u>know what you have to do</u> and (you have) the <u>tools to accomplish the task</u> with <u>teamwork</u> encouraged. We have the most <u>up-to-date equipment</u>.

The <u>empowerment</u> levels have risen in my department, and for that, I say thank you. Nothing is more encouraging than being able to say to a customer, "I can do that right now for you," or, "I can get it done by tomorrow no problem," and mean it.

We have the <u>tools and ability to really produce dynamic, cutting-edge solutions</u>. I love working for an organization...that accomplishes many great results and has great care and compassion for people.

The survey data discussed in Chapter 1, "What Workers Want—The Big Picture," which portrayed how workers feel about their ability to get their jobs done, showed variability in two ways. First, organizations differ greatly from each other. For example, although on average, 57 percent of employees rate their organizations favorably on the overall effectiveness with which they are managed, the range is enormous: 24 to 92 percent. Obviously, some organizations are seen as highly effective and in others, from the employees' perspectives, it is a wonder that anything ever gets done! Workers dislike the latter intensely because they have little or no sense of accomplishment—indeed, working there embarrasses them—and because an ineffectively managed organization does not bode well for long-term job security or advancement prospects. A high degree of perceived effectiveness is a condition for worker enthusiasm.

Besides the differences between organizations, variability also exists in *what* hampers employees from getting the job done. Over the many companies we surveyed, the highest average percent favorable (84 percent) is obtained in response to the question, "I have a clear idea of the results expected of me on my job." One of the least favorable percents (39 percent) is in response to a question about bureaucracy interfering with getting the job done.

Therefore, the pervasive problem is not lack of information about what to do. It is getting tasks done in the face of the obstacles organizations erect, however unintentionally, to their accomplishment. The latter illustrates the law of unintended consequences such as a decision-making process that makes it excruciatingly difficult for *any* decision to be made, or made in a timely way.

Where in organizations do we find the most pervasive obstacles? We previously established that employees tend to be most positive toward two opposite poles of the organization: the immediate work environment and the total organization. Examples of the former are the clarity of the results expected from the worker, the immediate supervisor's technical competence, the skills and abilities of co-workers, and the job itself. The total organization level includes views of profitability, the quality of the products or services the organization produces for its customers, and the organization's ethics in the conduct of its business.

Although some organizations are viewed as dysfunctional from top to bottom, the tendency is for the major problems, as seen by employees, to be in the "middle" (below senior management and the organization as a whole and above the immediate manager and immediate work environment). It is as if the products produced and the profits achieved come *despite* what goes on internally (for example, the need for continual rework to be able to eventually ship a high-quality product). Consider this comment:

> *It is amazing that the (product) we deliver to the (government agency) is of such high quality considering the lousy tools we have, the politics in management, people finger-pointing and screaming at each other, and the unbelievable red tape and bureaucracy. The quality costs a bundle, of course, because of all the rework and waste, but that's what taxpayers are for.*

The "middle" is where coordination and control among the parts of the organization take place. When employees complain about "bureaucracy," they don't usually see the villain as their own boss or the CEO, but rather middle management and staff departments, such as Finance or IT. When they complain about a lack of cooperation, they most often see the problem stemming from departments other than their own and not being dealt with—in fact, sometimes magnified—by the middle managers to whom their and those other departments report. A complaint about disorganization is usually directed at inefficient work processes that cut across departments, such as the way staff groups and the line don't communicate or coordinate well with each other.

Because this chapter is about the ability of workers to get their jobs done, we focus largely on middle-organization issues because that is where, on average, the most severe impediments to performance originate. It is where, on matters of performance, organizations with enthusiastic workforces most differ from their counterparts.

Immediate supervisors are, of course, important, but in surveys they receive quite high ratings in just about all organizations. (This is as true in surveys done by others as in our own.) Our surveys show that 78 percent of employees are positive toward their managers' technical skills (knowing the job). Although the rating on their human-relations skills is lower (66 percent), it is still much higher than the ratings we obtain on issues such as bureaucracy. In almost all companies, only about 10 percent of managers receive ratings that can be described as unfavorable. That 10 percent can do much harm and require attention, but, by and large, we find first-line management to be bulwarks of organizations, even of those organizations that otherwise might be dysfunctional almost to the point of collapse.

It is telling that the attitudes of first-line managers toward levels above them and toward staff groups are often identical to those of their subordinates. Managers see themselves as "buffers" who protect their workers—and their performance—from the damage that those levels and groups can inflict.

A frequent theme in senior-management discussions and in the management literature is the presumed weakness of first-level management: they are blamed for various employee morale and performance problems. It makes sense intuitively to target those managers because they are in direct contact with the workers and might be relatively inexperienced in management. Yes, they are a big influence, but usually for the better! Therefore, intuition fails here and improvement steps, to the extent that they target the first level, are often misplaced.

Our focus on action in the middle does not mean that what happens at the top is unimportant. The CEO is often responsible for impediments such as excessive bureaucracy because he wants the organization to operate that way, and he chooses the middle-level line and staff people who gladly do what he wants, but his role in those respects is often invisible to the rank and file. He, therefore, receives unjustifiably high ratings. However, action to resolve the problems, although directed at the middle, must begin with him.

By and large, the key impediments to job accomplishment are a function of the culture set by senior management—especially the CEO—that is expressed operationally in the way the organization is structured and the way people interact within that structure. Our framework for discussing these matters will be "bureaucracy" because that encompasses much of what our survey data show as problems.

Ah, Bureaucracy! The Evil That Just Won't Go Away

I find it mind-boggling. We do not shoot paper at the enemy.

—Admiral Joseph Metcalf, U.S. Navy (Ret.), on the 20 tons of paper and file cabinets aboard the Navy's newest frigates.

The only thing that saves us from the bureaucracy is its inefficiency.

—Eugene McCarthy, Former Senator from Minnesota

Bureaucracy defends the status quo long past the time when the quo has lost its status.

—Laurence J. Peter, Former Educator and Author, and the Father of the Famous "Peter Principle"

In our surveys, employees see bureaucracy as the major obstacle to completing their jobs. What do employees mean by the bureaucracy they say they deplore? The issue is frequently mentioned in write-ins, as shown earlier, as well as in focus groups. A number of insights emerge.

One area that workers often cite as a bureaucratic obstacle is the decision-approval process, which is seen as needlessly delaying decisions (such as decisions about resources employees need to do their jobs), detracting from the quality of decisions (often because the ultimate decision-makers are far from the action), and reflecting a distrust of employees and their ability to make the right decisions.

Another bureaucratic obstacle is the perceived obsession with rules and the enforcement of those rules. Employees see this as diverting the organization from its objectives and its ability to respond to changing conditions. It is the seeming obsession on means rather than ends that rankles workers here.

Let's not forget good old-fashioned "paperwork" (whether it's really paperwork or new-age digital paperwork). Employees see much of the paperwork as utterly useless at worst, or simply shrouded in mystery at best ("What use is made of all these reports?"). All in all, much of it is taken to be a general waste of employees' time and the organization's resources.

Another facet of bureaucracy that's frequently mentioned is what's created by functional specialization, which is seen as narrowing the attention of units to only their own goals and creating boundaries between units that inhibit cooperation between them.

Of course, most people would prefer to operate with considerable autonomy, ignore the paperwork, and be able to rely on the cooperation of other units to effectively perform their jobs. That's not news. It seems that the term bureaucracy is rarely used in anything but a pejorative sense. Much of the disdain for bureaucracy is well-earned, but before we elaborate on its dysfunctions and recommend what an organization can do about them, we must first recognize why bureaucracy is, in a number of ways, simply *indispensable* to organizations.

Can an organization survive for long without a clearly defined authority structure? Can it survive well without executives who are unafraid to use their authority? Of course not. People who argue for the elimination of bureaucracy in organizations—much of which concerns eliminating or drastically reducing power differentials—are arguing for chaos and organization ineptitude.[1]

Only anarchists and theorists with no practical experience advocate chaos. *Workers certainly do not.* Therefore, although the majority of comments about bureaucracy concerns its downsides, we also receive complaints in a number of organization surveys about *under*-control (i.e., too little bureaucracy)! Take these comments, for example:

I feel that the structure is disorganized, and I don't feel as if I can get a clear answer.

We are completely disorganized and have no real planning when we roll out new products and services!

This "matrix" structure here is very confusing—everyone seems to think they can give me orders and they conflict with each other. How do I satisfy many masters? Who am I accountable to?

This place seems completely disorganized. Every change seems to be a knee-jerk reaction, and it seems that leadership usually has to go back and change things after they see that it hasn't worked. There's no stability. This place needs an over haul. There are too many old Band-Aids over old wounds.

Who's in charge here? Nobody seems to want to take responsibility for anything. It's a spineless management, starting at the top. No leadership, all CYA.

There's little documentation when programs change—it drives me crazy. We need at least a little paperwork! When people leave, the most elementary knowledge of what's been done leaves with them.

We are not arguing for the bureaucracy overkill that we have all come to know and hate. However, chaos is not the only alternative to that type of bureaucracy. In their studies of group functioning, social psychologists make a useful distinction between three types of leadership: autocratic, laissez-faire, and democratic. We call the last of these "participative" because democracy usually means that the leaders are chosen by the led and that concept has little applicability in the employee-management relationship. The key criterion is not how leaders are chosen but how they lead.

An autocratic style of management is characterized by domination of employees, inflexibility, and a belief that discipline and punishment are the most effective means to get most workers to work. This characterization can be applied to individual managers, such as compulsive, micro-managing autocrats, and to the formal structures and processes that constitute excessive bureaucracy: approvals required for even the smallest decisions, a multitude of rules rigidly enforced, and work divided into extremely narrow tasks. Both at the individual manager and structural levels, a fundamental assumption underlying autocratic management is a distrust of workers and their ability or willingness to do their jobs without a high degree of top-down control.

Autocratic management is not necessarily a malevolent management in the sense of unconcern for the economic well-being of workers. Some paternalistic organizations treat their workers well—in pay, benefits, and job security—but because of the "father knows best" attitude, their managements are normally highly autocratic. These organizations are benevolent dictatorships.

At the opposite extreme from autocratic management is a laissez-faire style, which means "to let (people) do (as they choose)." Laissez-faire managers are divorced from their employees, uninvolved in what they do (either in a directing or helping sense). These proverbial "weak" managers can, in their way, frustrate employees as much as autocratic managers.

On a structural level, laissez-faire management is the "anti-bureaucracy," with few or no approval processes, rules, paperwork, or specialization by task. We know of no organization that is laissez-faire in its pure form, but those companies that even approximate this management style cannot endure: they soon disappear or are overhauled in order to survive. However, individual laissez-faire managers can survive for a while, especially in prosperous times when no one pays much attention to a department's mediocre performance. When times get tight, these managers can no longer be tolerated and are removed.

Unfortunately, new executives brought in "to get this place under control," usually go to the opposite extreme: the pendulum swings and they turn what was chaos into what employees feel is a virtual prison. The assumption is not just that things need to be tightened up—of course, they do—but that workers somehow enjoy chaos and must therefore be managed with an iron fist. So, the frustration of employees formerly working under laissez-faire management turns into resentment because of the severity of the controls that have been imposed and the view that employees are untrustworthy.

The alternative to laissez-faire and autocratic management is participative management, whose key characteristic is *mutual influence*. Figure 7-1 shows the three management types depicted in terms of influence patterns.

Autocratic management is top-down, laissez-faire is bottom-up ("the inmates running the asylum," as the joke goes), and in participative management, influence goes both up and down. The point of two-way influence is *not* that there is no boss or that everyone is boss. That is a laissez-faire environment, and it is not what we mean or what workers want.

Figure 7-1   Three styles of management.

In Figure 7-1, the arrow pointing down in participative management symbolizes the importance of certain traditional, top-down management principles. These principles are important to both the organization and its workers because both the effectiveness of organizations and worker satisfaction require that there be clear and decisive direction from leadership; clarity of responsibilities, authorities, and accountabilities; authority that is commensurate with responsibility and accountability; unified command (each employee has one boss); and a clear approval process and rules governing acceptable employee behavior.

These principles are familiar and uncomplicated, and they encompass key aspects of what is normally termed bureaucracy. Although they are familiar, the principles deserve to be repeated because they are fundamental and, as we have said, they are seen by some influential modern theorists as largely out-of-date and dysfunctional, especially in the "new economy" or "post-industrial age" and with so-called Generation X workers. These theorists talk about recasting traditional hierarchical organizations into all kinds of new forms, such as "spider's webs," "starbursts," "wagon wheels," or "shamrocks."

To seriously advocate the destruction of any semblance of hierarchy shows a lack of experience with the debilitating consequences of working in a directionless organization, or getting conflicting instructions from different bosses, or being unable to decipher who is responsible for what, or not having the authority to carry out one's responsibilities. *These severe obstacles hinder the performance of workers, whether they work in the "new" or "old" economy and whatever their "generation."*

However, the fundamental top-down principles can be taken to the opposite extreme, and that is the nub of the problem created by the bureaucracy and the bureaucrats that we abhor. For example, being decisive can sometimes mean rejecting all the subordinates' input into decisions. Also, providing direction to an organization can turn into micro-management: instructing trained and experienced subordinates on how to do their jobs in every detail and requiring them to seek approvals for even the most minor deviations and decisions. So too, making responsibilities and accountabilities clear can result in rigid boundaries between departments, which makes collaboration impossible (the familiar problem of organization "silos").

These examples depict the slippage of common-sense organization principles into a rigid machine model of bureaucracy. A machine cannot function without "a place for everything and everything in its place" and without external initiation and control. That's the nature of an inanimate machine. But, people are not machines or parts of machines: they can exercise judgment, do more than one task simultaneously, and initiate activity. And they have emotions, such as feeling disrespected and angry when they're treated as if they cannot exercise judgment, do more than one task at a time, or initiate activity.

Workers want, and organizations require, just as much order as is appropriate to the need, and no more. Workers in a machine shop do not pretend that they can set corporate or divisional strategies, so they want leaders who know how to do that and do it well. But, they can run the machines, and they are a rich source of ideas for how to make those machines run better and how to improve many other aspects of their work environments and work processes to increase performance. Managers who obsess about how their employees do their work, and about minutiae such as the exact amount of time they take for rest breaks, are not only doing what they shouldn't be doing (meddling), they are not doing what they need to be doing: the planning, expediting, counseling, and coordinating that truly help employees get their jobs done.

The consequences of autocratic management—by an individual autocratic supervisor or a system that is excessively bureaucratic—are twofold in terms of worker performance. On the one hand, spurts in performance can be obtained by such top-down methods, but unless the pressure is continually applied and employees are supervised closely (and the supervisors are supervised closely) performance will soon dissipate. In other words, achieving performance becomes completely dependent on outside forces applied on resistant employees instead of on their internal motivation to do well and be proud of their work.

A second major consequence of autocratic management is an enormous loss of brainpower: the ideas and ingenuity that the people who know the jobs well (the workers) can apply to improving performance.

Autocratic management—whether by an individual manager or by an oppressive bureaucracy—makes the very costly mistake of assuming that wisdom is related directly and almost entirely to hierarchical level.

A Management Style That Works

Although autocratic and laissez-faire managing are different styles, both demotivate the overwhelming majority of workers, and both place severe obstacles in the way of their getting their jobs done. The research done in this area strongly supports a third approach, which is participative. This approach is not simply a middle ground between the other two styles of management (a little less of this, a little more of that); it is really an entirely different method.

When moving away from autocratic management, some people adopt a laissez-faire attitude; this is an abandonment of leadership, not a leadership style. Participative leadership is an active style that stimulates involvement, not a passive style that forfeits leadership. In an effective participative organization, no one is in doubt as to who is in charge. But, that person expects employees to *think*, to exercise judgment, and not just do. Judgment is expected from workers in performing their specific tasks and in identifying and implementing ways to improve the organization's performance as a whole. That is the environment in which impediments to performance can be removed and in which employee enthusiasm can flourish.

Our advocacy of participative management is based on more than theory or a democratic ethic. A great deal of research evidence demonstrates the superiority of participative management for *performance*. The evidence comes both from laboratory experiments and from field studies in real organizations. It has been collected in systematic ways since the 1940s. Also, contrary to what is commonly assumed, its value is not limited to America or other societies with a long history of democratic traditions.[2]

Over the last two or three decades, participative management has found widespread acceptance in industry, so our arguments, which were perhaps once considered radical, might now strike some readers as unsurprising, almost truisms. Unfortunately, much of the acceptance of this management style has been superficial: in our studies, we find significant gaps between what organizations and managers say—and even believe—and what they actually do, as their employees report it.

However, many managers are consistent: they not only practice an autocratic management style, they advocate it! They reject all arguments or evidence that participative management is anything more than a naive wish or fad. This is management's "old school," command-and-control types who believe that work is inherently distasteful to most people and that getting people to work and work hard requires a tough, autocratic approach.

Other skeptics employ a more sophisticated argument, asserting that the effectiveness of any approach to management depends on the conditions in which it used. Their contentions range from the obvious (for example, in case of a fire, does a manager engage his employees in a discussion of what to do?) to the less obvious, such as arguing that entire categories of work are best handled with autocratic methods.

Of course, specific conditions exist, such as many emergencies, where people don't want to be asked for their opinions; they just want to be told what to do. It is ludicrous to think otherwise, and nobody does. Who would suggest that new and untrained employees be given latitude as to how to do their work? *The workers themselves* don't want that latitude—they want training and direction. Being left on their own greatly frustrates them, and it is an example of laissez-faire, not participative, management. Finally, there are those few employees who simply don't want to exercise judgment or give opinions under any condition; they are most comfortable taking and following orders and that is how they need to be managed.

These are exceptions to the usual circumstance, such as trained and experienced employees working under normal, non-emergency conditions with a strong desire to exercise judgment while performing their jobs and to be asked for their views on how to improve performance. The exceptions do not negate the validity of the assertion about the overall superiority of participative management; they simply point to the need to avoid unthinking, mechanical application of this—or any—principle.

More serious and sweeping than the obvious exceptions to the rule (such as emergencies) is the argument that *entire categories of work* suffer if the management style and structure are participative. It is argued that autocratic management and hierarchical bureaucracy are better suited than participation to work that is simple and stable. "If the work is relatively simple and there is little need for coordination and problem-solving, it is possible that the control-oriented approach [what we are calling autocratic] will produce better results...The control-oriented approach also works well if the type of work is highly stable so that it can be programmed to be done in the same way for a long period."[3]

In other words, when there is no apparent need to think, don't ask workers to do it.

The reasoning, if correct, would make participative management inapplicable to most blue-collar manufacturing jobs. In the most widely quoted paper employing this reasoning, "Beyond Theory Y," the authors compare the effectiveness of authoritarian and participative styles in two manufacturing and two research laboratory settings. They conclude that:

> Enterprises with highly predictable tasks [the manufacturing plants] perform better with organizations characterized by the highly formalized procedures and management hierarchies of the classical approach. With highly uncertain tasks that require more extensive problem solving [the two research laboratories], on the other hand, organizations that are less formalized and emphasize self-control and member participation in decision making are more effective.

They term this reasoning *contingency theory*, which is that the effectiveness of a management practice is contingent on other factors, such as the nature of the task.[4]

Contingency theory certainly makes intuitive sense, but it has a serious problem: it is contradicted by the legion of extraordinarily successful participatory initiatives in manufacturing plants throughout the world. For example, what is one to make of the extensive use by Japanese manufacturing companies of worker participation in shop-floor decision making and the extraordinarily positive productivity and quality results that have thereby been achieved? The best-known of these applications have been with assembly-line workers in Japan's automotive industry—hardly a condition of "highly uncertain tasks."

Because of their success, the Japanese have been emulated in many countries, most frequently in manufacturing settings. That is where a change to participation has been most needed because manufacturing workers have been traditionally among the most autocratically managed. We don't pretend that manufacturing workers can ever approach the kind of autonomy that, say, research scientists or sales representatives enjoy. The nature of manufacturing work, the need for standardization and precise coordination, for example, doesn't allow for it and *workers don't expect it*. But, that doesn't mean that participation by workers is irrelevant or even harmful in manufacturing, as the contingency theorists appear to argue. For one, no matter how routine a job might appear, there is almost always room for worker judgment.

Second, although work may be highly standardized to the point where a company wouldn't want individual workers to deviate too much from the prescribed method, improvement opportunities invariably abound that workers can spot. These potential improvements can be fully discussed and carefully planned before they're implemented. The results are encouraging and, sometimes, astounding.

> One of this book's authors, consulting with a plastics manufacturer, heard workers in a focus group comment on the enormous amount of "trim waste" in the plant. A participant said that he had long had an idea for a device to be attached to the cutting machine that would reduce the waste by at least half. The consultant reported this to the engineering department and after innumerable meetings, the engineering department decided to try out the idea; it was made and installed on one cutting machine, and the trim waste was reduced by 82 percent! The device was installed throughout the plant. When asked why he hadn't mentioned the idea before, the worker simply said, "Nobody asked me."

Jeffrey Pfeffer writes of a department in the Eaton Corporation where "…workers tired of fixing equipment that broke down and suggested that they build two new automated machines themselves. They did it for less than a third of what outside vendors would have charged and doubled the output of the department in the first year."[5]

Tom Peters reports on an experience in the Tennant Company where the engineers devised a system to increase the efficiency of a welding department. The system, designed to reduce the need to store units during the welding process, would cost $100,000, which the company deemed too costly. "A small group of welders tackled the problem. They designed an overhead monorail that could carry welded parts from one station to another so a frame could be welded together from start to finish without leaving the department…They discovered a supply of I-beams in a local junkyard and bought them for less than $2,000. In two days, they installed the monorail. In the first year of its use, the new system saved…more than $29,000 in time and storage space."[6]

Anyone who has worked with manufacturing employees and kept his eyes open would not be surprised by these and the many thousands of other instances of the contributions these people can make—if only they were asked! The moral of our story, for the theory and practice of management, is that there is often too much emphasis on human differences and not enough on human similarities. We hear of the differences between occupations, between generations, and between nations. (We used to hear much about differences between the sexes and the races, but those views are no longer acceptable to express.) Many of the presumed differences make intuitive sense because they confirm long-held prejudices. But, they usually cannot withstand empirical tests. For example, Japan was historically a highly authoritarian society, and yet industrial democracy has been flourishing there for half a century. Isn't it so, the prejudice goes, that most blue-collar workers don't have the will or the ability to use their minds to improve work operations? We know that assumption is dead wrong, and outstanding managers have known that for a long time.

With the few exceptions we have cited, participative management works under all conditions and for all segments of the workforce.

Layers of Management

Central to a discussion of authoritarian and participative management is the matter of "steep" or "flat" organizations. Organizations that workers feel to be excessively bureaucratic are typically steep: there are many layers in the management hierarchy with each level supervising relatively few employees. A flat organization is, of course, the opposite: fewer layers exist in the management hierarchy and, generally, a larger number of employees report to each level.

In steep organizations, workers' comments about the number of management levels are notably caustic and cynical. The criticism does *not* indicate that workers don't want to be managed—they do. They simply see no added value—they see value *subtracted* by the many management layers. In addition to problems of over-supervision (because the boss supervises only a small number of employees, what else does the boss have to do but supervise?), their major gripes concern the large costs to the organization of so many managers (salary, expensive office space, and so on), the way these steep hierarchies inhibit timely decision making, and the way they inhibit clear communications up and down the organization. Here are some typical employee comments about management layers. They are in response to the question, "What do you like least about working here?"

All these levels of management and their cost! What are their jobs but to be messenger boys and work like crazy to keep their jobs? They have very few people to supervise so they're all over their employees.

The unneeded multiple levels of management and the politics that exists. Managers that only care about themselves and not the process or the people are useless. I see very little value add of all these levels. If you asked me who my real manager was, I would say two levels above the one they call my immediate manager. Essentially, I don't know why they need him and his manager.

There is a lack of clear communication between all these multiple levels of management, creating confusion about goals and achievements. It's like the telephone game. By the time the message gets to us, it's garbled.

A question we often see asked, in answers to open–ended survey questions, is the caustic, "What do all these people do?" It is actually a good question, and one that is occasionally asked by the people who occupy the multi-management layers!

Two major reasons exist for steep organization structures: control and functional specialization. It's interesting that the number of employees reporting to a supervisor is referred to as *span of control*. The more control that is desired (in other words, the less people are trusted to control themselves), the fewer the number of people that report to managers at each level, and thus the greater the number of management levels that is required. In that sense, the steep organization consists of checkers upon checkers.

In addition, the role of managers in each layer of the hierarchy is to coordinate with other managers of interdependent departments. The finer the division of labor ("functionalization") in an organization—the more each individual or department performs just one function rather than being responsible for the "whole thing" (e.g., a whole product or a whole customer)—the greater is the interdependence, and, consequently, the greater the need for coordination among the parts and for layers of management to do the coordination. In a completely functionalized organization, no one is responsible for the "whole thing" except the very top to which all the functions report through their individual, and usually multi-layered, hierarchies. We return to this matter in detail in the section, "The Benefits of Self-Managed Teams," where we show how a team can within itself perform a variety of functions and make more possible very flat (and effective) organizations.

Not much research has been done that systematically and directly tests the relationship between the number of management layers and organization performance. One study, performed by A.T. Kearny in 1985 that covered 41 large companies, found a strong relationship between the number of management layers and long-term financial performance. The organizations with outstanding performance had an average of 7.2 layers versus 11.1 for the others. They also had 500 fewer staff specialists per $1 billion in sales.[7] In another study, researchers found that companies with average spans of three (necessitating a steep hierarchy) spend almost four times as much to manage each payroll dollar as do firms that have average spans of eight.[8]

Many case studies reinforce the quantitative research findings. Again, companies with records of outstanding long-term performance frequently have extraordinarily flat structures. Nucor Corporation is a leading example of this. As F. Kenneth Iverson, the chairman of Nucor, has said, "The most important thing American industry needs to do is reduce the number of management layers...(It's) one thing we're really fanatical about. We have four management layers. We have a foreman, and the foreman goes directly to the department head, and the department head goes directly to the general manager, and he goes directly to this office."[9] Another example is The Dana Corporation, which went from 15 management layers (and barely profitable) to five layers (with greater profit).

Many organizations with flat structures, such as Nucor, are characterized by a strong sense of purpose and principles. A powerful company culture built on a belief in the importance and value of what it does and shared norms as to what is acceptable behavior is in itself a control mechanism that lessens the need for external controls such as layer upon layer of management.

It's of a piece and the process is circular: organizations with committed and enthusiastic workforces require fewer controls and the fewer those controls, the greater the commitment and enthusiasm.

Perhaps a major reason companies with enthusiastic workforces are more successful is simply that it is so much less costly to manage them. Steep structures are especially costly, but not only because of the compensation and expenses of the occupants of the many hierarchical layers. Time and manpower spent responding to the checking and meddling of managers and their staff groups, directly or through endless report requests, is another expense source. Yet another is the inherent delays in the flow of needed information through the hierarchy and in decision making; these delays reduce the timeliness and quality of response to problems and to a changing business environment. Last, but by no means least, is employee frustration and demotivation. There is no such thing as an enthusiastic workforce in an excessively layered organization.

The Benefits of Self-Managed Teams

A goal of every organization should be to flatten the structure as much as possible, probably to somewhere between 5 and 7 levels for the total organization, and just three levels in any single facility.[10] Flat organizations lend themselves to decentralized decision making because managers have less time to get involved in the minutiae of day-day-to-day decision making. Organizations that don't take advantage of this—that simply cut managers and management levels without consciously and deliberately moving authority down the line—find that the workload of the remaining managers has increased enormously, the quality of their work has likely decreased, and their work lives have become correspondingly miserable. These organizations eventually add back managerial staff, which causes costs to balloon once again. They accomplish worse than nothing because reorganizations and re-reorganizations are expensive and pendulum swings in structure foster (or reinforce) a cynicism in employees about their management's competence.

The decentralization that allows for effective flattening of an organization (not just head chopping) is, by far, best accomplished by establishing self-managed teams (occasionally known by the acronym SMTs). SMTs are teams of workers who, with their supervisors, have delegated to them various functions and the authority and resources needed to carry them out. Ideally, the team does the "whole thing," builds a whole product or provides all the services for a defined customer or set of customers.

You could go so far as to suggest that SMTs are required for effective flat organizations, if for no other reason than some of the work performed by the eliminated management layers actually does need to be done!

Increasing control by, not of, employees is the essence of the SMT approach to management. This self control is a product of less need to obtain management's approval for many decisions because these have been delegated to the team ("vertical" autonomy) and less need for the group to interact with other units to obtain their assent to decisions because so many functions—traditionally distributed among a number of departments—are performed within the team and, therefore, under control of the team ("horizontal" autonomy).

Performance is further enhanced in well-run SMTs by the emergence of "group norms," in which members exert a strong influence on each other's behavior. This is especially pronounced in the case of nonproductive employees who are subjected to internal group pressure to perform, thus reducing the need for management's intervention.

There is considerable variability in the number and kinds of management tasks delegated to the teams. Any SMT worthy of its name will have a great deal of input over work methods, work scheduling, production goals, quality assurance, and relationships with the team's customers (external or internal). But, some organizations have gone considerably further and delegate human-resources decisions, such as hiring employees, to the teams.

Large differences exist in the degree to which a team performs the "whole thing." At one end of the continuum are organizations such as Volvo, which experimented with workers building an entire car. At the other end are organizations such as Toyota, which has given teams a lot of authority, but the actual work done is still highly fractionated.

In looking at the research in general on the effectiveness of SMTs, it seems that the ideal SMT is one that:

- Produces the whole thing for an identified customer or set of customers with whom the team interacts.

- Has clear goals for which it is accountable.

- Contains within it all the skills needed to get the job done.

- Has access to the information and has control over the resources it needs to complete the job.

- Receives rewards based on team performance.

In other words, under ideal circumstances, the team operates like a small business whose members are highly involved in its management and in the sharing of its rewards.[11]

Of course, all this can be taken to an illogical extreme. Should each small team in a company have its own computer specialists for programming, computer repair, and so on? That would be quite a luxury. For the sake of efficiency and depth of resources, some degree of centralization (sharing) of IT services is required. Should a team of employees in an automobile-assembly plant assemble an entire car, rather than use the traditional mass-production method? The idea sounds enticing and it has even been tried in a few places, such as in the Volvo plant in Uddevalla, Sweden. The research on this manufacturing model, such as that done by Dr. Paul Adler of USC, concludes that it can never achieve the levels of well-run mass-production automobile-assembly plants.[12]

The Toyota paradigm is instructive because it does have teams and it strongly encourages—in fact, is famous for—employee participation: employees are encouraged to suggest ways to improve the manufacturing process to increase quality and reduce waste and inefficiency. Furthermore, they have responsibility and authority as teams for various duties, such as quality control, scheduling shifts, maintaining and repairing equipment, record keeping, measuring performance, and ordering supplies. Workers have the authority to stop the line when they see a defect or problem. One of the four principles of the Toyota production system is that people are intelligent and motivated to do a good job and that they will do that and more if they're given the right tools and adequate authority.

Nevertheless, Toyota's assembly lines are still highly fractionated and standardized. The teams in that company are each responsible for a few stations on the assembly line, not the "whole thing." Volvo represents a rejection of the scientific management principles that govern the structure of the traditional mass-production assembly line. Toyota, for the sake of efficiency, accepts those principles, but puts workers as a team largely in charge of the line.

Manufacturing the "whole car" is an example of taking the SMT concept too far. But, the number of organizations in which the concept doesn't go far enough outweigh such examples. These are the instances where SMTs and other participative mechanisms are largely antithetical to the organization's real culture and outside the mainstream of its business.

Participative programs are too often like ornaments—worn by organizations to enhance their image (and even self image) but bear little relationship to the organization's reality. Office or plant walls display signs and slogans that preach participation and the importance of people, but the treatment of workers day to day, even when there are SMTs, makes these signs appear to be nothing more than company propaganda. In a study of the General Motors plant in Linden, NJ, for example, Ruth Milkman found that the company had introduced a number of participative philosophies and methods. However, despite company slogans calling for involvement and empowerment, workers at Linden "...were told they could pull a cord and stop the line to prevent defective products from proceeding, but those who did so were criticized by foremen and eventually stopped trying."[13]

The situation in Linden is reminiscent of other participative efforts, such as many formal suggestion programs that fail or just limp along because of the gap between their promise and what employees experience in practice. It has been said that suggestion programs raise morale at two times: when you put them in and when you take them out. Who can dispute the worthiness of soliciting improvement ideas from workers and paying them for the ideas that the company adopts? Despite the promise, suggestion programs often frustrate employees.

By contrast, Toyota's suggestion system has been fabulously successful. Toyota employees, on the average, are reported to contribute 50 or more ideas per person per year, and 80 percent of those ideas are implemented. Essentially, all employees participate. In the U.S., however, the participation rate in suggestion programs is about 8 percent (2.4 ideas per person per year), and only about one-third of the suggestions are implemented. Toyota has a highly participative culture and its suggestion system is integral to its continuous improvement efforts.[14]

The lesson from Toyota lies not just in the mechanics of its suggestion programs or the way it structures teams. It is that, for this company, the programs are not add-ons or symbols of the way Toyota wants the world to believe that it manages people. It is not public relations. *It is the way Toyota actually treats its workers, day in and day out.*

It is critical, furthermore, that participative mechanisms be at the heart of the *business,* not just the culture. Self-managing teams do best when management gives them clear direction with high performance goals and clear accountabilities.[15] You might recall that participative management— as contrasted with laissez-faire—contains an "arrow down," which is direction from above. That arrow ties the team to the goals and strategies of the business.

Therefore, we prefer the term "self managed" to "self led" teams. We have never observed an effective SMT with a weak leader or one whose top priorities did not include the priorities of the business as a business. Therefore, it's not all fun and games. In fact, what is really not fun for workers is to work on things that don't really matter. In some applications of SMTs, one gets the feeling that the team, with its endless team-building exercises, becomes almost an end in itself rather than a means for the achievement of business ends. "I've seen too many groups go off on wilderness excursions or use 'structured team-building experiences' to try to turn a group into a team. These approaches don't work because they're not focused on business and performance issues or the broader organization context and focus. They don't get any real work done."[16]

To summarize, self-managed teams and other participative mechanisms can achieve more than brief bursts of enthusiasm and performance only if they do not stand alone: they must be exemplars of—not exceptions to—the broad organization culture, and they must clearly and directly support the achievement of business objectives. Failing those, they will shrivel and, to all intents and purposes, die. But, when they are an integral part of the organization—not something tacked on for show—they are, by far, the most effective way to organize.

CHAPTER 8

Job Challenge

---

*"The greatest analgesic, soporific, stimulant,
tranquilizer, narcotic, and to some extent even
antibiotic—in short, the closest thing
to a genuine panacea—known to medical
science is work."*

—Thomas Szasz, M.D., Psychiatrist, Author

The previous chapter focused on enablement, which is creating an organization where workers can get their jobs done and the positive impact that such enablement has on their satisfaction and pride. But efficient, even high quality, performance is not sufficient. The *work itself*—what is done—is also critical.

For example, for many workers, doing simple, repetitive work for long periods of time (no matter how well done) can be highly unsatisfying, even intolerable. Here are some comments from employees in these jobs about the work itself (in response to the question about what they like least in the company):

> *(I dislike) waking up in the morning to come to this boring job...my skills are being wasted daily!*

> *Dealing with the repetitiveness. My job is always the same in my case. I don't have much of a variety of things to do, so sometimes things can be mind-numbing, frustrating, or even stressful.*

The type of work we do is very tedious and it is very hard not to get in a rut. Sometimes, the pressure of the job can get to you. You can feel the anxiety building up as soon as you enter the building.

This job is monotonous. After say, three months, there is no longer any challenge. Just being able to sit at a desk for hours at a time is the most challenge I face.

My job is mundane. It can be very boring, so it is a challenge to enjoy the actual work I do, even though I enjoy the company as a whole.

My job does not require much grey matter. I think my 12-year old sister could do it.

Those comments are from people for whom challenging work is important and whose jobs don't provide it. As previously stated, the literature is full of social commentary on the presumed debilitating and dehumanizing nature of routine work. We are all familiar with the depiction of much work as so boring that only a trained monkey could bear it.

Therefore, we would expect a large percentage of people to be unhappy with their work. Even more broadly, as we have said, it is widely believed that people are inherently averse to work anyway, no matter how it is structured. According to this view, job satisfaction is a contradiction in terms; we work because we are forced to, not because we want to. It is a widely held, in fact ancient, notion.[1] But, it is a misconception.

Our research disproves the notion that most people are unhappy with the kind of work they do.

As reported earlier, 76 percent of millions of surveyed workers say they like their jobs. Only 8 percent report dissatisfaction. Furthermore, the range of responses from the most positive to the least positive organization on this point is from 95 percent to 52 percent. Therefore, even in the organization with the employees least happy with their jobs, more than half of the workers are nonetheless still favorable. These results, as we have pointed out, show surprisingly little variation by the type of work people do. For example, while 76 percent of salaried employees express satisfaction with their jobs, 72 percent of hourly employees do so as well.[2]

Is This an Aberration, Are Workers Delusional, or Are They Lying?

None of the above. You can gain insight into how some people view the work itself from this not atypical interchange, which is abstracted from a focus group of puckers in a cookie and cracker factory. These women do extremely routine and repetitive work.

> *Focus Group Moderator*: What is it that you particularly like about working here?
>
> *Worker 1*: We get good pay and this company has been here forever so I feel secure here.
>
> *Worker 2*: Our pay has kept up with the cost of living—that's really important to me.
>
> *Worker 3*: I like the fact that we are making a product that people really enjoy. It makes me feel good to know that what I do makes people happy.
>
> *Worker 4*: We can have as much product as we like for free at lunch and coffee breaks but we shouldn't be eating so much. [Laughter] But the cookies really are so good.
>
> *Moderator*: Now, what do you particular dislike about working here?
>
> *Worker 1*: The equipment. It keeps breaking down. They only have two maintenance people left. It's crazy! We lose so much production waiting for maintenance to show up.
>
> *Worker 4*: My forelady—she is always looking over my shoulder, trying to make sure I'm working and doing my work right. I've been here 27 years, for goodness sake, doing the same thing, and she wants to make sure I know how to do it?
>
> *Worker 3*: I don't think that management thinks we're very smart. They almost never ask for our opinions and we could help. There's a lot of wastage now.
>
> *Moderator*: For example?
>
> *Worker 3*: For example, we see when a machine is running so fast that it's sure to break down. And it always does. I've stopped telling them because they don't listen.

(Additional dislikes were then mentioned such as sometimes being asked to work overtime on too short notice, heating and air conditioning that don't work well ("it's either too hot or too cold"), a co-worker who "gets away with murder," and the factory general manager who "just looks straight ahead and never says 'Hello'").

Moderator: Nobody mentioned the actual work you do, packing cookies and crackers. Do you like this kind of work?

Worker 1: It's fine; it's a job. I'm happy to have it and I do it well.

Worker 2: Well, really, the work is boring; I'm doing the same thing over and over again. I'd rather be doing something else. Sometimes, I feel like I just can't do it anymore. I feel like a machine, but I'm too old to change jobs now.

Worker 3: It's not very interesting, it's the same thing every day, but to tell you the truth, I don't much care. Because we don't have to think on the job, we can talk to each other. We really socialize; I love that, with all the ladies.

Worker 4: Look, I'm lucky to have a steady job. My father was always getting laid off, always worried.

Worker 5: Frankly, although I wouldn't say I hate the work, it does get boring. I'd like to do something more interesting. I want to do bookkeeping and I'm thinking of going to night school for it.

Worker 6: This job is good enough for me. I couldn't be a book-keeper, numbers make my head spin.

Worker 7: As (name) said, it's a job and a pretty good one when you consider that I don't have much education.

Moderator: Would any of you be interested in a promotion to a management position, such as forelady?

Worker 2: Not interested—who needs all those headaches? When I leave work, I don't want to think about it.

Worker 7: And we'd lose our union membership and overtime pay. It's more work for very little more pay.

Worker 6: I couldn't stand managing people. They're a headache. And I'd lose my friends because of the things I'd have to do, like discipline them. I'd be terrible at that.

> *Worker 5*: Me, I think I could do it. I would certainly like to try if they would give me training. I'm a good organizer. But I've never been asked.

Notice the two different reactions to the routine nature of the work: Worker 2 felt like a machine sometimes, but most of the others had different reactions. Although the latter workers were not particularly positive ("it's a job"), they were certainly not particularly negative. Judging from their other comments (about equipment, the forelady, and so on), these women were not reluctant to express the negative views they did have. Their opinions about their jobs stand in great contrast to the earlier ones cited, selected from employees in a number of different companies who expressed great unhappiness with the routine nature of their work.

The divergence in views supports what is obvious to us all: *people differ enormously in what is attractive or unattractive to them about the content of jobs.* Although there are also individual differences in the other needs we have discussed in this book, such as the importance of job security or camaraderie, these differences are small compared to the great variations in the kinds of jobs people prefer.

The differences are of two kinds. One concerns sheer preference for a type of work based on interest or personality or upbringing. Some people, for example, prefer outdoor to indoor work, office work to factory work, working near one's boss to being "on one's own" (such as a salesperson), working in the private to the public or not-for-profit sector, 9-to-5 jobs versus jobs with often long and uncertain working hours, or predictable to unpredictable job routines.

Given a Choice, Few People Volunteer to Fail

A second set of differences comes from people's sense of what they can do *well*. Being a professional athlete is awfully appealing to many youngsters, but they learn quickly whether they have the rare talent to be successful at it. Few without that talent continue trying for long.

As we know, workers want to be proud of what they do. If the job involves managing others, for example, and an employee doesn't feel she is good at that, she keeps away from management positions. If someone is poor in math, he keeps away from engineering studies and engineering jobs. If he is clumsy, he naturally keeps away from jobs requiring a lot of manual dexterity.

This is why we don't see more dissatisfaction with the work itself in our surveys, even among those who do repetitive and routine work. Many of us could not do repetitive work for long without feeling great frustration. But, although we choose not to do repetitive work, others *do* choose to do it. They are not, by and large, unhappy with their choice.

Some workers feel that they're good primarily at doing the same thing over again. In addition to the cookie and cracker factory workers, consider Melvyn Reich, who's known as the buttonhole man:

> Would you want to make buttonholes day in and day out? *The New York Times* recently ran an offbeat article on Melvin Reich, Manhattan's premier buttonhole man. "Buttonholes are what we do. We do buttonholes and buttonholes and buttonholes. I am specialized, like the doctors," said Reich. "You think it's nothing. Just a buttonhole. But it's something. It's not nothing." And the clincher: "Zippers are a totally different field. It's a different game. A man can do so much."[3]

Note that, in the group of cookie packers, only one worker expressed interest in a management position. Many workers share the view of "who needs the headaches?". Other workers, however, thrive on those headaches. So, you might sensibly ask, "Who is the more rational (or less neurotic): workers who just want to do their jobs with minimum problems and stress and leave work without thinking any more about it, or people who can't live without work-related stress 24/7?"

We are being facetious to make the point that understanding workers requires that we put ourselves in *their* shoes, asking what *they* want from a job. We do not argue that people who prefer routine work and don't want to be bosses have greater emotional health than the rest of us. What some workers avoid as "stressful," others seek out as "challenging." To put ourselves in other people's shoes requires suspending evaluative judgments— such as judging to be demeaning the kinds of work that millions of people choose to do—and feeling that they must (or should) be unhappy with it.

Although a free labor market allows for the diversity of individual preferences to be matched by the diversity of jobs, it doesn't always work that way. In our surveys, an average of 8 percent say that they are dissatisfied with their jobs; so, some people obviously do find themselves doing a job that they dislike. This group is only a minority of the workforce, but the consequence of that unhappiness for their overall morale is huge. For example, 65 percent of employees who are dissatisfied with the work itself express dissatisfaction with the company overall, while only 10 percent of those satisfied with their jobs express such dissatisfaction. Table 8-1 shows the relationship between satisfaction with the work itself and overall satisfaction with an organization.

Table 8-1   Relationship Between Job Satisfaction and Overall Satisfaction

Job Satisfaction	Overall Satisfaction		
	Satisfied	**Neutral**	**Dissatisfied**
Satisfied	74%	16%	10%
Neutral	32%	44%	24%
Dissatisfied	13%	22%	65%

Given the importance of the work itself and the diversity of jobs available, why do some people wind up in jobs they dislike?

For one, mistakes can be made in job choices, especially in initial choices. For example, people might misjudge their abilities or be wrong about the abilities a job requires so, early in their employment, they search for other, more compatible opportunities. This is why most voluntary or mutually agreed upon turnover occurs within the first year or so of employment. (That is healthy turnover because people should not stay in jobs they dislike and organizations should not want them to stay.)

Sometimes, however, people get "stuck" in a job that it is difficult or impossible to leave, often for financial reasons. The need to earn a living can lead people to take and keep a job that is disliked, sometimes intensely. That is truly a sad situation, spending eight hours a day being miserable, and is most pronounced in times of economic downturn (when work is scarce) and in a person's middle and later career stages when leaving an organization to search for another job can result in significant financial loss. The latter is the familiar case of the "golden handcuffs": pensions, stock options, and the like hold employees in jobs with which they are unhappy and in which they might remain for a long time just for financial reasons. Certainly, man does not live by bread alone, but bread is important, especially with mortgages, college tuitions to pay and, later in life, the need to retire with financial security.

Push and Pull Forces

It's interesting to view the area of job choice, retention, and satisfaction as the result of motivational *push-pull forces*. Pull forces are the factors that make a job choice (or any choice) feel attractive, like the interest a person has in the job, its challenge, and the promise of excitement.

On the other hand, push forces feel like coercive influences coming from behind, in the sense of driving or forcing us against our will toward the choice, such as the need to please other people ("I promised my parents I would be a doctor!") or because it is the lesser of two evils ("I dislike this alternative the least."), or perhaps the need to just make a living ("I have to eat."). A mixture of these two forces controls many job choices.

When the pull forces predominate, you arise each morning and look forward to going to work. When only push forces exist, your action of choice when the sun rises is hitting the snooze button.

Now, let's complicate it a bit. Sometimes, the type of occupation is perfectly desirable, but it has been structured by the organization, or managed by a manager, in a way that makes it onerous for the job occupant. Although only 8 percent express dissatisfaction with "the job itself—the kind of work you do," the results are considerably less positive on other questions regarding the job. For example, about 20 percent of our surveyed employees say that their jobs do not make good use of their skills and abilities.

The kind of work might be desirable, but not the way that the job is structured or managed. Consider these views, which were abstracted from an interview with Terry, a sales representative in a telecommunications company:

> Terry loves sales work, but finds his sales job in the company to be a miserable experience.
>
> Terry loves the challenge of selling. He is most happy when he is with customers, either pursuing or servicing accounts. He is a salesman's salesman. He derives great pleasure from landing accounts and doing the things necessary to keep customers loyal. The money is important to him as it is to other salespeople, but Terry absolutely loves the activity itself. He believes in his product and in himself. He genuinely likes people, and people seem to like Terry. He is highly motivated to deliver on each promise to his clients and he does not sleep well if he misses any.

Give him a territory, a challenging quota, a clear, accurate compensation plan, and a smart leader who points him in the right direction, and he is a happy employee who will deliver the goods. What else would someone want from a salesman?

Unfortunately for Terry and the company, Terry's day is significantly consumed by something other than selling. Paperwork is the bane of a salesperson's existence. Some of this administrative activity is seen as an unavoidable and necessary evil by salespeople and is absolutely required to keep track of important outcomes.

Terry also unfortunately reports to Mr. Pitz, a former top salesman, who also fashions himself an innovative administrator. Mr. Pitz established an elaborate database that tracks every interaction each salesperson has with each customer contact. He calls it TCTS (Total Customer Tracking System). The level of detail of his database grows every month and, thus, its attendant burden on his salespeople. In fact, part of the performance evaluation of his people is the thoroughness of their data input. Mr. Pitz presented his system to top management and they were impressed.

Terry and his colleagues must track each contact they have with customers and record the nature of the customer's business (its gross revenue, number of employees, geography, and ten other demographic characteristics); details of the conversation (whom they talked to and their job title, whether they bought, if so how much, the tone of the conversation); and the reasons of those who didn't buy (budget issues, satisfaction with current supplier, reputation of Terry's company).

Despite the fact that some of this information could be useful, Terry feels that he has been relegated to doing the job of a clerk rather than a salesman for a significant part of his day. It interferes with his ability to sell. Terry would like to leave the company, but he feels he can't because of his pay and pension; he feels that he cannot duplicate them elsewhere.

Terry loves the work itself—sales, but not his sales job in this company. Of course, some people just won't put up with a job in which they're miserable, no matter what the financial impact of leaving; witness the following write-in comment from a survey:

People are leaving this company for the competition and cannot believe the difference in stress level and how much better they are treated at their new job. We are constantly being pulled into internal conference calls, district calls, training, etc. Sixty percent of my time is spent on internal non-value work. Valuable people will continue to leave the organization unless some of the non-value internal initiatives are eliminated. This company is burning people out! I'm going to leave even if I can't immediately find a job elsewhere. I'll just take a little time off to recover and look for something else.

When employees are unhappy in their current situation, it's fortunate if they also feel able to leave it. However, many employees are like Terry; for whatever reason (financial, lack of self confidence, and so on), they feel stuck. Terry very much wants to be a salesman—it's his dream career—but it has become a nightmare. We will continue this discussion of job structure and what organizations should do about it later in this chapter. But we must elaborate first on the near-universal need people have to feel proud of their work.

Although large differences exist in the kinds of work (occupations) people prefer, almost everyone wants to be proud of what they do. Pride in the job comes from three sources: *performing well*, *using valued skills*, and *doing something of significance*.

Performing well.   The criteria a worker uses to judge his performance usually have both external sources (such as what the company or immediate boss wants) and internal sources (how the worker himself judges his performance, which, in turn, almost always has past external sources, especially the standards emphasized in training). Although the two primary and nearly universal criteria to evaluate performance are quantity and quality of work, it is the quality of the work that is the more important cause of worker pride. Turning out a lot of work is just not as meaningful in terms of self-esteem as doing something well.[4] This underlies much of the frequent conflict between workers and management about the amount of work expected. It is not just workers' resistance to a pace that will leave them physically exhausted or even harm their health. Those are, of course, important, but workers also fear the impact of undue production pressure on their ability to produce quality work and provide quality service to customers. The issue, in other words, is a matter of their *pride*. The following comments represent this point (in response to the question of what you like least about working here):

> *The ongoing facade that quality is so important, when in actuality, very little value is placed upon it; with the vast majority of emphasis placed on the all important numbers, the quantity, the production, etc. My over 100 percent quality means absolutely nothing in comparison with my low numbers. Poor quality is OK, low numbers are not! But poor quality is not OK with me!*

> *The incredible fast pace that everyone works at this company is a problem. I can't help but wonder if people at other companies work at such an incredibly fast pace. Things cannot keep speeding faster and faster, which seems to be the plan. We can't do the high quality work we are capable of because there is not enough time to read, think and make smart decisions and plans.*

> *There are so many customer complaints due to layoffs and outsourcing of systems, which result in poor quality and slow response times. Supposedly it saves money, but down times are increased and clients and customers are given poorer service. I hate hearing customer complaints but there's nothing we can do. No matter what we say, we are budget driven rather than quality driven.*

It is easy to interpret resistance to production pressure as proof of workers' laziness. However, few workers want a lax, laissez-faire environment — there is no pride in that. They object to an emphasis on quantity when it becomes excessive and detrimental to their physical well being, the quality of their work, and the organization's reputation with its customers.

Using valued skills.   Self-esteem flows not just from performing well, but doing so in a way that uses what the employee considers her valued skills. In a broad sense, the importance of quality derives from this because quality is associated with traits that workers value, traits that are distinctly human, such as craftsmanship, dedication, and judgment. Sheer production, on the other hand, is most closely associated with the non-human world, such as robots and the proverbial "trained monkeys." In fact, for speed of output, usually nothing human can beat a machine.

Within the human world—the world of workers—there are numerous kinds and levels of skill. Most workers become frustrated when their jobs do not make use of their skills:

> *This organization must work on utilizing the abilities and brains of the administrative staff. It's very difficult doing exactly the*

same tasks over and over every month. Just because you are very good at something does not mean it's all you are capable of!

My management does not have sufficient tech skills to manage me in a technical environment. They do not use my skills properly. I work more as a technician than an engineer. It's galling not to be treated as a professional.

The bureaucracy is stifling. I have a management title and believe I have strong management abilities, but I'm not allowed to function as a manager. I am micro-managed every step of the way. My manager constantly goes around me directly to my employees. When he goes through me, I'm just a messenger for him.

I was hired here to run Sales. The CEO was head of Sales at one time and still acts that way. I get almost no latitude. I was told when I was hired that he wanted new ideas because things were stagnant. That was just talk. I'm really his A.A. [administrative assistant]. He's not going to change and it's time to get out of here.

I feel like a trained monkey on this job. It's so routine and predetermined that there is absolutely no room for using my judgment, my education. It's really debilitating.

My greatest challenge is surviving the day. I feel there is way too much emphasis on administrative activities, rather than satisfying customer needs. My customer service skills are atrophying.

On the other hand, when workers feel that their skills are being fully used, it becomes a source of joy:

I like the autonomy given me by my leader to use my professional skills and experience to accomplish my daily tasks. I am especially pleased about my leaders' confidence in me as a person and in my abilities. This empowers me with the motivation and pride to perform my job at this company with 100 percent dedication to my client and my employer.

I am really using and further developing my skills—I just love it! Who would have believed that I would have fallen into a job like this at my age—they trust me with major assignments such as managing relationships with pretty big customers.

It's very pleasurable not having a pigeon-holed job. Instead, things here are dynamic and new skills are learned every day.

I feel blessed to have the opportunity to succeed, learn, grow, and enhance my current management, HR, conflict resolution, and sales skills.

When a worker has a skill that is both important and unique or unusual in his workplace, it is a source of *great* joy. Being considered the expert in your field of work is such a terrific feeling:

I hate to boast, but I don't know what they'd do here without me.

My leadership and technological skills have increased immeasurably over the last five-plus years. I am extremely grateful to the company. It is a source of great pride to me to be regularly sought out and asked by other managers what to do in particular situations.

Many workers are interested in improving their current skills and gaining additional valued skills through training. Training, of course, has many positive consequences for a worker in addition to a heightened sense of competence and pride, such as higher potential income within and outside the organization and greater job security. The importance of training, especially in fields that rapidly change, has been demonstrated in many studies. For example, in a survey of the goals of technical employees in 25 countries, we found that receiving training—continual training—ranked at or near the top in every country in what employees say they want from their jobs.[5]

Doing work of significance.   In addition to performing well and having their skills used, most everyone wants to feel that what they do makes a difference, especially to their organizations and to the organization's customers. Professional employees are also often interested in having an impact on the status and progress of their professions.

We are not referring to Nobel Prize–type contributions. The workers at the cookie factory were pleased that the product they packed "made people happy." The following comments help illustrate the point:

I like the fact that you are recognized for your contributions, and rewarded for them. I have had a really good year and made the company a lot of money. I'm proud and lucky enough to be able to go on the [destination] trip for Outstanding Contributors.

My boss told me that I am essential to this department. That's the kind of boss he is. Compliments like that keep me going.

The best part of my job when all is said and done is providing good service to the customers. Pleasant and satisfied customers make the work seem like fun.

It is important to me that I feel I am contributing to my customers' success. It is especially gratifying when a customer lets me know that I have helped him or her. I feel that's why I'm here!

In this company, they don't make you feel small. They make every employee feel important, that he or she is a key part of the company's success. That works like magic for our morale.

Employees' interest in doing high-quality work comes, in part, from their concern for customers. Customer satisfaction is mentioned frequently in employee focus groups: on the positive side when workers feel that they served customers well, and with frustration and disappointment when they feel they have not, usually because, as they see it, their ability to provide quality service was severely hampered by workload or other obstacles.

Making a difference to customers again brings us to the matter of workers doing the "whole thing" rather than each worker being responsible for a fragment of a product or service. Although it's usually discussed in terms of products, such as producing an entire automobile engine, let's apply it here to servicing customers. Our first example is a bit far-out: the "customers" are laboratory animals.

One of this book's authors was engaged by the chief veterinarian of a pharmaceuticals company to help the veterinarian understand and do something about the morale of his laboratory-animal caretakers. He said that the caretakers were lethargic about their work, such as not cleaning the cages well, feeding the animals late, and coming to work late. In his words, "They are a really unenthusiastic crowd." His continual exhortations to them to improve did little good: things changed for a few days and then returned to their previous mediocre level.

On the basis of in-depth interviews with each of the caretakers, we concluded that the key issue for these people was their highly fragmented work. They were happy with the basics of their employment (pay, benefits, and job security) and liked their supervisor, but found their jobs dull and almost without meaning. But, they also said that they enjoyed animals and saw the work done in the laboratory as important. How, then, could it be dull and meaningless?

The heart of the problem was that each caretaker was responsible for just one function: filling the food and water dishes, or cleaning the cages, or administering medications, or keeping daily records (of food intake, weight, and so on). The work became routine: cleaning out the cages in the same way every day with little or no use of higher order skills and little or no sense of responsibility for, or impact on, the "customer," the *whole* customer. As one caretaker put it, "My job is not to take care of the animal; it's to shovel s...."

Unlike the cookie packers, the animal caretakers greatly disliked their fragmented jobs. The solution was obvious and was put into effect; each caretaker was given his own group of animals and almost all the responsibility for their care. This required some training of the caretakers in their various functions, including instruction in rudimentary diagnostic techniques to help them know their animals and their condition. The training and brief learning curves on the job were about the only costs incurred in making the transition to the enriched jobs.

Follow-up interviews uncovered significantly improved job satisfaction, including the feeling that their caretaker work was now more professional. The veterinarian reported that, with the exception of one caretaker who continued to be a problem and was eventually dismissed, the performance problems had almost evaporated.

Almost by definition, a sense of accomplishment means *completing* something, doing a job from beginning to end so that you can see the fruits of your labors. But, as previously pointed out, this is not always easy to accomplish because doing the "whole job," on an automobile assembly line, for example, can result in severe efficiency losses.

As a general principle, every effort should be made, within the constraints of maintaining efficiency, to design work so that workers have a sense of completeness to their tasks. A second principle is that it is almost invariably desirable—and especially when efficiency issues severely limit providing complete tasks for individuals—to organize by *self-managing teams* (SMTs) that do have beginning-to-end responsibility for significant operations. As noted in the previous chapter, SMTs are delegated responsibility for tasks such as scheduling, assigning work, improving methods, maintenance, on-the-job training, and quality control. These are a complete and enriched set of responsibilities in which individual workers participate and from which, as a team, they obtain a sense of achievement and pride.

To the extent possible, the team should also be responsible and accountable for *relationships with customers*. This is important because it is primarily through the customer relationship that people learn whether their work has, indeed, made a difference. Of course, many employees do not have contact with external customers, but everyone in an organization can be said to have a customer, if not external, then internal. For example, on an assembly line, those who machine parts have those who assemble them as customers. The customers of product development are manufacturing and sales. The customers of staff groups, such as Human Resources and Information Technology, are the line divisions.

Chapter 10, "Teamwork," details the relationships between an organization's units, and between them and the external customers. For now, suffice it to say that effectiveness and job satisfaction are greatly enhanced by organizing the teams, when possible, around identified customers (whether they're external or internal), and setting the primary goal of the teams to meet the needs of their customers.

Organizing around customers allows employees to not only focus on customers and their needs, but it permits them to know the extent to which those needs are being met. We have said that making a difference—to customers, their organization, perhaps to their profession—is important for job satisfaction. What we have largely omitted from the discussion is how employees know that they have made a difference. They might feel that they know based on self-evaluation, but that is usually inadequate. Clear and regular feedback is absolutely vital from those the work is meant to affect. Such feedback provides both the information workers need for evaluating and improving their performance and the recognition for good performance that is so crucial for maintaining a high level of worker motivation and morale. The next chapter discusses feedback, recognition, and reward.

CHAPTER 9

Feedback, Recognition, and Reward

"I can live for two months on a good compliment!"

—Mark Twain

The previous chapters have focused on the satisfaction (or dissatisfaction) that's intrinsic to the work itself. Now, we turn to the external sources of satisfaction. Here, we refer to that sense of achievement and accomplishment that comes from the opinions of others, especially the opinions of those whose views we respect or can influence our careers and earnings. Feedback from others enables us to improve how we do our work, and so we obtain an even greater sense of achievement.

Do Workers Get the Feedback They Need?

When asked to rate their own organizations with regard to feedback, the survey data are, at best, lukewarm. Remember that the great majority of employees (84 percent) in our surveys say that they know what's expected of them. However, only 53 percent claim to receive sufficient feedback on how well they do their work. Similarly, only about 51 percent say that they are satisfied with the recognition they receive after a job well done. Most interestingly, only 38 percent of surveyed workers *disagree* with the statement, "I get criticized much more quickly for poor performance than praised for good performance," which means that the performance of most employees is more likely to be "recognized" in a negative sense when it is perceived to be sub-par than when it meets or exceeds a manager's expectations. The following comments, which respond to the question, "What do you like *least* about working here?" exemplify the data:

> *Having to deal on a daily basis with my manager since every time he gives feedback, it is always negative. That is the only thing I think in the mornings when going to work. Am I going to get more of his negative feedback? I leave my house with a negative feeling, drive to work with a negative feeling. When I finally get here, my motivation is sapped.*

> *I will never, never, never—I repeat never—hear anything good from my supervisor about my work. It's as if praising an employee somehow lessens him. He simply has to be the only one who matters here. But make a mistake and he's on your back immediately.*

> *My manager is a pretty good guy and certainly knows his job but has to learn that you don't only give feedback to an employee when something goes wrong. He praises very, very rarely.*

It's unfortunate that many managers appear to have trouble giving good feedback. By this, we mean constructive feedback; it need not always be positive to be effective, but it must always be helpful. Considered most broadly, performance feedback is a vehicle for the following:

- **Guidance.**   The improvements an employee must make in his performance, and the steps he can take to improve. This is among the most basic of a manager's responsibilities.

- **Evaluation.**   How the organization regards the employee's performance in relation to expectations and to others. Is the employee doing well, poorly, or average?

- **Recognition.**   Expressing appreciation for a job well done.

- **Reward.**   Recognition translated into something tangible (usually money).

- **Direction.**   Communicating or reinforcing what the organization needs, values, and expects from employees.

These five aspects and outcomes of feedback are vital to employees and the organization. Although most people have a sense of responsibility and want to do their jobs well, that motivation wanes rapidly *if no one seems to care.* On the other hand, if no one seems to care except when something goes wrong, motivation can quickly turn into resentment.

We are told that some people are entirely "inner-directed." They don't care about the opinions of others, and they don't need external impetus or feedback to be productively engaged in their work. Where these people are, we don't know! But, common myth says they exist, and we're sure that one or two of them must be running around making it difficult for the rest of us mere humans. Wouldn't it be terrific if all of us were so "inner-directed" that others' reactions to our work were irrelevant? Unfortunately, that is not human nature. Aside from the usefulness of feedback in providing direction to employees and helping them improve, human beings require attention and appreciation from others to perform at their best levels. When that performance is taken for granted by management, as in, "that's what we expect, why mention it?," employees and the company lose.

Managers must be concerned with each function of feedback: guidance, evaluation, recognition, reward, and direction. Let's look thoroughly at each of these.

Guidance: Cognitive Feedback

Guidance refers to the cognitive functions of feedback. It is the process of providing employees with empirical, factual (and hopefully objective) knowledge about their performance and how to improve it. This is not the same as *affective* feedback, which relates to evaluation, recognition, and reward. In real life, of course, cognitive and affective feedback are not so easily separated: it is difficult to communicate the errors a person makes without also conveying an evaluation of her performance. That is one of the major problems in providing the kind of feedback that employees accept and use rather than resist. We will return to this problem shortly, including suggestions on to how you might overcome it.

At its most basic level, nobody can function in life (much less at work) without factual feedback. We do something and want to know whether what we did had the expected or desired effect. The source of feedback does not have to be human: we learn whether we combed our hair to our liking from a mirror; whether we're speeding from a speedometer; whether we get to work on time from a clock; whether we're exercising too hard from a heart monitor. Feedback allows us to modify our behavior: for example, we can decide to take a faster method of transportation when late for an appointment, and the next time we have the same appointment, we can decide to leave home earlier.

Critical to us as humans is feedback from other humans. Some feedback requires human intervention to give it real meaning, such as a doctor interpreting the results of a medical test for a patient. Some feedback can only be from other humans, like much of the feedback people get on the appropriateness of their behavior in daily life (whether, for example, their behavior conforms to basic civility and "good manners").

At work, the most crucial feedback people can receive concerns their performance. Without feedback, there can be only a limited sense of achievement and opportunity to improve performance, and at work, it has both nonhuman and human sources. Almost all organizations have numerous performance measures: profitability, sales, costs, delivery time, customer defections, productivity, defective parts, absenteeism, and so on. Ideally, those measures are designed into the business or work process so that they are provided automatically and frequently—sometimes continuously—to the organization and its employees.

Even the most comprehensive and most automatic measurement systems almost invariably require human intervention. By themselves, numbers have limited meaning within organizations. What matters is how management and employees *interpret* those numbers. How do the numbers, for example, stack up against management's expectations? Are the changes observed in the measures, improvements or decrements, considered significant by the organization? Do other events, such as the introduction of new equipment or a change in general economic conditions, account for variations in the measures? How do the measures compare to each other (say, an increase in quality accompanied by a decrease in productivity), and what is the significance of that comparison? In general, what is the relative importance of the various measures (they are rarely equally important)?

The answers to these questions are vital to make sense of the numbers and to enable both the organization and the employee to decide on a proper course of action. If, for example, the productivity of an employee declines soon after the introduction of new equipment but declines less than what's expected, it's likely that no action would be required of that employee and management might even reward him in some way. If, on the other hand, an employee's performance improves but is less than what's expected (say, months after the use of the new equipment has been fully integrated into the employee's work), that could signal the need for corrective action. The action might include greater clarity in what is expected from the employee or additional coaching on using the new equipment.

Both the employee who performs well and the employee whose performance is below expectation need feedback, not just from the "numbers," but from a manager capable of interpreting the numbers and conveying their meaning. Part of what is also being conveyed to the employee is, of course, direction: what really matters to management in the employee's performance and behavior. (At the end of the chapter, we return to that function of feedback.)

Giving performance feedback is easier said than done. Many managers consider it among their most difficult tasks. Here is a comment about giving performance reviews from a manager's perspective:

> *The annual performance reviews I am required to conduct with my 12 direct reports is the one thing I hate about this job. I always put it off until I'm called by the HR Department and am forced to do it. My employees often can't take the criticism...they argue with me. They say they're surprised at what I said and all they want to know is about the size of their salary increase. I try to make them as brief as possible, get them over with as soon as possible. Sure, I slant them toward the positive. Who needs the trouble? Yes, I'll put in something that "needs improvement" so I won't be bothered by my boss or HR; it's just a game.*
>
> *By the way, I haven't ever been appraised by my manager, who is the VP of Manufacturing, since I can't remember when. He hates to do it, too, but HR won't get after him about it.*

This comment is not atypical: by and large, managers dislike (even dread) giving performance appraisals; they want to get them over with as quickly as possible and with as little trouble as possible. Some managers claim that it is a problem of time and onerous paperwork, ranking up there with organizing file cabinets.

The problem, however, is about as common in providing informal day-to-day feedback throughout the year. Comments such as this one are often heard:

I would like to hear from my manager now and then. You know, informally about how he feels I'm doing—might be with a few tips on how I can improve and might be a compliment from time to time. But we only speak about my performance at my annual performance appraisal, when I'm often surprised about what he likes and doesn't like about my performance. The only time I hear from him other than appraisal time is the rare occasion I have screwed up royally. He reads me the riot act and I probably deserve it, but it always takes me by surprise. When appraisal time rolls around, I expect the worst. It usually goes okay, but I'm always nervous before we sit down and go through my appraisal numbers.

A Short Course on Giving Guidance

Performance feedback is done much less frequently than it should be. When it is done, it is often poorly handled. It does not have to be so. A large amount of research has been done on the conditions that make for effective feedback.[1] From these studies, numerous specific guidelines for managers have emerged. Adhering to these guidelines makes performance feedback much less onerous for managers and more helpful to employees. Here are the key guidelines:

1. **Do not equate performance feedback with the annual performance appraisal.** Many managers make this big mistake. Aside from the fact that many such appraisals tend to be somewhat perfunctory and, to avoid unpleasantness, are positively biased, reserving feedback for that time (even when it is comprehensive and unbiased) violates a basic principle of learning and change, namely, that feedback should be given *as closely in time as possible to the actual situation*. If an employee is performing unsatisfactorily in some way, it should be obvious that he needs to know about it then and there so that the behavior does not continue. (This is also true of recognition and the reinforcement of good performance; we discuss that later in this chapter.) Many of the difficulties encountered during performance appraisal sessions come from employees being surprised by what they hear.

The extent to which employees learn something entirely new about their performance during the appraisal review is a measure of the *failure* of the performance-review process. The purposes of an annual review are to summarize, in the form of ratings and commentary, the employee's performance over the year; to more fully discuss that performance and the effectiveness of the improvement steps the employee has undertaken to improve (including what the *manager* must do to help the employee); to discuss the implications of the performance for salary increases and other rewards; and to plan for the next year, such as setting the employee's performance goals.

The formal annual appraisal session, then, is a mechanism for closure on one year and for planning the next. Also, it provides time away from immediate job pressures to simply talk about topics of relevance to the employee and his manager. In many organizations, this is a rare opportunity for a conversation that is more than perfunctory. Managers should be *required* to do it, and do it with the attitude and tools that these guidelines suggest.

2. **Don't assume that employees are only interested in receiving praise for what they do well and resent having areas in need of improvement pointed out to them.**   People enjoy being praised and prefer praise to criticism, but it is a myth that they have no interest in learning what they don't do well and what they must do to improve. This is not a hypothetical statement or wishful thinking. Take a look at some common types of write-in comments:

> *I love my supervisor. He is one of the best managers I have had since I have been here. He encourages us to do well and keeps us well informed of what we need to do, and he gives us feedback in a calm, helpful way when we do something wrong. I find what he says very helpful and I listen very carefully*

> *My manager assists me with an actionable plan for my current job, things I can do better, as well as my career/professional development. He provides avenues for growth and development. In fact his manager and he make up a great management team. It's a real education working for them.*

*My supervisor is...fair and willing to listen to our feed-
back, but she also doesn't hold back when she feels something needs improvement. She readily tries to find solutions
to any and all situations or problems and is more than
willing to join us in resolving issues. I feel fortunate to
have her as my supervisor. She is a good manager and
friend.*

*For the last three months, my team has a new...leader who
is dedicated and honest and provides us with all the information we need to measure our success. Before, I was
never given any [feedback during the year]; I was always
told by my previous supervisor my job was great. The big
surprise was at the end of the year when I was given what
I considered a marginal rating. There were obviously
improvement opportunities nobody ever made me aware
of. Thank heavens this will not happen with my current
team leader.*

It should not be a surprise that employees really do want feedback. Employees naturally want to know how they can do their
jobs better because improvement will give them a greater sense of
achievement and pride. Why, then, do managers so often assume
the opposite and hesitate to point out to employees opportunities
for improvement?

One reason is that a few employees are extremely thin-skinned
and find even a hint of criticism intolerable. They might even see
criticism where none exists. Such employees are difficult to deal
with in this respect, but fortunately, they comprise just a tiny percentage of any workforce. As with the small numbers of people
"allergic to work" (discussed in a previous chapter), you should
not generalize to everybody else based on these few employees.
Although many employees do seem to resist feedback and to be
overly sensitive to criticism, that is not primarily because of
employees' psychological problems, but rather is a result of the
way *management handles feedback*.[2]

A second reason, therefore, for managers' hesitation in providing
feedback, is that many managers simply do not know how to discuss needed improvements in their employees' work without

irritating or discouraging them. So they tend to either avoid it
entirely, deal with it through vague and indirect communications,
or, most commonly, oscillate between saying little or nothing and,
when that is no longer possible (as in "the last straw"), overreact
in a harsh way that surprises and angers employees.

Of course, some managers neither hold back nor oscillate in their
criticism: these managers don't much care what employees think,
and they can be unrelenting in finding fault with the performance
of their employees. These managers are inclined to believe that
workers don't want to work (or are careless or stupid) and that
their performance will always be deficient unless they are continually reminded of what they are doing wrong and the consequences of not improving. Interestingly, we find this management
style to be as common—perhaps even more so—in the way managers treat other managers (especially in the treatment meted out
by high-level executives) as in the way non-managerial employees are treated by their managers. In some companies, managers
are subject to much verbal abuse, including humiliation in front of
their peers. After all, senior management argues, isn't "being able
to take it" one of the reasons managers are paid a high salary? "If
they can't stand the heat, they should get out of the kitchen." But,
how do these people actually react? Here are just three examples
from managers:

> *My manager treats all his direct reports equally, that is,
> without respect and dignity. He's like a tyrant who only
> gives feedback when he is unhappy with something. He
> rants and raves, and doesn't do this in the privacy of his
> office. He doesn't care who is around, even the people who
> work for me.*

> *There is a total lack of respect and a general condescend-
> ing attitude by our management. This is a daily and con-
> stant reminder of managerial incompetence and the lack of
> direction in which this establishment is headed. What is
> preached, respect, is blatantly not practiced. I and my col-
> leagues don't behave that way with our employees. How
> did these upper-level managers get where they are?*

> *He [the CEO] treats the workers with kid gloves, he's like
> their father. With us, he's usually a first-class [expletive*

deleted]. He even blasts us for doing something he asked
us to do because he changed his mind. Nobody dares
answer back or question him; he's the king.

Whatever the pattern, managers rarely have good role models
when it comes to giving feedback. As they observe employees'
and their own reactions to the process, their belief is reinforced
that performance feedback is a difficult and unenviable job. We
know that some mangers are good at it: they don't procrastinate in
getting it done and they get the performance results they want
with little distress for themselves or their employees. It comes
down to a matter of skill (to be discussed in detail later in this
chapter) and to the fundamental assumptions that managers make
about people at work. Do managers assume that their employees
want to do the best job possible and would *appreciate* management's observations and guidance about their performance? Or,
do they believe that employees don't care about doing a good job
and so they have to be bludgeoned into doing any work at all or
doing the work correctly? Or, do they believe that employees care
about doing good work so much and their egos are so fragile that
pointing out any performance problems would be considered a
mortal wound?

Our view is that besides a small minority of employees (those
"allergic" to work and those inordinately sensitive to criticism),
the first assumption is valid: employees want to perform well and
learn how they can improve. If a manager operates on the basis of
that assumption, he will succeed, provided he follows the few
basic guidelines we spell out here. But, without accepting that
basic premise, these guidelines become meaningless.

To summarize, feedback needs to proceed from a manager's
intentions to help and guide his employees. The goal should be
learning, not venting, shaming, or lambasting.

3. **An employee whose overall performance is satisfactory and
appreciated by the organization needs to be made aware of
that.**   In the course of an employee doing his job, the work is
usually satisfactory, and even outstanding at times, but occasionally will not be good enough. That pattern is true of the overwhelming majority in every organization, and it is vital that an

employee understands that management sees his performance that way. In other words, most everyone is good, but nobody's perfect and it is to the employee's and organization's benefit that striving for improvement be *continual and normal*. (We discuss the case of poor performers who should never have been hired into their jobs or into the organization later in this chapter.)

In the statistical data, we saw that most employees agree with the statement, "A person here gets criticized much more quickly for poor performance than praised for good performance." That management style makes people uneasy about management's view of their *overall* performance and contribution to the organization. It is then difficult for an employee to feel anything but insecurity and resentment when criticized on any aspect of his performance, no matter how valid and needed the criticism is and how small the object of criticism is relative to the employee's total performance.

It is easier to accept the need for improvement—in fact, many employees welcome it—when they believe that management basically likes what they do and is helping them to do it even better. To believe that their contribution is genuinely appreciated requires more than being told from time to time in general terms, "We are happy with your work here." To be accepted as genuine, general comments and evaluations require a factual basis that is achieved by recognition of *specific* accomplishments, such as, "That report you wrote is great. I especially liked the part where you...."

Being specific in your praise diminishes the feeling that the praise is given for effect (a sort of public-relations gesture). It is helpful in pointing out the areas of performance that the employee needs to maintain. This brings us to the importance of specificity in dealing with improvement opportunities.

4. **Comments about areas that need improvement should be specific and factual rather than evaluative, and directed at the situation rather than the person.**   Positive feedback and feedback about improvement needs are similar in that both require the manager to be as specific and factual as possible. Although comments on positive aspects of performance should, indeed, convey a positive evaluation, it is better to avoid a negative tone when pointing out a need for improvement.

It is helpful to say, "You did a good job on this," but it is not help-ful to say, "You did a poor job on this." Instead, you might say, "Here is something that I think needs to be done differently." Terms such as "good," "great," "excellent," and "first class," espe-cially when accompanied by the specifics that support those eval-uations, build pride in employees and reinforce the performance so that it is sustained. But, is there any point to saying to an other-wise satisfactorily performing employee that she did a "poor," "shoddy," "unprofessional," or "below standard" job on some-thing? She already knows that a problem exists because a manag-er has told her and is being specific about the problem. Adding an evaluative comment is likely to discourage or offend the employ-ee and, in the long run, diminish her motivation and performance.

It gets worse when the negative evaluative comment is directed at the person rather than the person's performance. This is seen most commonly in critical comments about the supposed disposition or intention of the employee, such as, "You must not have been pay-ing attention when you did that," "You must find it difficult to change and do it a different way," or even, "You must have gotten up on the wrong side of the bed this morning." Although the man-ager might feel he is being "helpful" with these remarks, the employee views them as attacks on his character and reacts with defensiveness. Furthermore, managers are not being paid or asked by the organization or their employees to be psychologists. Engag-ing in amateur psychology is often a power-play anyway (it says, "I can see into you") and employees feel that and resent it. To sum-marize, stick to what the employee *does* rather than what he *is*.

There are exceptions to the recommendation to avoid negative evaluations of the employee's performance. First, the formal per-formance appraisal is a time where the manager needs to rate the employee on various dimensions of performance, and these might not be favorable: "You did well on this aspect of your perform-ance, but not on this." Obviously, we all would like to receive pos-itive rather than negative performance evaluations, but because the formal appraisal sums up the year and can be the basis for rewards such as salary increases, in our view, you can't escape their neces-sity. Furthermore, employees expect and want to know how their performance over the course of the year stacks up in manage-ment's eyes. The negative effects of unfavorable ratings are greatly mitigated if, per our guidelines, the evaluations have a factual basis and are unsurprising because they are, indeed, a summary of the feedback the employee received throughout the year.

The second exception to the recommendation regarding unfavorable evaluations is the case of the truly unsatisfactory employee; he has to know and must know early. (We discuss this situation later in this chapter.)

5. **Feedback needs to be limited to those aspects of employee behavior that relate to performance.** In their performance feedback, some managers dwell on aspects of employee behavior that are personally objectionable to the manager but are unrelated, or only marginally related, to the employee's performance or to the organization's success. These aspects might be completely outside the work situation, such as the way the employee spends her leisure time, gets along with her spouse, or raises her children. On the job, some managers are overly concerned and critical about employees' dress, even when it is wholly within the bounds of appropriate work attire. One employee bitterly complained in an interview about his manager's dislike of his southern accent.

Indeed, many aspects of what an employee does on the job or the way he lives are truly none of the manager's business or are trivial and reflect little more than a manager's personal preferences and prejudices. Some managers see themselves as parental figures who provide "helpful" guidance to employees about all things, whether it's wanted or not, whether it's related to job performance or not, and whether it's important or not. The manager must try to stick to the job and those factors that significantly affect job results. Advice on other matters should be given only when the employee seeks it (assuming the manager has knowledge in those areas).

6. **When giving performance feedback, encourage two-way communication.** When giving feedback, it is almost always sensible to involve the employee in determining what the problem is and what to do about it rather than simply instructing the employee. Obviously, this isn't wise when the employee is so new on the job that asking his opinion adds no value. It also shouldn't be done those few times when the manager is absolutely certain she knows what needs to be done and just wants the employee to

do it. Engaging the employee in a participative conversation at that point—other than to clarify what the manager wants—is seen as manipulative by the employee. Other than those occasions, the manager needs to ask the employee what he thinks and should genuinely listen to him. After all, the employee is on the job and his experience and observations must be taken into account to determine how a performance problem is to be overcome, including what the manager might be doing to harm the employee's performance. A real conversation also makes the employee more of a "partner" in the improvement process rather than simply a target of criticism. It helps create an atmosphere in which the employee feels comfortable initiating questions of his manager that will help him improve his work. In this regard, the most propitious time for performance feedback, of course, is when the employee requests it.

7. **Remember that the goal of feedback is action that improves performance.** This guideline is obvious, but it is violated in a number of ways. One major example is where the manager assumes that the issue is the employee's will or character, in which case he simply admonishes the employee to, "Pay attention to what you're doing!," or "Get moving, we need more from you!," or "Stop talking with everyone!" Those comments are appropriate for only a few workers, the ones for whom insufficient motivation is indeed the problem. However, they are unhelpful to the great majority of employees and convey disrespect for them. What is needed is a specific, doable action plan that attacks the problem, not the person, as shown in the following example (which is fictionalized from actual events):

> *Manager*: I'd like to talk to you about meeting deadlines for reports that my boss asked you to prepare. I think you missed a couple of deadlines recently.
>
> *Employee*: I didn't realize these requests had specific deadlines. He just dropped by my desk and, in a low-key manner, asked me to obtain some information.
>
> *Manager*: That's his style. Please remember to translate any request he makes as urgent. I had the same problem early in my career. You might want to ask him when he

wants this. He's likely to say as soon as possible. This usually means he wants you to start on it right away and have it to him in a day or two. I realize this puts you in a difficult situation. Feel free to come to me when he makes his next request.

A second way this rule is violated is to request action that is not in the immediate control of the person to whom the feedback is given. Remember that the action must be doable; to make it so might require resources outside of the employee's immediate control. Here's an example of a manager really "going to bat" for her employee. This is what you want to see happen (and read in your company survey):

> *My leader is...open and honest, and I am able to be the same with her. She is always available to assist me and goes out of her way to assist with my development. For example, I didn't understand the new system changes well enough. She not only provided me some materials to read and forwarded the relevant training courses available, but also put me in touch with an expert to call whenever I had a problem. I don't think I would still be here if it wasn't for her.*

The third major way in which this rule is violated is where an employee is so overwhelmed with identified problems and action steps that he simply does nothing or does things in a superficial way. A good rule of thumb is to have the employee work on no more than two or three significant action items at any time. Arriving at these requires prioritization, which is governed by what is most doable and what has the most impact on performance.

8. **Follow up and reinforce.**   For most action steps following feedback, the manager needs to follow up with the employee to assess progress: whether action has been taken, what the results were, and what, if anything, still needs to be done. Follow up also gives the manager the opportunity to compliment the employee on the changes made, which positively reinforces the behavior. Furthermore, the act of following up—and the employee knowing that it will take place—emphasizes to the employee the importance that he take action.

9. **Provide feedback only in areas in which you are competent.**
   We leave the most obvious guideline for last: know what you are
   talking about. Our guidelines, as focused as they have been on
   how feedback should be conveyed, cannot substitute for inaccura-
   cies and gaps in *what* is conveyed to an employee. Only under
   duress will employees pay attention to feedback from managers
   who know little or nothing about the workers' jobs. We see this
   problem frequently where the organization hires recent college
   graduates into supervisory jobs. These new supervisors find themselves managing workers who have been on those jobs for years
   and who, in many respects, are more knowledgeable than their
   managers. We often see comments such as this one from this frustrated worker:

   > *This company must stop hiring these young hotshots into*
   > *front-line supervisory positions just because they have col-*
   > *lege diplomas. They come on the job and tell us what to do,*
   > *but they know diddly squat. They think they can learn the*
   > *job in a day or a week, but it takes years to know what's*
   > *really going on with the machinery, with who really knows*
   > *what's what. In the old days, the foremen rose through the*
   > *ranks. We respected them because they knew the job at*
   > *least as well as we did.*

   Be modest and honest about what you know and get the right kind
   of help for the worker. When we discuss advancement later in this
   chapter, we question the wisdom of most of the hiring that is done
   directly into managerial positions.

Before we leave this topic of "cognitive" feedback, we should mention a
technique increasingly being used, namely, "360" feedback. Thus far, our
focus has been primarily on feedback from managers to employees.
Through the 360 process, ratings on various aspects of performance are
gathered from a variety of sources in addition to the manager, especially
direct reports (if the employee is a manager), peers, and internal and external customers (hence "360" for 360 degrees, i.e., feedback from a number
of angles). Other terms for the technique are multi-source and multi-rater
feedback. 360 feedback is valuable precisely because it provides data
from a number of sources and perspectives. A manager may be personally

biased in his evaluations of employees but even if not biased may be unaware of crucial aspects of employees' behavior, such as the way they interact with their peers. There is quite a bit of research data supporting the effectiveness of 360 feedback in changing behavior, particularly when the process is facilitated and supported by well-developed counseling and follow-up activities.[3]

Evaluation, Recognition, and Reward

So far, we concentrated primarily on the cognitive side of feedback (feedback that is factual and non-evaluative). Now, we consider in detail the affective, evaluative side, which is the manager's and the organization's judgment of *how well* the employee does and the implications of that judgment.

In our previous discussion, it was impossible to ignore entirely the affective side because although it is desirable to avoid evaluative comments when the feedback concerns improvement needs, we *don't want* to separate facts from evaluation when the employee does something well. In that case, evaluation and facts are inseparable because nothing needs to change in the employee's performance and, therefore, there's no reason for that feedback other than to praise and thank the employee for good performance.

How important is employee recognition in terms of generating enthusiasm and maintaining good performance? On the surface, it would not seem to be terribly important. From the organization's perspective, isn't the company already *paying* the employee for good performance? But, providing such recognition is vital: *to receive recognition for one's achievements is among the most fundamental of human needs.* We see this early in life. Think of young children eagerly awaiting their parents' praise for their accomplishments in school. It continues strongly into adulthood, even if it's not always as visible. Just as parents do well by their children when they express admiration for their children's "work," so do managers when they praise their employees' contributions. In our interviews and the write-in questions on our surveys, workers tell us with deep feeling how much they appreciate a compliment.

On the other hand, when managers do not bother to acknowledge high levels of employee performance, the effect can be discouraging and even devastating to some employees.

The desire for recognition of one's achievements is neither childish nor neurotic. Freud, the pre-eminent student of both childhood and neuroses (and their relationship), is said to have quipped at his 80th birthday party that, "An individual can tolerate infinite helpings of praise." Sometimes, we hear people deny that recognition is important to them; a worker might say "forget the praise, just give me the money," but their behavior belies this assertion. Once, we did a study at a media organization in which a tough chief executive scoffed at high-priced workers in the organization who craved professional recognition. However, those employees noted that when the CEO was passed over for a prestigious industry award, there was much fulminating and stomping around his office.

Of course, the desire for recognition can also be extreme and dysfunctional. We see this in some people in the way their need for praise is insatiable: they require it continuously, often for achievements not particularly noteworthy, and become depressed or agitated when it is not forthcoming. Furthermore, they are not too discriminating about the sources of the recognition; they want it from everyone: from people they respect and from those they disdain, from those with power and from those with no influence over their careers. Often, they are the employees we see vying for the spotlight and grabbing credit for achievements that are either not theirs or not solely theirs. They tend to be noisy and visible (often whiny), but as with the other needs we have discussed, this extreme constitutes a tiny percentage of the workforce.

Psychologically healthy people want to be recognized for their genuine achievements and are concerned primarily with the opinions of those whom they admire and, because they are realistic, with the opinions of those who can help or hurt their careers.

Before we continue this discussion, we reiterate the difference between recognition for performance and respectful treatment of workers, which was the subject of Chapter 5, "Respect." As we use the term, respect is a matter of *equity* that's owed to employees simply by virtue of their employment, just as they are owed a living wage. It is, in other words, a function of who they *are*—employees and human beings. On the other hand, recognition is for what they *do*: their performance and contribution to the organization. The two are not entirely independent, of course. The term recognition has two meanings: to acknowledge someone's *performance*, and to acknowledge someone's *existence*. The latter is a mark of respect in the workplace, such as managers being sure to say "Hello" to employees and referring to them by name. As we have said, that is important to a worker, but is not the kind of recognition that is the subject of this chapter. For recognition, the parallel comment is, "Thank you!" Whether, how much, and how a worker is thanked varies with the worker's performance. That differs from respect, which dictates that everyone deserves a "hello."

The importance of recognition is evident in the panoply of awards (both financial and non-financial) dispensed by public, private, and non-profit organizations throughout America and, indeed, the world. The range is enormous, from Nobel Prizes, Oscars, and building and street names for the famous (or soon-to-be famous) to company pins, plaques, gold watches, and various cash awards for the obscure (and soon-to-be less obscure). These are the formal means of recognition, and organizations understand that they meet deep-felt needs. Unfortunately, they might be administered in a way that severely dilutes their impact or even boomerangs to the detriment of the employees and the organization. It is also unfortunate that when executives think of employee recognition for their organizations, they usually equate that with formal recognition programs and give not nearly as much attention to informal recognition, such as managers acknowledging good performance day-to-day on the shop or office floor. Or, they equate recognition with the compensation system—pay, pay increases, bonuses, stock awards, and so on. In that view, recognition programs, if they exist, are seen as "icing on the cake"—nice to have, but not really at the heart of what employees want, which is money.

There are four major means to recognize employees. No one vehicle, such as money, suffices to provide the recognition to employees that is most important to them and beneficial for the organization:

- **Compensation.** Providing differential compensation to employees based on performance.

- **Informal recognition.** Day-to-day recognition of performance, most importantly by the immediate manager.

- **Honorifics.** Special awards given for performance as part of formal awards programs and that may be accompanied by cash.

- **Promotion.** Advancement to higher-level positions for performance.

First, we consider compensation, informal recognition, and honorifics, all of which involve just the current job of the employee and require no criteria for their exercise other than performance. Then, we discuss the role of advancement to higher-level jobs.

Management can use compensation, informal recognition, and honorifics to recognize employees either individually or in groups. The three methods are, in certain respects, independent of each other and, in other ways, interdependent. They are independent because each is important in its own right and cannot be substituted for each other. In previous chapters, we took strong exception to the view that satisfaction with the work itself can be substituted for money, and the corollary proposition that when workers complain about pay, they are really complaining about unsatisfying work. We argue that workers want *both* (and more), and to neglect either significantly diminishes employee satisfaction and motivation.

Similarly, we take issue with those who argue that only money serves to give workers genuine recognition, or, at the opposite extreme, that what they "really" crave is "attention" or "esteem" (and that a focus on money is a displacement brought on by their frustration in not getting what they really want). Some suggest that the basic human need to feel appreciated can be satisfied by recognition programs and no-cost job-recognition devices.[4]

This advice might comfort managements trying to economize, but it is unhelpful—and even dangerous—because it ignores money's importance to people and can cause managers to believe that they can manipulate and "psychologize" people and save on labor costs. They can't—not for long, anyway. It doesn't matter that part of the power of money is its symbolic or psychological significance. Whether symbolic or practical, it is of great importance to most people and cannot be satisfied with non-financial rewards.

Psychological rewards are not a substitute for money, but managers should not make the opposite error, which is believing that money can be a substitute for psychological recognition. Both are important.

For example, a high-level executive in an investment bank told one of the authors about an experience he had with the bank's chairman. It was the end of the year, and bonuses were being distributed. The chairman came into the executive's office, gave him an envelope with his bonus check, and said, "This is for you," and walked out. The check was for $500,000. The executive was discouraged and angry. "Why didn't he say anything to me?" he asked. "I have no idea what he really thinks of my performance and whether he cares whether I stay or leave. He never tells me."

This sounds nutty. Shouldn't $500,000 be enough? Doesn't the amount of money speak for itself? No, it doesn't. It is terribly important that employees also *hear* from their management directly and personally that their performance is appreciated. Employees in that company describe the chairman as wanting to keep employees on a "slippery slope," perpetually anxious about his evaluation of them. When he meets employees in the hallways, he almost invariably "greets" them by mentioning something that *hasn't* gone well in their area of responsibility or something they haven't done. The chairman has a difficult time expressing appreciation to others, even when giving them large bonuses; that, of course, would be an ideal time to do so. The executive left the company about six months later because, as he put it in a private conversation, it was "an opportunity I couldn't refuse" and "I could no longer take [chairman's name]."

The needs for both money and non-financial rewards are important. Neither can replace the other. There are also, however, two senses in which they are interdependent. First, they are multiplicative—not just additive—in their effects. Put negatively, if one form of recognition is absent, not only is the total effect reduced, it is reduced by more than would be expected simply by its absence. This is because it also diminishes the impact of the other form of recognition. We saw this clearly in the previous example where not getting a "thank you" reduced the positive impact of a substantial bonus. By the same logic, *adding* one form of recognition to another increases the value of the latter. Consider honorifics, which are the formal awards programs of organizations. The lesson of our argument for those programs is that their impact on employees is usually increased when money accompanies them. Just as in the investment bank case, adding words of appreciation to the bonus would increase its value for the executive, so adding money to an award conveys to an employee that the organization really means it because it is putting its money where its mouth is. To be most effective, then, most formal awards programs require both "mouth" and money. Although the money involved is no substitute for basic kinds of compensation (salary increases, bonuses, and so on), it should be substantial enough to be seen as more than just a "token."

Our argument does not, of course, imply that day-to-day *informal* recognition be accompanied by money. But, what is said informally loses its impact if it is not reflected at the appropriate time in employees' compensation.

The three means of recognition are also interdependent in that they need to be consistent with each other in the criteria used for recognition. For example, if a company has embarked on a quality improvement effort—at least in its public statements—it is likely to use its formal awards programs to recognize employees for quality contributions and to do so in a public way. In day-to-day informal communications and recognition and in compensation (such as pay increases), the message might be different: if it is then really quantity that counts, the message is inconsistent and counter-productive. It's the kind of contradiction that creates confusion among employees as to what management wants and skepticism about management's integrity; those severely compromise the impact of an organization's recognition efforts. The criteria must be aligned and this should be achieved by aligning each with the organization's real goals and values. In that way, employees are rewarded, and the goals of the organization are advanced and its values reinforced.

To be most effective, organizations must think of recognition as a *cluster* of components that need to be used (and used consistently) with each other and with the organization's goals and values.

How is recognition best implemented? There are a number of basic principles here, which we summarize. We touched on some of these earlier:

- **Be specific about what is being recognized.** The employee needs to be praised for concrete achievements. This both reinforces the particular behaviors that the manager wants to see repeated and, in the eyes of the employee, increases the sincerity of the praise.

- **Do it in person.** Although this might sound obvious, recognition by long distance or proxy is not nearly as effective as face-to-face recognition.

- **Be timely.** Give recognition as soon as possible after the desired behavior. By and large, the more the time between the completion of a behavior and the delivery of a reinforcing consequence, the less effective is the reinforcement. This advice is wonderfully summarized in the phrase "catch them at being good." Catching people in the act, as it were, is usually reserved for misdeeds, but applying the same principle to good performance is exactly what managers should do.

  The guidance regarding timeliness is applicable primarily to informal feedback. The other forms of recognition—compensation and honorifics—normally cannot be done at the moment and on the spot. However, they are important to formally "reinforce the reinforcement" and to demonstrate to the workforce that the organization backs its words with money and public recognition. Taken together, as we have said, the three means of recognition constitute a powerful package.

- **Be sincere.**   This is an odd piece of advice; after all, a manager either means praise sincerely or he doesn't. We can do nothing to help a manager who does not genuinely appreciate her employees' performance. Some managers never do—they genuinely believe that only their efforts count—and this book is not an instruction manual in acting sincerely. Other managers, however, are sincere in their praise and yet it doesn't come across that way to their employees. They might be so general in what they say or so tardy in when they say it that expressing appreciation seems to employees like something a manager feels he has to do rather than something he genuinely wants to do. Or, they might give mixed messages about an employee's performance, such as, "You did well on that, but...," or "Thank goodness you finally got that right." Perhaps because of their own discomfort, managers might undermine the effect with "humor," saying something like, "You've done such a good job, you would never know that you had an MBA," or "He's so loyal to the company, he hasn't seen his family in months." Managers can overdo it, exaggerating the achievement with meaningless flattery, such as, "The most wonderful...," "the greatest...," "never in the history of the company...." Although much of the advice about how to give recognition—and perhaps recognition itself—might seem trite and even corny, be assured that *recognition is vitally important to employees and that employees listen carefully to every word that is said when it is given.* The simpler and more direct the compliment, the better, such as, "You did a great job on   and I want you to know that. I especially liked...Thank you very much." If the praise is exaggerated or too flowery, it won't be believable. If it is a mixed message, the employee most remembers the negative comment or implication, even if the manager finishes on a positive note. Simply stated, people want honest and deserved acknowledgment of their contributions and, when received, it is greatly appreciated. Don't spoil it.

- **Recognition should be given for both group and individual performance.** Chapter 4, "Compensation," suggests that, for most employees, pay for performance should be based on group accomplishments. We argue that individual reward schemes (such as piecework and merit pay) are usually administrative and employee-relations nightmares that result in many employees feeling no sense of reward and that they tend to diminish teamwork. But, we must still deal with the fact that in a group, some individuals contribute more than others (perhaps much more). Should—and how do—these people get recognized? In part, recognition is obtained from co-workers, especially when the pay or bonus is group-based. An outstanding contributor is valued by the group under that condition because his work is financially beneficial to all (which is in contrast to the "rate buster" within individual pay systems who is ostracized because his high performance is detrimental to his co-workers).

  Fully employing the three means of recognition allows both individuals and groups to receive due acknowledgment for their efforts. Although we suggest that for most workers compensation for performance be based on group performance, informal recognition by the manager will usually be given to individuals. As the occasion warrants, the manager will also bring the entire group together for a collective "thank you."

Honorifics, which are the formal awards, need to also be distributed to both individuals and groups. However, in our view, these must be largely reserved for truly outstanding achievements: the organization's "Nobel Prizes." We suggest dispensing with the multitude of recognition awards distributed by some organizations, such as gift certificates, reserved parking spaces, dinner-for-two, and employee-of-the-month. After they are in place for a period of time, our attitude surveys *never* show anything better than a lukewarm response to these programs. Indeed, they generate numerous complaints, especially about who is selected for the awards and the mystery that normally surrounds the selection process.

Programs of this type should be greeted with enthusiasm by the workforce—after all, they are designed to provide *recognition*—but they seem to have the opposite effect on most employees. Upon hearing of the complaints, management often revises the programs to distribute the awards more widely so people don't feel excluded. As recognition for performance, most of these programs then become increasingly meaningless.

As indicated, our suggestion is to have just one (or very few) programs and to limit these to truly outstanding contributions. The awards should be for both individuals and groups, and the choice of awardees needs to be made by a committee that includes the employees' peers. Including peers goes a long way toward reducing the mystery and enhances the perceived fairness of the selection process.

Promoting From Within

We have discussed recognition and rewards within the context of the employee's current job. However, one of the most powerful rewards for many employees is the opportunity for a promotion from a current job to a higher-level position within the organization. It is powerful because it delivers a number of rewards simultaneously: more money; more status; often, a more challenging, interesting, and influential job; and public recognition.

A major issue for employees is the degree to which their organizations are committed to promoting from within. In general, organizations can be categorized into two kinds: those that do their utmost to promote from within, and those for whom current employees are, in effect, "soiled goods." As one manager in a client company described his organization's philosophy when searching for a new high-level manager, "I guess we feel that anyone who works here can't be too smart so we'd better get someone from the outside." This theme is often repeated in write-in comments:

> *Current opportunities for personal growth through promotion...*
> *are severely limited...this company brings in many people from*
> *the outside to fill critical managerial and professional positions.*
> *I don't believe mechanisms are in place here to identify the best*
> *candidates within the company for positions when they come*
> *open.*

> *My biggest problems with this company are recognition, growth,*
> *and promotion from within as opposed to bringing so many peo-*
> *ple into leadership roles from outside the company.*

> *Despite messages to the contrary, I see no evidence that senior*
> *management in my business unit here are interested in promoting*
> *from within. Do they really think all the talent is on the outside?*
> *How about experience with our company and our products—*
> *doesn't that count?*

Organizations that do not adhere to a promote-from-within philosophy lose out in a number of ways:

- They send a message that they don't have much respect for their own employees' competence and so they lose out on the commitment and enthusiasm that respect for people generates.

- They lose out on the motivational impact of promotions and promotion prospects, which causes ambitious employees to feel stagnant and frustrated.

- They lose out on the edge that an experienced workforce—experienced in *that* business and at all levels—gives to an organization.

- They lose out in the stability of organizational goals and culture.

- They lose out in the recruitment and training costs that hiring entails.

Companies give three main reasons for not promoting from within to higher-level job openings: the most common reason is that the right persons for the positions do not exist within the organization or significantly better persons are on the outside. Another reason is that the organization is in such trouble—or is so stagnant—that "new blood" must be brought in. Lastly, "high potential" people need to be hired for whom the open positions provide "developmental" opportunities. These arguments make sense theoretically and are certainly valid in specific instances. If, for example, there is a need for a particular type of specialist that doesn't exist within the organization, that specialist will have to be hired.

However, the research that has been done overwhelmingly supports the proposition that, on the average, organizations that adhere to a promote-from-within policy perform much better than those that do not. For example, in *Built to Last*, Collins and Porras conclude from their research on higher– versus lower–performing companies that the former "...develop, promote, and carefully select managerial talent from inside the company to a greater degree than the comparison (lower-performing) companies...." In fact, the CEOs of the higher-performing companies were six times more likely to be insiders promoted from within.[5]

Some executives talk interminably about the flaws of the people who work for them. But, when they describe someone they are about to hire, that person seems to have no imperfections. It seems that "hope springs eternal." This, of course, is largely a pipe dream because the perfect executive does not exist, and this is discovered—sometimes with shock and dismay—after the new person is on board. The right—not the perfect—person for the job is usually under management's noses if only they look. If that person is not there, it was probably not for lack of raw material, but because that material was not developed as it would be if effective management succession and development programs had been in place, or because good people became so frustrated with the lack of opportunity that they left the organization.

It is imperative that the company first seek all possible internal candidates for an opening. To be fully effective, this policy obviously must be accompanied by programs for the identification and development of the organization's talent.

Should companies promote only the best performers? This is an interesting and troublesome question, mostly because of the perceived danger of promoting workers to levels above their competence. For example, the best engineer might not be the best engineering manager, or the best salesperson the best sales manager. But, if the best performing people are not promoted, wouldn't that impair the motivation and enthusiasm of those people? Yes, it would, and although it would be ludicrous to suggest that a promotion always go to the best performing employee (that employee might really be unsuited for the job), it needs to be always offered to someone *from among* the best performing employees. Selecting a "satisfactory" employee is a serious mistake when higher-performing employees are qualified for the job. The satisfactory employee might have all kinds of other attributes that would appear to make him more suitable for the promotion, *but he has not earned the right to it.* Put negatively, the high-performing employees—with the exception of the clearly unqualified—have earned the right to fail, and it is most unlikely that a reasonable candidate would not be found among those employees.

Dealing with Unsatisfactory Performance

From time to time in this book, we have referred to employees whose performance is clearly and continually unsatisfactory. Most of these people should not remain in the organization or, at least, in their current jobs. Such employees constitute a small percentage of any workforce (rarely more than 5 percent), but they consume an inordinate amount of management's time.

Employees who are clearly and continually unsatisfactory come in three general varieties:

- Those who, with competent guidance, clear goals, and considerable encouragement, can improve to a satisfactory level in their current positions.

- Those who are in the wrong job or organization and will not improve until they are correctly placed.

- Those who do poorly no matter how much guidance they receive or in what job or organization they are placed.

Not dealing with poor performers has morale consequences for their co-workers. In fact, among the largest and most consistently negative employee survey findings are those about the organization's approach to poor performance. When asked, "How do you feel about the extent to which (the organization) faces up to poor performance?" the percentages obtained, on the average, are revealing (see Table 9-1).

Table 9-1   Response to the Question "To What Extent Does Your Company Face Up to Poor Performers?"

Answer	Percentage of Respondents
Much too much	2%
Too much	5%
About right	52%
Too little	29%
Much too little	12%

It is not that 41 percent of employees (29 percent plus 12 percent) are seen as poor performers. The poor performers are typically a small percentage of any employee population, usually just one or two employees in an individual department. However, they aggravate many employees. What is especially discouraging is management's perceived unwillingness to confront this problem and do something about it. The problem is clear to everyone and there is usually no disagreement among the workers as to who the culprit is. In focus groups, they almost always point to the same person—sometimes literally!

For example, we once did a focus group in a government agency and the group consisted of all ten employees in a particular section. One of the major complaints expressed by many of the participants was that one employee in the section "loafed all day." The discussion about this employee went on and on even though that person must have been present because everyone in the section was there. The discussion finally shifted to another topic, and a worker who had been quiet up until then finally began to participate. The rest of the group in seeming unison nodded at the moderator; they had subtly let him know who the loafer was.

The consensus among co-workers is not just about the culprit, but also the reason for the poor performance and the solution. Employees are usually insightful when it comes to diagnosing the problems their co-workers have, such as a lack of training or a mismatch between employee and job (such as, "He's just not a salesman"). About others, they say simply that, "Nothing can be done about him." They want help given to those they feel can be helped and understandably have mixed feelings about what to do with employees they consider incorrigible. Employees typically do not want their colleagues fired, but become reconciled to it if they believe that management has done whatever is reasonable to help the employee improve and has otherwise treated him fairly.

Whatever the reason for poor performance, it is critical that it be dealt with *quickly, squarely, and fairly.* The first step is to provide guidance and, in a way that conforms to our previous suggestions, including, importantly, the opportunity for the employee to express what he believes the problem is and what the solution might be. Improvement goals need to be set and follow-up done to assess whether satisfactory performance—or at least sufficient progress—has been achieved. If not, and enough time has elapsed, the manager (in consultation with his management and usually with Human Resources) needs to decide whether the appropriate solution is to transfer the employee to another job in the organization or to fire him. Transfers should not be sought for two kinds of employees: those unlikely to have the ability for any job in the organization (why continue the torture?), and those who have the ability but whose personality (overly rebellious, overly passive, totally disorganized, just plain lazy, and so on) would make them a poor risk as an employee anywhere.

Here, we won't review the legal and administrative requirements that govern the firing of employees, such as providing sufficient notice to them of impending action and having adequate documentation. Suffice it to say that those requirements need to be followed, and not just to avoid lawsuits and penalties. Although it's time consuming and costly to abide by the rules, they exist to provide necessary protection to employees against arbitrary action by management and abiding by them reinforces confidence throughout the workforce in management's fairness.

Management frequently blames unions or civil-service regulations or Human Resources departments for delays in dealing with poor performers. To the extent we have been able to study this, our data do not bear this out. The problem of management's unwillingness to face up to poor performers appears unrelated to those variables. For example, our data show little difference between the way workers in unionized and non-unionized companies respond to the question about the company facing up to poor performers (see Table 9-2). The problem therefore appears to lie in *management*, not in the constraints imposed by unions.

Table 9-2   Response to the Question "To What Extent Does Your Company Face Up to Poor Performers?" by Union and Non-Union Workers

	Percentage of Respondents	
Answer	**Unionized Companies**	**Non-Unionized Companies**
Much too much	2%	3%
Too much	6%	4%
About right	48%	52%
Too little	31%	29%
Much too little	13%	12%

Feedback Sets Priorities

An extremely important function of feedback, both cognitive and affective, is to convey messages to the workforce as to what the organizational priorities are. Employees quickly learn that what organizations say in their formal pronouncements—such as in their vision and values statements—is less important than what they hear from their managers day-to-day at work and how their financial and other rewards are determined. If, for example, a company preaches customer service, but employees in a customer-call center hear from their managers only when the *quantity* of the calls they process is insufficient, they learn that it is quantity—not quality—that really counts. If the company talks about ethics, but winks at employees cutting corners as long as the numbers come out "right" (in fact, may *reward* them for those numbers), the message about ethics to employees is clear: don't take them too seriously. If the company talks about "excellence in everything we do" and does nothing about poor performance, "excellence" then becomes a high-sounding word with little relevance for how the organization actually runs.

An explicit vision and values statement can be beneficial if the company takes it seriously, which means bringing the messages conveyed by performance feedback and recognition into line with that statement. That is the reason why, in Chapter 6, "Organization Purpose and Principles," we emphasized the importance of implementation. It is only through the implementation of overarching goals and values that employees learn what the organization really cares about. Having serious gaps between words and deeds is worse than having no words at all because the gaps breed employee cynicism about management's competence or motives.

PART IV

Enthusiastic Workforces, Motivated by *Camaraderie*

CHAPTER 10

Teamwork

"We must indeed all hang together, or, most assuredly, we shall all hang separately."

—Benjamin Franklin

"When he took time to help the man up the mountain, lo, he scaled it himself."

—Tibetan Proverb

Human beings are profoundly social animals. Characterized by a need for membership and identification with others and getting pleasure from giving and getting help, it is natural that healthy people cluster into groups, spending most of their lives in association with others, especially family members, friends, and work associates.

This book is about the workplace, not about relationships per se. Yet, the quality of social relationships in the workplace—its "social capital"— is of enormous importance, not only because of the general need people have for camaraderie, but because cooperative relationships are critical for effective performance and, therefore, for a sense of achievement in one's work.[1]

A Look Back

In a sense, it is almost comical to consider a time when the great majority of businesses deliberately and forcefully discouraged social interaction among workers, fearing that it would lead to wasted time, and be nothing more than an opportunity to "goof off." Once, in a survey we did in an industrial setting, we received the following comment:

> *If you try to talk, the forelady comes running over with a lot more work to do, or she yells, "Why aren't you finished yet?"*

It sounds like something out of a comedy routine, but it nonetheless represents the state of human relations at work not all that long ago.

The field of industrial and organization psychology emerged in the 1920s and 1930s, largely in reaction to these jaundiced views of worker motivation and behavior. On the basis of the famous Hawthorn studies, Elton Mayo, who is widely considered the founder of the "human relations" movement in industry, made the social needs of workers central to his theory:

> Man's desire to be continuously associated in work with his fellows is a strong, if not the strongest, human characteristic. Any disregard of it by management or any ill-advised attempt to defeat this human impulse leads instantly to some form of defeat for management itself.[2]

What did Mayo mean by a "defeat for management?" He refers to two manifestations: first, the negative impact on employee morale; second, the reduction of the cooperation required for the effective performance of almost every job.

The field has come a long way since the "human relations" movement and, although its theories and prescriptions have been broadened to include other human needs, such as those addressed in this book, you can't deny the importance of social relationships for both the satisfaction and performance of people at work.

Are We Doing Better Now?

Having been schooled in human relations, many of today's managers do not readily admit to concerns about workers who socialize on the job. But, the unease persists, even at the highest levels. For example, in the course of an in-depth interview with the CEO of a large computer-services corporation, the executive shared these views regarding his top managers:

> *There is one thing that bugs me, not so much my immediate team but some of the people who work for them. It's their lunch habits—I'm told they can take two hours or more for lunch. I know sometimes it's with customers, but they also take each other to lunch and, believe it or not, they charge the company, they put it on their expense accounts. That can happen a few times a month. They say they're talking company business but I don't know….*

The interviews with those managers revealed a sharply different picture. They said that they didn't just socialize over lunch and that they usually got an enormous amount done (by being "away from the phone," "away from the boss," and so on). These lunches were mostly work sessions, they said, and claimed that the company was getting more than its money's worth. Besides, considering their 60-plus hour work weeks and their level, they wondered why anyone would worry about the time they took for lunch.

Would a CEO of a major corporation fret over a matter as apparently trivial as whether senior executives took unduly long lunch breaks? You bet! When it comes to human relationships and emotions such as recognition, fairness and trust, the fundamental issues are amazingly consistent from level to level. Pettiness is as prevalent in the executive suite as it is on the shop floor, as any senior manager can tell you.

Do employees want to waste time? Some surely do; those few would spend the whole day socializing if they were allowed. But, the overwhelming majority of employees are *frustrated* when time is wasted. They don't like to waste time on the job (such as in unproductive meetings) or in excessive work breaks. Of course, they don't want to—in fact, they cannot—work every minute of every day. Work breaks are no more a waste of time than vacations.

We are not referring to situations where the work or work environment is so onerous that socializing is an escape from it or a way for employees to express resentment of the company. That is, when workers are apathetic or angry, breaks are more than simply needed pauses in the workday. They are then also likely to be excessive, which causes managers to crack down on the "malingerers," which further alienates the workforce. This vicious circle harms the organization and its employees.

In organizations that incorporate the practices we describe and recommend in this book, employees are motivated to work hard. Taking time to rest and socialize is nothing to worry about; in fact, should be encouraged. Such breaks are needed because they add to overall employee performance and provide a sign of management's concern for employees' well being, including their health.

Socializing While Working

Although employees derive pleasure from associating with others, such as during breaks, *their greatest satisfaction comes from interacting as a team on the job in the service of common performance goals.* That is a tremendous source of morale for employees. In fact, a good deal of the interaction while socializing is work related. In organizations with good teamwork, the boundary between work and breaks becomes blurred and, even when the conversation is about non-work related matters, socializing helps cement relationships among team members. In effect, through teamwork and simple and repeated social interaction, a *work community* is established: people who enjoy each other's company and have a shared commitment to each other and pride in the group's achievements.

It is fortunate that social relationships are as important as they are to people because practically all work requires a high degree of social cooperation. This seems too obvious to mention, but some managers and management theorists still maintain that there are numerous jobs where teamwork is simply unnecessary. The example most frequently cited is that of assembly-line workers performing highly fractionated jobs. What would teamwork add to performance on jobs so simplified, standardized, and segregated into individual tasks, other than time wasted in meetings? We previously discussed the similarly skeptical view about the value of participation in decision making on routine jobs. We showed that skepticism is belied by the many successful participative experiments that have been conducted in precisely those environments.

The same holds true for teamwork. In fact, the participative experiments have, to our knowledge, always involved a *team* approach, such as self-managed teams. The technique requires that people work collaboratively (within and between units) to solve problems and make decisions. This, as has been repeatedly demonstrated, is an enormously effective approach to management and organization.

Why should this be true for work that has been standardized and structured—like a machine—into minute tasks performed by individuals? It is true because the reality of such work situations is different from the theoretical conditions suggested by the machine model. The fact is that when work is highly fractionated, the interdependence among the parts is actually greater than when a job consists of doing the "whole thing." The performance of a worker assigned to just one step of an operation depends on receiving work product from the previous worker on time and with the quality required to perform the task. Workers in a multiple-shift organization depend on their co-workers doing the same job on other shifts for a smooth "hand off" of the work. There is great dependence on various support departments to provide the resources that enable workers to do their jobs (such as tools, machine maintenance, and so on). Changes (such as in specifications, procedures, or equipment) are likely to be frequent, and workers need others to distribute information to them about the changes and provide any training that might be required.

Therefore, *enormous* interdependence exists among workers doing even the most highly fractionated work. Although you could argue that the more finely divided the jobs, the greater the interdependence, teamwork is needed for just about every job at every level. Things don't happen automatically, they require cooperation. *Cooperation—not job descriptions, not organization charts, not formal procedures—is the glue that binds the parts of the organization.*

The Negative Effect of Uncooperative Co-Workers

When a co-worker doesn't cooperate, the effect is not simply a reduction in effectiveness in proportion to the degree of that person's non-cooperation. The impairment is exponential because it almost always results in a diminishment in the cooperation from others. Furthermore, lack of cooperation can lead to serious conflicts that are fueled by paranoia, such as,

"You're not helping me because you'd like to see me fail, so I'd better defend myself and the best defense is a good offense."

If these battles are ignored by senior management, they escalate as a matter of course and can be costly. The costs are not just the time spent in battle, but also not being able to exploit opportunities collaboratively.

Just as a lack of cooperation can escalate into a large-scale problem, good cooperation can have a significant synergistic effect. When organizations are managed as more than a collection of individuals, the resulting whole is typically greater than the sum of its parts. Although groups are often derided as promoting dull conformity ("groupthink") or conversely, bizarre solutions ("a camel is a horse put together by a committee"), the research evidence shows that the quality of group performance, such as in problem solving, is by and large superior to that of an individual working alone. In addition to the esprit de corps they generate, groups, when structured and managed correctly, allow for the emergence and consideration of different perspectives, which is vital to solve problems and make good decisions, and they generate greater acceptance by the members of the outcome.[3] Our own analyses almost invariably show strong positive correlations between teamwork in organizations (as perceived by employees) and organization performance.

At the obvious extreme, there is absolutely no way the Manhattan or Apollo projects and thousands like them could have succeeded without high-functioning teams. For those cynical about doing work "by committee," keep in mind such well-known products of committees as the U.S. Constitution and the King James Version of the Bible. Committees or teams fail when they are not structured and managed properly (more on that later), or when they are devices put in place to avoid, rather than make, decisions. Those are not the committees or teams we have in mind.

Contentious Workgroups Are a Drag

As we said in Chapter 1, "What Workers Want—The Big Picture," our surveys reveal that teamwork tends to be good within work units (73 percent satisfied), but considerably less so between units (51 percent satisfied). It's favorable within units because there is a natural inclination to cooperate and, unless management acts in a way that disrupts those relationships, people find ways to work together. Take this example, which is from an executive interview in a retail corporation, of a senior manager disrupting naturally forming cooperative relationships:

> He (the manager) keeps telling us that we don't work well to-gether. He's right, we're always arguing, but it's mostly his fault. For example, someone gets an assignment in a meeting and then, after the meeting, he gives someone else the same assignment without telling the other person. We're all running around—and our people are running around—trying to get it done and we find out others are doing it, too. So we assume that the others are invading our turf and we're p.o.'d at each other. And it's a great waste of high-priced time. Another thing: he's always bad-mouthing us to each other.

When it occurs, conflict within units is often the result of a manager's par-ticular style or the quirks of one or two individual employees. Conflict between units is more frequent because, in addition to individual factors, broad organizational forces at work can create discord. Organizations are divided, by necessity, into business or functional units, and the members of the units focus primarily or exclusively on the achievement of their own goals. They are convinced that achieving their own goals is beneficial not only for them, but for the organization as a whole and for the units with which they interact. In practice, however, they are often at odds with those units.

For example, many organizations are beset by serious and continuing disputes between "line" and "staff" functions. Line functions, such as product development, production, and sales, are directly responsible for accomplishing the end purposes of the organization, while staff groups, such as information technology, human resources, finance, and legal, exist primarily to assist the line in its work. (The term "staff" derives from the rod or stick that assists walking, and it comes from a Sanskrit root mean-ing "support.") Although staff personnel firmly believe that they are dedi-cated to supporting the line and should therefore be welcomed by the line, the opposite is often the case. As the saying goes, "with such 'friends,' we don't need enemies."

Probably the most frequent example of this kind of conflict is the one between information technology and the line. We detail that relationship later in this chapter. Perhaps the second most common type of conflict is the relationship between the Human Resources department and employees—yes, employees! Shouldn't the Human Resources department *help* employees? Well, take a look at some of these comments:

> *After choosing (a benefits package), I found there was misinfor-mation from HR, which caused much stress. I found that our Human Resources department was useless. It feels as if we are left out to dry when it comes to benefit issues.*

> *I am never able to find the right people to talk to when we have questions related to human resources. I go in circles being trans-ferred to multiple people who know less than the next one.*

> *I am completely frustrated talking with Human Resources about payroll issues, changing benefits, and getting reimbursement for time or business expenses.*

> *I hate dealing with Human Resources regarding a range of issues. Either I can't reach the proper person or the person gives me wrong advice and answers. I think each division of this company should have a qualified representative on site that can assist with your needs and that really wants to assist.*

> *It is difficult adjusting to Human Resources and compensation policy changes that are enacted by the leaders of the company without a true warning, such as the elimination of overtime/ compensatory time right at the beginning of the busy season. HR is not an advocate of the employee but nothing more than the mouthpiece of higher management.*

> *They [the Human Resources department] are just a bunch of bureaucrats—everything is forms, forms, forms and the answers are no, no, no. We call them Inhuman Resources.*

Inter-unit conflict is not limited to line-staff relationships. Consider the tensions between production and sales, which are two line organizations. From the sales side:

> *I am in a position of selling to willing customers but our produc-tion organization doesn't handle my orders in the time the customers want them. Not a few of my sales opportunities are therefore lost. How can we get them to respond in a timely man-ner? They seem completely resistant to trying out new ways that*

> *will speed things up. Also, it often takes days for them to return*
> *my calls. It's much easier dealing with other companies.*

From the production side:

> *Our sales people should understand what we can produce and*
> *how fast we can do it. Promising the customer something we*
> *can't deliver in a time we can't deliver it frankly drives us crazy.*
> *Before making a commitment, it would be great if they checked*
> *with us first. By not doing this, escalations are the norm rather*
> *than the exception. We are not working as a team.*

Working together is a natural human instinct and yet much internal discord exists. The work community we spoke of earlier seems not to extend,
in many cases, to the organization as a whole. Ironically, the problem is
magnified by the need for camaraderie. Here's the downside of the desire
for strong relationships with others: it might be satisfied at the expense of
relationships with those not in the immediate group. Whoever's not in the
immediate group can be viewed as competitors and even as the "enemy
camp." Employees frequently refer to a "we-they" atmosphere within their
organizations: "they" might be the people in another department on the
other side of the hall or a group in corporate headquarters on the other side
of the country or world.

Conflict, of course, is not inherently detrimental. On the broadest
level, conflict and its corollary, competition, are at the heart of our economic and political systems, and they yield great rewards. Companies in
the same industry, for example, need to compete aggressively with each
other. But such aggressive competition among entities within a company
does serious harm to the organization's effectiveness. The damage has
three major elements: the resources that need to be expended to pursue the
battle, the loss of collaborative opportunities, and the negative impact on
employee morale. Regarding morale, although the "we-they" phenomenon can temporarily boost in-group identification in relation to the
"enemy," few employees enjoy such conflict over the long term. It inhibits
their performance, the organization's performance, and it is tiring. Most
employees want to battle the competition—that can be exhilarating—not
each other.

Besides being wasteful and debilitating, much of the conflict in
organizations is needless and irrational. It is needless because it's resolv-
able: the parties can be brought together in a collaborative or win-win

relationship. It is irrational because it's driven by misperceptions of the inevitability of conflict between them. Yes, inherent conflicts of interest exist where one party's gain equates to the other party's loss. Numerous issues in labor-management relations are of this kind. No one should expect workers to participate gladly and collaboratively in being downsized, outsourced, or offshored. Such an incompatible situation can usually be settled only through a traditional adversarial process, which is basically a matter of the relative power of the two sides, their skill in employing that power, and an appreciation of the costs of not settling the dispute.

Much of the discord between groups in organizations does not stem from an inherent incompatibility of interests, but from a perception that such incompatibility exists. For example, does an inherent conflict of interests exist between an IT function and its "user" divisions? The parties might *act* that way, but doesn't IT exist primarily to help its users do their work, and don't both groups exist to further the organization's success? The parties don't act that way because that's not how they see it: each group sees the other as acting solely in its own selfish interests and often in ways that are detrimental to the other party. Therefore, each group protects itself and, as the conflict continues, it generates intensifying perceptions of malice in each other's intentions. In fact, the perceptions then *do* become grounded in reality since each party, because of its assumptions, *does* begin to act in ways that seek to undermine the other. It is no longer a distortion for each side to see the other as untrustworthy and dangerous: the conflict process has made the perceptions a reality. In other words, if the parties believe a conflict exists, it does—or soon will.

Building Partnership

Other than those few managers who believe that conflict between individuals and groups within an organization is beneficial (as in "good old American competition"), most managers understand that conflict of that kind is extraordinarily and needlessly costly. In fact, they detest it, like almost all of their employees; people don't want to come to work to fight! *It is important to understand this fundamental desire to work collaboratively—this fundamental goodwill—because that is the basis on which teamwork is built after the layers of suspicion and resentment are removed.*

As we have said, conflicts differ in how real or psychologically based they are. Approaches to reduce conflict must take this into account and there are two basic strategies:

- **Conflict management.**   The parties agree not to fight and to establish mechanisms to help avoid and settle disagreements.

- **Partnership building.**   The parties agree to actively collaborate in the achievement of mutual goals (that is, to establish a relationship aimed at adding value and not just minimizing discord and its costs).

Conflict management is most appropriate when the conflict stems from a real divergence of interests; partnership building is appropriate when the root cause is misperceptions. The labor-relations arena provides good examples of the two approaches. An antagonistic and costly relationship between labor and management can be converted, through conflict management, into one where workers and the company agree on mechanisms to prevent and handle disputes, such as an orderly and relatively non-contentious grievance procedure and commencing bargaining well in advance of contract expiration to prevent strikes. That happens when the parties, despite their different specific financial interests, recognize that the mutual interest of the parties is served by containing or reducing the costs of conflict that can only shrink the economic pie that's available to both groups.

However, the parties can agree to go beyond this result to consider how they can work together to increase the economic pie that they share. They can do this by improving efficiency, quality, and the like. That is the difference between a relationship of respectful adversaries and one of active allies.

Getting management and labor to cooperate in areas such as improving quality first requires successful conflict management. Antagonism between the parties on basic equity issues makes a collaborative relationship on other matters difficult. But, managing such conflict well does not guarantee that the parties will move to the next level. Another hurdle must be overcome: the misperceptions the parties usually have of each other regarding their interest in matters such as quality improvement and their interest in establishing a truly collaborative relationship to achieve those ends. With regard to quality, for example, management tends to assume that workers don't really care about quality, while workers tend to assume that all that management wants is production, no matter what the quality. These beliefs are rarely accurate or, at least, they are distorted by a significant amount. Unless misperceptions are clearly identified and acknowledged, the parties have no chance of becoming allies in a sustained way to improve quality. The foundation for success (like that of the self-managed teams described in Chapter 7, "Job Enablement") is both parties trusting that they share a common goal.

How Can the Misperceptions Be Uncovered, Confronted, and Corrected?

The first step toward resolving organizational conflicts is simply to get the perceptions of the various sides "on the table." This is best done through survey methods, whether through interviews or questionnaires. This phase of the process is one of the most helpful because it shows in no uncertain terms just how *similar* the two parties actually are: in many of their fundamental interests, in their positive assumptions about themselves, and in their negative assumptions about each other. Such data, if analyzed well and reported candidly, are an immensely powerful catalyst for change.

To illustrate, let's thoroughly examine the relationship we uncovered between the IT function and its "user" divisions in a large financial-services company. The reason for the study was expressed strong user dissatisfaction with internal IT functions. Complaints included errors, excessive costs, and especially "attitude," a sense that many IT personnel were indifferent to providing genuinely good service to its users. The senior management of the company, which was largely sympathetic to the users, asked us to determine, in essence, what was wrong with IT and how it could be fixed.

In-depth interviews were conducted with all the managers in those units and with samples of non-managerial personnel. What we found was more complex than originally thought: the villain was neither party individually, but the relationship between them.

To start, each group considered itself to be competent, committed to serving the interests of the company, and highly dedicated to doing its job well. Contrary to how they were viewed, IT employees felt themselves to be dedicated to providing users with high quality, timely, and cost-effective work. Each side, however, saw the other as committed only to its *own* success (that is, unconcerned with either the company or the other party). The IT employees typically considered users to be unreasonably demanding, continually changing their minds about what they wanted (disregarding the impact such mid-course changes had on IT and its ability to do the job), and oblivious to costs (unless the costs were billed to them, in which case they felt they had been overcharged). This was compounded by IT's view that many users' ignorance of technology was matched only by their ignorance of their ignorance. It was further compounded by IT's conviction that users were unconcerned about IT's frustrations, especially the way that function was bombarded with "the highest priority" projects, all of which required timely and error-free completion that IT just didn't have the resources to provide.

The user divisions had an equally jaundiced opinion of IT personnel's characteristics. The IT department was typically seen as having little sense of urgency in doing the work (hence, the frequent lateness in delivery), failing to understand the users' objectives (even though, according to the users, these objectives were clearly spelled out), being resistant to user ideas and suggestions, being frequently careless in the quality of their work, being unresponsive to the users' daily needs (including not returning phone calls, which was a tremendous frustration), and grossly overcharging for their work. In parallel with the IT function's view, the users saw IT as ignorant of (and quite unconcerned with) the company's mainline business and its changing demands.

In essence, the views were mirror images of each other: each party saw itself as dedicated and competent and the other as largely self-absorbed and ignorant.

Although these perceptions might have had some degree of validity (for example, the users typically did not fully appreciate the pressures on the IT function), they were, in essence, misperceptions because of their assumptions of a basic incompatibility of interests and the other party's incompetence. There was an assumption of conflict, for example, in the users' views that IT made mistakes because it didn't care about serving users well rather than because of inordinate pressures on them or misunderstandings as to what the users want. Also, there was an assumption of incompetence in the view that users change the project specifications continually because they really don't know what they want rather than because of changing demands on them.

You might be tempted to ask, "Why don't these people grow up? They're acting like children, 'You did this to me,' 'No, I didn't—you did that to me.' Why don't they just get down to business and stop the incessant bickering and blaming?"

If only getting down to business was that simple. Childish or not, we know that emotion is rarely absent in people's relationships, including mature businesspeople, and that misperceptions and misunderstandings frequently arise. These feed on themselves, which causes increasing, needless, and serious damage to everyone's interests and morale. Although at times these problems can be resolved by the parties themselves, they usually need help from a third party: a skilled facilitator.

We now describe in detail an approach to partnership building that has been used successfully in numerous settings. It assists the parties to achieve mutually beneficial and collaborative relationships. The approach has been successfully applied to a variety of relationships, such as between business units, line and staff groups, home country and overseas units, acquirer and acquired company employees, and the members of senior-management teams. It has also been applied to a company and its key external constituencies, such as suppliers, customers, and community groups.

A facilitator manages the process, and its centerpiece is an intensive partnership-building workshop that uses survey data as its springboard. Although the approach must be tailored to the objectives and conditions of the organization in which the work is being done, the following sections describe a fairly typical set of basic steps.

A Short Course on Effective Partnership Workshops

Orientation and assessment of readiness. The facilitator meets with senior leaders of the organizations to gain an understanding of the situation from their perspective; understand their goals in a partnership-building effort; review with them the method to be used and its perceived appropriateness for the problem, the personalities involved, and the organizations' culture; and determine whether they are prepared to devote the required resources and time (including their own) to achieve genuine and lasting collaboration.

Planning. Having determined that the process is appropriate and the organization is ready for it, the process's objectives, procedure, schedule, and specific expected outcomes are finalized.

Communication. The partnership-building objectives and plan are fully communicated to all employees in the organization who will be affected by the process.

Diagnosis.   Through interviews, or a combination of interviews and questionnaires, the organization's members are surveyed. The surveys yield in-depth profiles of the views the members hold of themselves and the other party; what they see as the key components, causes, and consequences of the lack of collaboration; the suggestions they might have to increase collaboration, and what they deem to be the potential benefits of increased collaboration in terms of specific business problems and opportunities.

Establish Workshop Ground Rules

Following the diagnosis, a workshop is conducted that aims to establish the basis for a productive and lasting partnership between the parties. The workshop normally lasts about three days and the participants are those whose work will significantly benefit from collaboration improvements. As long as the participants follow a number of ground rules, the workshops almost invariably succeed. They basically succeed because the participants want them to succeed: they want to collaborate and they want the high levels of performance that teamwork can produce. The key workshop ground rules, which are sustained throughout the workshop by the facilitator, are as follows:

- **Business orientation.**   Unlike some team-building efforts, the process employed is clearly and directly business related. The goal is not to build relationships per se, but to build relationships that promote business objectives. This type of workshop rarely uses simulated exercises to get people to work together; they work collaboratively on business issues and opportunities that are real, significant, and best dealt with as a team. The human-relationship issues are identified and resolved within this business context and, as appropriate, the workshop takes the time needed to assess, discuss, and resolve those issues.

- **Open atmosphere.**   It is important that the workshop participants feel free to express their views. This is aided immeasurably by the diagnostic attitude data collected prior to the workshop that assess the viewpoints people hold of themselves and the other party. At the beginning of the workshop, the facilitator presents these data and initiates a discussion to bring issues into the open that, at least initially, the workshop participants might be reluctant to bring up themselves. The issues then become "safe" topics for discussion and help set an open atmosphere for the remainder of the workshop.

- **Constructive atmosphere.**   The open exchange of views should take place in an atmosphere of mutual respect. Mutual respect is demonstrated by a visible effort to appreciate the situation of the other party, showing an intention to work collaboratively on the issues, and demonstrating trust in the other party's intention to do so, and avoiding rude or abusive language.

- **Action orientation with follow up.**   The outcome of the workshop is a jointly developed action plan that involves close and continued collaboration between the parties and will contribute significantly to achieving their mutual business objectives. The plan includes mechanisms for following up to ensure that the agreed-upon actions are being taken and recommendations for structural changes, such as changes in the reward system of the total organization that reinforce inter-unit collaboration.

- **Flexible approach.**   Although certain general principles govern the partnership-building efforts, the specifics are often modified as the workshop proceeds. The interactions in the workshop are dynamic and unpredictable in many respects, so it is vital that adjustments be made on the spot.

In summary, the keys to a productive workshop are timely preparation of the participants, an open and respectful expression of views, an unyielding focus on the business objective of what is transpiring, disciplined action planning, and a willingness to make adaptations to the agenda as the situation warrants.

A Typical Workshop Agenda

1. Senior management and the facilitator review the objectives, agenda, and ground rules of the workshop.

2. The participants present their views of the relationship between the parties, covering key strengths and improvement needs and the specific business activities that could benefit from increased collaboration.

3. The facilitator presents the findings from the diagnostic survey. These tend to be more focused than the participant presentations on sensitive relationship issues.

4. The participant presentations and the diagnostic findings are discussed, starting with the human relationship concerns (for example, the misperceptions that cause friction in the relationship) and concluding with the substantive business issues.

5. The participants reach an agreement on a limited number of priority business issues that will benefit from collaboration. They then decide how best to tackle the key issues in the workshop (for example, those that need to be dealt with by the group as a whole and those best handled in sub-groups).

6. The participants carefully define the priority issues and develop action plans to deal with those issues.

7. The workshop concludes by establishing mechanisms for the following:

   • Reviewing, finalizing, and implementing the action plans.

   • Determining how the collaborative relationship between the parties can best be sustained. Unless this is addressed, it is almost inevitable that, over time, the teamwork the workshop produced will largely dissipate as the participants resume their normal routines and are subjected to pressures that generate friction and discord.

In addition to the business sessions of the workshop, various social activities are scheduled (usually in the evenings) to provide an opportunity for relaxed and informal interaction.

Action Example: IT and Its Users

We previously described the contentious relationship between the IT function and its users in a financial-services company. The following summarizes what they accomplished in their team-building workshop and in follow-up meetings.

The workshop participants decided on the following basic objective for their work:

> To help IT become a truly user-focused organization, every user must feel that IT is doing its best to help him or her do the job; every user must feel that IT is concerned about him or her individually; every user must be satisfied with the services he or she receives from IT. This will be accomplished both by changing attitudes and processes within IT and by changes among the users to help them become more involved and informed consumers of IT services so that IT can assist them more effectively.

Here, in the participants' own words, are excerpts from their actions plans:

1. Establishment of a company-wide IT-User Partnership Council to assure smooth working relationships; will meet monthly with an agenda consisting of:

    -   Specific problems that have been encountered; Council will decide how to resolve them.

    -   Consideration of basic changes that still need to be made to assure a good working relationship.

    -   Opportunities for additional collaborative undertakings between IT and the users.

    -   Review of the results, as they are available, from regular measurements of attitudes and performance of IT and user employees.

    Individual user organizations may set up their own Partnership Councils to assure adequate attention to their specific issues.

2. Individuals will be appointed by IT to serve as the interfaces with each user organization. These persons will be the primary—but not sole—points of contact between IT and the user organizations. Through communications and coordination, these persons will work to assure that the users' expectations of IT are satisfied, including helping set realistic user expectations.

3. Communication and involvement:

-   Within each user organization, communication sessions will be held with IT in which:

    -   The relevant aspects of the user's business will be fully described for IT.

    -   The relevant IT processes will be fully described for the user.

    -   Guidelines will be presented for the kinds of behavior— on both sides—that constitute a cooperative working relationship.

    Enough time will be allowed for questions and discussion, with time for socializing and interaction. Each session's agenda will be developed jointly by IT and user representatives to assure clarity and relevance.

-   All projects will now begin with a full discussion between IT and the users of the project's objectives and requirements; requirements will be recorded, but as a working document that will likely change (versus a legalistic and static document); will be followed up with regular meetings reviewing project status, changes, etc.; also, electronic notification will be provided to users regarding project status; "no surprises" billing: costs fully detailed and explained at beginning of project; when modified, detailed explanation will be given to user with opportunity to question and negotiate.

-   IT projects that are not initiated by a user but will affect that user will be discussed in detail with the user to assure understanding and to obtain user input.

-   Telephone inquiries from users will be answered within two hours.

-   Monthly newsletter will be published (electronic) for both IT and user personnel (accomplishments, new developments, etc).

4. Training to be scheduled:

- For IT personnel (including help-desk personnel) in basic communication and customer-relationship skills.

- For IT personnel in new technologies (both on- and off-site training).

- For user personnel in systems that have been developed for them.

5. IT internal structure and processes:

- Will reduce needless bureaucracy: a lengthy approval process to be shortened considerably by reducing the number of approvals required, especially in the applications development process; a "destroyer" task force will review all paperwork and eliminate paperwork that is no longer useful.

- Cross-functional communication mechanisms (meetings, etc.) will be strengthened within IT.

- New and transparent prioritization process will be developed (combination of time of request, urgency, and amount and availability of resources).

Action implementation began. A follow-up interview survey conducted eight months after the workshop revealed sharp gains in most respects in collaboration-related attitudes. Here's a typical comment from an interview with a user:

> Things have changed for the better here. Most of them (IT employees) have a different attitude now. They actually return my phone calls and right away. Most seem to *want* to help. A big change is how we now plan development projects together and we don't have to worry about dotting every "i" and crossing every "t" because we know that things will change anyway, and we'll have to keep communicating and working together. Also, if things will be late, they tell us; if they don't understand what we want, they ask us. The only real problem is with one small group of programmers who are stuck in the past. It's their manager—he's still the same arrogant (expletive deleted). Also, I think their internal approval process is still a little too bureaucratic and time-wasting.

This comment is taken from an IT employee's interview:

> I enjoy my work more now—the haggling is much less now. We understand each other much better now. I used to think they were not so smart—that's the way I always thought about bankers: expensive suits, not much else. They're still not really up on technology, but I see now a lot of dedication and business sense on the part of most of them. It's great working together to solve their problems and I've gotten more interested in the business. We still have problems with them wanting too much too soon, and they get frustrated with us. But, the anger isn't there like before and they now almost never go around us to top management to force us to give in to their demands. One guy still does. We talk more face to face about the problems and we work most of them out. We understand more the pressures on each of us.

The partnership-building process does not result in Utopia. Certain issues remain and must be dealt with and, given the forces in an organization that pull people and units apart, attention must be paid continually to the relationship or serious problems will certainly recur. Therefore, it is a good idea for the parties to periodically meet offsite for a day or so to examine fully and candidly the state of their relationship. This examination usually leads to further changes to reinforce and enhance collaboration; some changes might be quite basic and some might be painful to individuals.

For example, the parties might decide that structural modifications are in order, such as decentralizing segments of a staff function into the line organization. Certain relationships might lend themselves to modifications in compensation to make pay more reflective of teamwork and not just individual effort. Personnel changes might be needed, such as moving an employee to another job, or even firing those individuals who, despite counseling and time to change their behavior, simply will not or cannot conform to the new collaborative norms. These measures make partnership-building more than a passing fad or a temporary fix for a problem. They serve to institutionalize and sustain a genuinely collaborative culture.

PART V

Bringing It All Together: The Total Organization Culture—and How to Change It

CHAPTER 11

The Partnership Organization

"As they say on my own Cape Cod, a rising tide lifts all the boats. And a partnership, by definition, serves both partners, without domination or unfair advantage. Together, we have been partners in adversity—let us also be partners in prosperity."

—John F. Kennedy, June 25, 1963, West Germany

"I have found no greater satisfaction than achieving success through honest dealing and strict adherence to the view that, for you to gain, those you deal with should gain as well."

—Alan Greenspan

In this book, we have enumerated the specific components of management behavior that produce employee enthusiasm and high performance. Our aim is to provide guidance to managers and executives that seek to change themselves or their organizations. We hope that individual managers find our suggestions helpful in dealing with their own people. But, to bring about truly significant and lasting organization change, we must think of the components not just individually, but together as a *system*, one that is governed by an organization *culture*.

By a system, we mean that the parts interact so that changing one element without changing others significantly reduces the impact of the first.

In fact, changing just one element might overall negatively affect the other elements, as when a company seeks to create a "participative" environment for a workforce that feels seriously underpaid. Management is then viewed not only as miserly, but as hypocritical. It's better to be seen as a genuinely miserly boss than one who is also a phony.

By culture, we mean the standards and values that define how people in an organization are expected to behave, especially in their relationships with each other. It is not sufficient to put in place good practices, such as an effective compensation system. To have maximum impact and be sustained in their fundamentals as conditions change, the practices must be supported by deeply felt and explicitly stated values ("We do this because…," "We will change this, but not that, because…."). A good illustration of this is the Johnson & Johnson Credo, discussed in Chapter 6, "Organization Purpose and Principles," which has guided the company in its policies and practices for more than 60 years.

Partnership and Its Alternatives

The essence of the system and culture we describe in this book is a "partnership" relationship. Chapter 1, "What Workers Want—The Big Picture," explains that partnership is a business relationship *plus*. The plus is the human dimension—the trust and goodwill that allows people to go beyond what is required by strictly monetary calculations, formal contracts, and short-term interests. We have offered considerable evidence to demonstrate that a partnership relationship generates the highest level of long-term performance for organizations. Partnership has both a vertical dimension, which consists of the relationships between workers and management, and a horizontal dimension, which is the relationships between individuals and between work units. *It is people working together—up, down, and across—toward common goals.*

Partnership has both psychological and economic components, for example, employees' confidence that they make significant contributions to the organization's success, and that they also share in the financial gains of that contribution. It is a high involvement model: involvement in what the workers give to an organization and in what they receive from it. Both parties' interests are being served.

More specifically, here are the hallmarks of a successful partnership:

- **Win-win.** The parties recognize that they have key business goals in common and that the success of one party depends on the success of the other.

- **Basic trust.** The parties trust each other's intentions.

- **Long-term perspective.** The parties are committed to a long-term relationship, one that survives short-term vicissitudes of business.

- **Excellence.** The parties set high performance standards for themselves and for each other.

- **Competence.** The parties have confidence in each other's competence.

- **Joint decision-making.** The parties make key decisions jointly on matters that affect each of them.

- **Open communications.** The parties communicate fully with each other.

- **Mutual influence.** The parties listen to and are influenced by each other.

- **Mutual assistance.** The parties help each other perform.

- **Recognition.** The parties recognize each other for their contributions.

- **Day-to-day treatment.** The parties routinely treat each other with consideration and respect.

- **Financial sharing.** To the extent that the collaboration is designed to generate improved financial results, the parties share equitably in those results.

These criteria can be applied to any business relationship: between employees and management, between work units, and even to relationships with other business entities, such as suppliers.

Some might argue that the term "partnership" does not fit the employee-management relationship. For these people, the term implies a fundamental equality between the parties that is rarely present in any practical sense in the employee-management relationship. Applying it to that relationship therefore might seem dishonest and manipulative—an attempt to subtly convince employees that their power is more than what it is.

However, that is neither the objective nor the point. Power inequalities exist in every organization: almost everyone has a boss, even CEOs who answer to boards of directors. But, bosses vary greatly in what they *do* with their authority, and those differences lead to hugely diverse outcomes. In that sense, the use of power is a central concern of this book. So, although it is true that a large discrepancy in power between workers and management exists, it is also true that workers accept the legitimacy and the necessity of this. They are, in fact, disturbed when leaders don't lead, such as when they are unduly hesitant about making decisions. But workers do not accept the legitimacy of being treated as lazy and dumb (that is, unable or unwilling to significantly contribute to the success of the enterprise) by their bosses. Employees respond well when authority is properly exercised.

Analogously, workers do not bridle at pay differentials. To some people, partnership might imply pay equality, but in our formulation, it is pay *equity*. We have never heard workers objecting to senior management being paid more than them. They complain about senior management pay only when the gap with their pay is enormous, it appears to be unjustified by the performance of the organization, and that performance has caused the workers' pay to suffer. These complaints are exacerbated when that poor performance is seen as being caused by senior management ineptitude. Otherwise, they think, "Let the brass make as much as they can— I'm doing well."

The partnership organization stands in contrast to three other major organization types. As with all typologies, no organization fits any type perfectly and all are, to one extent or another, mixtures. This is especially evident when organizations are in the midst of change because of changing business conditions or the advent of a new top management bent on changing the organization's operations and culture. Also, different strata of a workforce, such as salaried compared to hourly employees, might be treated differently, and individual managers and managements might act differently depending on the circumstances of the moment. Although we therefore never find complete consistency, strikingly strong tendencies allow us to identify most organizations, and the major units within them, as closer to one type or another (or, at least as moving from one type to another).

In addition to partnership, the major organization types are *transactional*, *paternalistic*, and *adversarial*. The following paragraphs describe these types in detail.

Transactional.   The last two decades or so have witnessed the emergence of an explicit philosophy and set of management practices wherein employees are treated essentially as commodities that have a "price" and are owed nothing but that price (that is, nothing beyond their paychecks). We discussed this management style earlier, especially in Chapter 3, "Job

Security," and depicted it as emerging in response to a more competitive world and as a reaction to the costs and inflexibility of paternalism. Its most visible manifestations have been the downsizings, restructurings, re-engineerings, rightsizings, outsourcing, and offshoring of the last two decades (all terms usually signify getting rid of workers). These have occurred most notably in companies that had previously been well-known bulwarks of employment security, such as IBM, Kodak, Xerox, and GE. The transactional approach also manifests itself in the greatly increased use of temporary employees, independent contractors, and subcontractors who can be hired and fired at will.

Personal responsibility and personal accountability are among the buzzwords that describe and ideologically justify a transactional approach to management. These terms are contrasted with an entitlement mentality assumedly bred in employees by organizations that are operating paternalistically.

As we have pointed out, to be treated as a faceless commodity—an interchangeable part to be disposed of at the first whiff of less-than-sterling profitability—has consequences for employee morale and performance. The employee response is not so much anger as it is resignation and an indifferent attitude toward work and the company, such as "This is the way it is these days—company loyalty is dead, so why should I care?" Transactional management should not be confused with a "cruel" management that seeks to squeeze every last dime and ounce of sweat from its workers. Transactional organizations generally pay at or near the going wage rate and, as far as workload is concerned, are not, by and large, throwbacks to the infamous era of sweatshops. Essentially, it is an *indifferent* management—indifferent to the value of people other than to perform the specific tasks for which they are being paid. They don't expect more than that from a worker and, if they get less, the worker can be fired. There is, in the purest form of transactional management, no other connection or obligation to the worker, not even a negative connection. Why get aggravated and pressure the worker when he is not performing or is often absent or late? A manager might talk with him once or twice, and if the worker doesn't improve, the manager just fires him.

A transactional orientation is not limited to the shop or factory floor; it might occur as frequently in the executive suite. Chapter 9, "Feedback, Recognition, and Reward," relates an anecdote about a corporation where the executives of the company felt themselves as being on a "slippery slope;" their past performance seemed almost irrelevant to the CEO: it was, "What have you done for me today?" In interviews conducted with

senior management of a Midwest manufacturing company, the attitude of
their CEO was described this way by an interviewee:

> Let me tell you something: he does not give a damn whether we
> stay or leave. He thinks he is the reason for any success the com-
> pany has had and he can buy anybody to carry out his orders.
> Sure, when you're hired, you get a big sales job, you're a big hero
> then, "we really need you," but you go "from hero to zero" in just
> a few months. He just can't stand the competition from anyone
> who works for him. We're like a commodity. He's the only one
> with value.

All the other members of senior management expressed similar views.
The turnover rate in this group was 80 percent, with only one executive
having been with the company more than 18 months. They had all left voluntarily and were, by all reports, highly competent executives.

Paternalism.   As the term connotes, this is a relationship between a
company and its employees similar to that between caring parents and
their children. In the U.S., it dates largely from the late 19th and early 20th
centuries, the period that saw a great upsurge of industrial growth in the
U.S. accompanied by a tide of labor-union activity, but had for the most
part died out by the last decade of the 20th century. As we have indicated,
it has been replaced, in large measure, by companies with a transactional
orientation.

Above all else, paternalistic organizations provided security for their
employees in the form of protection against job loss and the provision of
benefits that freed employees from medical and retirement financial wor-
ries. Additional amenities often included educational programs, recreational facilities, subsidized cafeterias, company loans, and, in its earliest
days in "company towns," low-cost housing. The great majority of
employees joined such companies with the prospect of a lifetime career
for themselves.

Companies that were labeled paternalistic were not all alike, not by a
long shot. Most important was the difference between companies that
indeed treated their workers well and those in which paternalism was a
façade to conceal exploitative, even inhumane, management practices.
The latter was especially characteristic of many "company towns," where
the company owned just about everything—housing, stores, schools—and
employees had little alternative but to rent lodging, buy goods, and so on
from their employer. Pay was low and the company, in all its beneficence,

would allow employees to draw a portion of their wages before payday in the form of scrip. The scrip coupons, however, were redeemable only in company-owned stores and once an employee began using scrip, it was difficult for him to get out of debt to the company. A worker might owe 95 percent of his check to the company.

That kind of management must be distinguished from the paternalism of other corporations whose practices were truly benevolent and made these companies employers of choice for their workers, such as IBM, Eastman Kodak, Sears Roebuck, Corning, and Johnson & Johnson. These companies provided their workers with above-average wages, excellent fringe benefits, employee stock ownership or purchase plans, good working conditions, and, of course, job security. But despite, or rather because of, their benevolence, these companies were also subject to sharp criticism from a number of sources.

We already discussed one line of attack, namely, that paternalism is too costly and too inflexible in a highly competitive and rapidly changing business environment. This criticism comes from those who bemoan almost any worker "entitlement" and any constraint on management's ability to manage for the highest efficiency.

The other attack came from the opposite end of the ideological spectrum: the left, especially the labor movement that advocated checks on management and argued that paternalism was but a ploy, an insidious instrument for maintaining control over workers.

There is no question but that a major goal of paternalistic companies was control, in two senses. Through paternalism, employers attempted to prevent unionization of their workers and to govern their morals and social behavior.

Regarding unionization, paternalistic companies sought to provide for their employees at least as much as—and usually more than—they could obtain by joining a union. That was the basic economic reckoning, but the economics gave birth to strong emotions as well: great trust in, and loyalty to, the organization. Two of the authors of this book worked for IBM—a non-union company—toward the end of its paternalistic era and can attest to the enormous loyalty that company was able to engender among the great majority of it employees.

It could be argued that, on economic grounds alone, it made no sense for these paternalistic organizations to fight unions. After all, the things they did for employees to avoid unionization might have cost more— perhaps considerably more—than a union could have obtained for the workers. Cases can be made on both sides of that argument, and we won't get into that here. But the fact that the economic benefits of benevolent paternalism are not that clear brings us to non-economic motivations for paternalism. Many of the people who founded and ran these paternalistic organizations also genuinely believed they had a mission: not only to care for financially, but also to *morally elevate*, their employees. In other words, they really did see themselves as parents.

To today's students of management, the degree to which business leaders of an earlier era were driven by moral and religious impulses is truly amazing. These employers saw it as their duty to regulate workers' activities outside, as well as inside, the workplace.

> David Humphrey, founder of Humphreysville, Connecticut, made his "mill girls" go to bed early and eat plenty of fresh vegetables. The Merrimac Mills in Massachusetts invented a boarding-house system, with girls living in supervised boarding houses run by housekeepers. The company also made the girls sign a contract that demanded everything from "propriety at all times" to regular church attendance.[1]

Parental control evidenced itself as well in the way the firm was managed. When "papa knows best," his control is rarely limited to employee relations. Paternalistic companies tended to be highly centralized in all manner of decision making, just as are paternalistic families. The independent exercise of judgment by employees was not particularly valued: all major, and often the most trivial, of decisions, normally went to the boss for his approval. This centralization of power and authority—epitomized, too, by large central staff groups serving the boss ("the king and his court")—added to the rigidity of paternalistic organizations.

The importance placed in paternalistic organizations on the carrying out of the wishes of "papa" also resulted in an emphasis on loyalty as a criterion for advancement and other rewards. It would be a mistake to say that performance was not valued, but the "court" of the "king" had a large proportion of what can best be called retainers, persons who achieved their positions by showing absolute fidelity to the CEO and his wishes and views. Although high performers could also obtain high-level positions, their chances were limited if they were viewed in any way as too independent. Therefore, these organizations tended to be less attractive places to join and stay for persons with talent, ambition, and independent dispositions. Family members of employees often were given preference in hiring.

Another factor diluting the average ability levels in these organizations was their hesitation in facing up to poor employee performance. In part, this was a result of the fear of unionization, but it also stemmed from the emphasis on loyalty rather than performance. There was much less hesitation firing—or otherwise penalizing—an employee who violated one of the organization's moral codes. Despite the performance issues inherent in paternalistic organizations, they survived well—some even thrived—when they faced little significant competition in their industries or regions. Many were virtual monopolies. The onset of international and domestic competition made this management style largely obsolete.

Adversarial.   The paternalistic pattern arose to a significant extent to avoid unionization and most of them did. Say what one will about dependency, conformity, and the manipulation of workers, the workers in these companies—the benevolently paternalistic companies—thought they were getting a terrific deal. Although they often had complaints about matters such as excruciatingly slow decision making by management, their own lack of involvement in decision making, and the criteria used to select employees for advancement, lifetime employment, excellent fringe benefits, and other amenities were powerful inducements to stay with the company until retirement and not make too many waves.

Of course, many other companies had employees who did make waves—big ones. These were companies whose employees fought to organize into unions to improve what they considered to be deplorable employment conditions. Once organized, they felt they had to continue battling to maintain what they had achieved and to further improve their conditions. This is the adversarial organization where workers believe that their company's management gives them nothing unless they're forced to and, if conditions are right, they organize into unions to get what they feel workers need and deserve. Among workers in these organizations, there is a sense that they and management share no common objectives; they are destined to be implacable and perpetual foes.

The "win-lose" view of workers in adversarial organizations invariably has its genesis in the beliefs and behavior of *management*. Workers work to earn a living and get some sense of achievement from their jobs and satisfaction from their association with their co-workers. They certainly don't come to work to fight. The few who do are quickly marginalized by their co-workers if there's nothing to fight about. However, if a strong sense of unjust treatment exists, those workers can become the leaders of an incensed workforce.

Management also doesn't come to work wanting to fight, but in adversarial organizations, many do come with an extremely jaundiced view of workers and they act as if a battle is inevitable. Workers must be fought, they believe, if their outrageous economic demands, desire to do as little work as possible, and wish to "run the place" are to be restrained. It's necessary to be tough, very tough, with workers or "they'll run all over management." Workers usually respond with their own toughness; in their views and behavior in these companies, *they are a mirror image of management.*

Adversarial organizations differ from each other in how much conflict and travail they generate. These differences mirror the extent to which workers feel ill treated. At one extreme are the reactions of workers to employment conditions in the company towns previously described (the malevolent form of paternalistic management) or in the sweatshops of cities. These were the scenes of some of the most bitter and violent labor conflicts in American history.

At the other end of the adversarial scale are companies where labor relations can be described as tense, but not explosive. There is no love lost between the parties, but they learn to co-exist and contain the costs of conflict. This relationship is more characteristic of today's adversarial organizations than the bitter confrontations of the past.

In fact, over the last five decades or so, there has been a remarkable decline in the U.S. in the manifestations of conflict between labor and management. For one, there has been an enormous reduction in work stoppages. Twenty-five years ago, more than one million workers were involved in 298 stoppages. Ten years ago, there were 35 work stoppages involving 364,000 workers. But in 2003, there were just 14 major work stoppages involving less than 40,000 workers. That was the lowest since the Bureau of Labor Statistics started keeping records in 1947.[2] The decline comes as no surprise to those familiar with what has been happening to the labor movement in general in recent decades. Today's workers are less prone than in the past to join unions: the percentage of the total labor force in unions in 2003 was just 12.9 percent compared to approximately 35 percent in the 1950s.

What accounts for this extraordinary quiescence on the labor front, this near disappearance of visible adversarial behavior? Many reasons have been proposed for the decline in union membership, such as the shrinking percentage of the workforce engaged in manufacturing, which historically has been more heavily unionized than the service sector; the greater ability of companies to move operations to other parts of the country and overseas, thus heightening the dangers to workers of joining a union or engaging in militant union activities; the increased participation of women in the labor force, many of whom hold part-time or temporary positions and are more difficult to organize; and weaker enforcement in recent years of the laws governing the rights of workers to organize.

But, one systematically conducted study attributes the decline in union membership almost entirely and simply to the waning interest of workers in unions. Reviewing attitude surveys conducted from 1977 to 1991, they find that the percentage of workers responding affirmatively to questions about their interest in joining a union dropped significantly in that period. This was paralleled by an increase in their satisfaction with their conditions of employment. Because interest in union membership and dissatisfaction correlate highly both with each other and with actual union membership, and because union membership has been declining in the U.S. since the 1950s, it is probably safe to assume that interest in unions has also been declining since then and that satisfaction has been increasing.[3]

What accounts for these trends in union interest and satisfaction? First, employment conditions for workers are, on the average, much better than they were in past decades. Other than conditions in benignly paternalistic companies (always a small percentage of the economy), there really is no comparison between then and now. American labor has won a lot through their unions, such as higher pay, better benefits, more time off, better and safer physical working conditions, and other employers, in part to avoid unionization, have had to improve the conditions they provide their own workers.

Furthermore, the government protects workers in the form of wage and hour, occupational safety and heath, and anti-discrimination laws. Workers also receive financial support in the form of unemployment insurance and welfare benefits. Unions have fought long, hard, and successfully for these measures but, ironically, that very success has reduced the need for unions in the eyes of potential members.

Few of today's transaction-oriented companies are unionized—even those that aroused some anger in employees as they shed paternalistic practices. The loss of labor's clout has allowed them to move to a transactional mode without too much worry about being organized.

These companies are still pretty good places to work. There is an important difference between adversarial and transactional management as these modes play themselves out day-to-day in the workplace. The sins of adversarial management in the workplace can be described as largely sins of commission—what they do in their relationship with workers—while those of transactional management are those of omission—what they don't do. In transactional organizations, managers don't pay enough attention to workers as human beings; in adversarial organizations, they pay all too much attention and of the wrong kind because they are told that there is no other way to get high levels of production from workers than to *drive* them through close supervision and punitive measures for not performing. Employees of a transactional manager complain, in frustration, "He doesn't know I exist," but those of an adversarial manager want the manger off their backs. Workers don't join unions to get more attention from management; they join for protection from behavior that they consider abusive, and there is just much less of that in American industry today.

In a word, in the current environment, union representation is, by and large, no longer perceived to be as valuable as it once was. We reiterate that part of this is a result of the labor movement's own success in elevating the employment conditions for its members and for workers generally throughout the country. Unions appear to have been working themselves out of a job.[4]

Much of American industry has reached the point where neither the confrontational pattern of adversarial relationships nor paternalism appears to suit current conditions. Today, the choice facing organizations in managing their workers is between an arm's length transactional relationship and an arm-in-arm partnership relationship.

It is tempting to choose the transactional path. Why assume the commitments that partnership requires if management doesn't have to?

Well, management doesn't have to, but our basic proposition throughout this book is that committing to employees pays off big time. In considering our argument, we ask that you keep in mind that our reference is to the commitment that partners have to each other, not to that of parents to children. A major difference between partnership and paternalism is that partnership is a business relationship, so performance counts. If one party can't or chooses not to perform as agreed over a period of time, the partnership dissolves or significantly changes to reflect the performance difference. Thus, performance matters greatly in partnership but it's not defined by the question, "What have you done for me today?," as in a transactional relationship.

If a collaborative approach is so clearly preferable, why is it characteristic of such a small minority of companies (one estimate is about 10 percent)? Why has the dominant tendency in the U.S. been toward trans-actional relationships? A corollary question is why collaborative compa-nies have *always* been in a small minority when the superiority of the approach has been demonstrated for decades. First, the answer lies in the attractiveness among American executives of avoiding commitment to workers because this allows management to shed workers with minimum cost and travail (to the company). And other aspects of commitment might seem to be more trouble than what they are worth, such as the need to communicate and listen in meaningful ways to workers.

The need to listen brings us to a second reason that partnership is often unattractive; many senior executives' strong belief in the need for control through top-down management. Partnership differs from all three other models of management in its willing, in fact, deliberate, distribution of authority to the workforce. Although it is inaccurate to speak of equali-ty of power, in a collaborative setting the worker's influence on the way the job is performed and on the decisions made in the immediate work environment is much greater than within any of the other three models. For some executives, distributing authority to the non-management work-force is, at best, silly—after all, what can workers contribute?—and to others, it's frightening because they equate such decentralization with organizational anarchy (the unstable laissez-faire management described earlier). There is, of course, no evidence that most workers want authority outside of their work areas; they want a leader steering the ship, but a leader who recognizes that the day-to-day workings of the units of the ship are best left to those most knowledgeable of the work in those units.

A third impediment to the acceptance of the partnership approach is the short-term orientation of many senior managers as they seek rapid gains in profits and in the company's stock price. The collaborative model is a commitment to *long-term* performance. The research evidence we present in this book about the positive impact of collaboration on business performance concerns long-term results.

Fourth, the attractiveness of transactional management is enhanced by its compatibility with an anti-entitlement ideology. As we have pointed out, collaboration is often confused with paternalism where performance is, indeed, often secondary to entitlement as a criterion for rewards.

Therefore, strong forces militate against a partnership approach, and these are buttressed by the viewpoints of some union leaders who deeply distrust any approach that is not adversarial. Unions are still a force to be reckoned with in certain industries and companies.

A number of unions and companies, however, have chosen a collaborative path and have achieved impressive results. In these cases, the parties recognize their common interests, such as improving product quality, and establish mechanisms that enable them to work together on those while reserving areas of contention for the collective bargaining process. Research suggests that positive union-management relations are, in general, associated with higher organization performance.[5] Bringing that relationship to yet a higher level—actively working together to identify and solve performance problems—can yield truly dramatic results.[6]

Labor-management collaboration, which began in earnest in the United States in the late 1970s and early 1980s, is particularly relevant to our broad argument because it underscores the growing inappropriateness of highly adversarial relationships in a fiercely competitive business environment. The collaborative approach in the American automobile industry, for example, received its impetus from the enormous threat to that industry posed by Japanese automobile manufacturers. In effect, the union and the companies allied to meet this threat, with a heavy emphasis on collaboration to improve the quality of the product.

There is no inherent contradiction between being unionized and establishing a worker-management partnership. A good example of this is Southwest Airlines. Southwest is not only unionized, but it has the highest percentage of unionized workers of any airline in the U.S. President and Chief Operating Officer of Southwest Colleen Barrett says the following:

> We treat all as family, including outside union representatives. We walk into the room not as adversaries but as working on something together. Our attitude is that we should both do what's good for the company...[Unions] have their constituency, their customer base. We respect that. We have a great relationship with the Teamsters and they have a reputation for being tough negotiators. We try to stress with everybody that we really like partnerships.[7]

Marcie Means, a customer service agent and union activist at Southwest, offers a worker's point of view:

> Southwest has helped me make a wonderful contribution in my world. I am not looking to abuse the company or take advantage. I just want the right thing. There are things we need to have represented. But there is no need to threaten the company....It's fine to strike if you can't settle your differences any other way. But we

don't need to strike....We don't want to fight. We *belong* to this
company. It's a system that works that's been working for years.[8]

The spirit suggested by these comments starkly contrasts with most U.S.
airlines where the relationship between management and unions has frequently been highly adversarial. Any objective analysis of this history
quickly reveals that the quality of labor-management relations has largely
been a consequence of the attitudes and behavior of management. When
management treats workers and their organization as enemies, they are
treated as enemies in return. It's as simple as that.

We mentioned earlier that American Airlines management is seeking
to change its traditionally adversarial culture into one that emphasizes
partnership and collaboration with the workforce. Central to this is involving workers in the company's efforts to reduce costs. The results have
been extraordinary.

> Once it started asking, American got lots of ideas from controllers
> and pilots, flight attendants, and company managers. A dispatcher
> who was also into drag racing figured out that if passengers are
> seated toward the rear of a plane that isn't full, the plane's center of
> gravity moves toward the tail. That improved the airplane's aerody-
> namics, saving millions of dollars a year in fuel. An American pilot
> figured out that because of the 42-cent difference between the high
> price of jet fuel in Los Angeles and the lower price in Dallas that
> planes going to LA should carry enough fuel on board to get back
> without refueling there. Savings: $50,000 a day.[9]

Partnership does not require a complete identity of interests between the
parties. There can be differences, but what partnership does—what an
atmosphere of *trust* and *mutual respect* does—is allow these differences to
be settled in more realistic, constructive, and often innovative ways that
serve the interests of both parties.

Application to Other Constituencies

The partnership concept is powerful. It can be applied to the relationships
of an organization with all its key constituencies. For example, consider
suppliers. Suppliers can be treated as untrustworthy adversaries who must
be continually and closely monitored, and from whom every last nickel

needs to be squeezed. Or, they can be treated as "transactions;" that is, not poorly, but to whom the company owes nothing but payment for their goods, and who need to continually re-bid for work with the company. Or, they can be treated as genuine partners. Studies of supplier relations reveal tremendous benefits from a partnership relationship, especially in the quality of the products or services the supplier provides to the customer and in the timeliness of delivery. In part, this heightened performance is caused by increased supplier capability because of better two-way communications with the customer and the experience gained in a long-term relationship. In part, it stems from the extra effort the supplier applies to its work for a customer that treats it as a partner.

Let's return to Southwest Airlines. How does Southwest Airlines see its relationship with its suppliers? Here is a comment from a director of an airport; airports, of course, comprise a key group of suppliers of services to airlines:

> [Southwest] makes the airport part of their team. We make a presentation to them, and then they turn around and make one to us, saying here's how we see us working together. That's unheard of. It gives you the impression that this is a group I really want to work with, as opposed to [other airlines] where you wonder if you can get them to call you back. With Southwest, you want to see what you can do for them. I think it pays huge dividends. My reaction to how I'm handled by Southwest is that it makes me want to bend over backwards.
>
> —Kevin Dillon, Director of Manchester (NH) Airport[10]

The spirit of this remark is not much different from what we hear from enthusiastic employees whose companies treat them as partners. People, especially employees and suppliers, don't expect that kind of treatment from a company. When it happens, the positive effects—the willingness of people to go all out in their performance—are profound.

CHAPTER 12

Translating Partnership Theory into Partnership Practice

We advocate a partnership culture as the surest path to a high-performance organization. Partnership works because it harnesses the natural motivation and enthusiasm that is characteristic of the overwhelming majority of workers. Other management modes dampen—even destroy—that motivation and enthusiasm. The partnership organization is effective precisely because it is based on the assumption that the great majority of workers are, by nature, motivated. Rather than a vicious circle (assume and expect the worst and you get the worst), a partnership philosophy creates a virtuous circle (assume and expect the best and that's what you get).

But, does partnership always work? Nothing that we know of *always* works, and some conditions make partnership inappropriate.

First, there is the matter of individual differences. Throughout this book, we've noted that there are some individual workers who cannot be treated as partners. They are either naturally too lazy, hostile, or dishonest to participate in collaborative endeavors. It is self-defeating for management to try to do so because they will not respond positively; these workers, who are almost always a small number of individuals, must be dealt with separately, by dismissal from the organization or by placing them in jobs that minimize their impact on co-workers and the organization.

It is an unfortunate reality that there are workers with whom it is impossible to establish a collaborative relationship. Also, there are managers with whom this is impossible. The problem tends to be more one of philosophy: managers who simply do not accept the notions underlying partnership, the assumption, for example, that workers want to work or that they are reasonable in what they expect in their employment conditions. Sometimes, this problem can be overcome by training and counseling from experienced managers with a partnership approach, but sometimes it cannot. Organizations that have moved to a partnership culture have always had to deal with managers who could not (or would not) change, and they have had to remove them from managerial positions. Otherwise, they create cross-currents damaging to the installation of a partnership culture.

We come now to senior management. The issue here is not whether senior management expresses agreement with the partnership concept and methods—if they don't, it won't happen—but whether they genuinely believe what they say. In many companies, senior management has initiated (or, more precisely, allowed to be initiated) programs that sound good but have little substantial follow-through. To genuinely believe in partnership means more than just words, it means taking the *actions* that we've described throughout this book and sticking with them. Changing an organization's culture in the direction of partnership should never be attempted in a superficial way, such as with slogans instead of deeds or with isolated deeds that are unconnected to the reality of what goes on in the daily lives of employees. These efforts, which usually soon disappear ("programs of the month"), do nothing but generate or reinforce workers' skepticism about management and its intentions. If senior management, especially the CEO, does not genuinely commit to partnership by demonstrating its willingness to take serious action, forget it! (We return to this crucial matter of senior management commitment later in this chapter.)

We have not qualified the use of partnership by occupation or by national culture. There is no evidence that the approach does not work when it's applied to certain types of work or in certain cultures. Obviously, adaptations must be made, but the fundamental concepts are, to our knowledge, applicable everywhere. Is there an occupation where collaboration for the achievement of common ends is not desired? Is there a country where that is not the case? We think not. It's time to shelve the stereotypical portrayals that we apply to large groups of workers, stereotypes that can, in part, function to allow blame for problems to be placed on the "character" of workers instead of on the way they are managed. As we have said, individual employees might have character issues, but for the great majority, whatever they do and wherever they are, the proper injunction is, "Management, heal thyself."

Throughout this book, we've suggested specific best practices that can translate key partnership concepts into action, such as "rings of defense" to help avoid or minimize layoffs and group incentives that promote team work and share performance gains with workers. We didn't make these up; they come from organizations that took serious action based on partnership ideas and researchers that carefully assessed these efforts. These are what the best organizations (in our terms) and research studies have taught us. In describing these actions, we also paid some attention to the methods by which ideas can be converted into action, especially in the discussion of the translation of "purposes and principles" into practices such as Total Quality Management (which is discussed in Chapter 6, "Organization Purpose and Principles"). This chapter gathers these strands into a more comprehensive statement of a process for advancing an organization toward a partnership culture.

It Starts at the Top

Many partnership organizations didn't have to change to that form; they started that way with a visionary founder and CEO who strongly believed that is the way people should be managed. Frederick Smith of Federal Express and Herb Kelleher of Southwest Airlines are good examples of this. But, other organizations that have long operated with an entirely different management mode have consciously and deliberately undergone profound culture change to a partnership pattern. Good examples of these are Gordon Bethune's massive culture change and turnaround of Continental Airlines, and F. Kenneth Iverson's similarly highly successful efforts at Nucor.

A major lesson from these examples of partnership organizations is that *action must begin with, and be sustained by, senior management.* This chapter's goal is to help interested senior management implement partnership concepts and practices.

There are executives who, without reading this book or perhaps anything like it, naturally operate in a partnership mode. That's the way they *are*. Take the following excerpt from an interview with Gordon Bethune in *Human Capital: Strategies and News* about the way he engineered the turnaround of Continental Airlines:

"Continental Airlines was just three weeks away from failing to meet its payroll in 1994, losing about $55 million per month. After churning through 10 CEOs in 10 years, the airline only occasionally got passengers to the right place at the right time—maybe with their luggage.

"This was a crummy place to work. The culture at Continental, after years of layoffs and wage freezes and wage cuts and broken promises, was one of backbiting, mistrust, fear and loathing," says Bethune. "People, to put it mildly, were not happy to come to work. They were surly to customers, surly to each other, and ashamed of their company. And you can't have a good product without people who like coming to work. It just can't be done."

HCSN: How important is company culture and morale to the turn-around of Continental Airlines?

Bethune: It's everything. You can't quantify it. I mean, how important is your liver? There isn't going to be any success if you don't have the right culture and morale. It just doesn't work.

HCSN: When you came to Continental, you concluded the employees were basically a good group of people despite all the messes. Why?

Bethune: All you had to do was walk around. If you've been in this business, you could see there was nothing wrong with these people's thinking; their tools were fine, we had our stuff. But if you're running an airline, why would you run a late one? You can't figure out what time of day it is? You don't know how fast the planes fly? I mean, this is sixth-grade arithmetic we're talking about here. The fact is, everybody kind of knew what to do, but nobody cared about doing it. If every time, for the last 10 years, no matter what you did you lost, then you quit trying.

HCSN: How were you able to gain employees' trust?

Bethune: You have to earn and develop trust. It's like dealing with abused children. They kind of like the way you talk and act, but every adult they ever met screwed them over—so they're going to be a little hesitant until you just patiently, with consistent behavior, show them that you're not just a new deal from the same old deck. It took time and some concrete changes around here for them to believe things really were different.

> *HCSN:* In your book, *From Worst to First*, you talk about the importance of dealing with employees honestly, of communicating with them, of clarifying expectations and of removing a lot of rules and policies. What else?
>
> *Bethune:* Most importantly, we showed them concrete examples of positive change for them. We became a no-smoking company the first week. We took the locks off the executive suite doors. We went casual on Fridays just to change our dress behavior. We started rewarding extra if we did our job better. When we did our job better quickly, their lives got better because when we were on time, they were on time. They started getting home to pick up their kids from school or whatever mattered to them.[1]

Bethune goes on to describe the other changes he introduced, such as a focus on customer satisfaction, monthly bonuses for on-time performance, and replacing the "authoritarian" employee manual with a set of guidelines that didn't "box them into ridiculous procedures for every element of their work." He also felt that he had to replace a number of middle managers.

Here's Bethune's comment on the source of his ideas: "Someone asked me…how come I know so much about people? I said, 'I used to be one.' So I think understanding your co-workers is kind of a prerequisite to success. You're not going to make it without their help, so you have to learn how to talk to them and how to appreciate them."

The Action Process

We discussed *what* partnership is, so now we come to *how* it can be introduced and sustained. We don't have a cookbook recipe; you can bring about culture change in many ways, and it is never a neat and entirely predictable process. Nevertheless, certain approaches seem to work better than others (a series of steps is described later in this chapter), and knowing what they are should help an organization take significant steps forward with minimum downside risks (when adapted to individual circumstances).

You might have one of four broad kinds of reactions to this book: this is nonsense; this is what we already do; this sounds interesting, let's explore further; or this is exactly on the mark, let's go! Of course, there can be all sorts of intermediate responses, such as "we do some of this and the rest is nonsense, or too radical," but let's stick to those four as a spring-board for our description of a process for deciding on and taking action.

If you feel that this is what your organization already does, we ask you to hold on for a moment. You might be right, but you might not, or you might be only partially right. Some executives believe that they run their organizations as a collaborative endeavor with employees because they communicate frequently to them, they have suggestion programs, they have an "open door," they call their employees "associates" or "team members," and so on. But, by using the diagnostic methods we suggest in this chapter, these executives might learn that the reality is much different. The only reality that counts here is the *employee's* reality, not senior management's.

If you feel that the ideas and practices we have been espousing can be useful to your organization, you might be inclined to start implementing them right away. We suggest, however, that the first step is not implementation, but assessing just how ready the organization—especially senior management and, most especially, the CEO—is for partnership. This is greatly aided by *data* at the senior level that help those executives confront how they really feel about partnership concepts and policies. Later in this chapter, we explain using a "readiness" questionnaire that senior management completes to get these views "on the table" so that the basic decision—is this really for us?—can be made

Here, then, is a process by which partnership can be considered and introduced into an organization. The recommended steps are largely designed to be applied to an organization that wants to change itself in its entirety (whether the organization is a total company or a relatively self-contained business unit). It can be usefully applied to segments of organizations, such as individual departments, but often with less marked results because what goes on in those units is usually heavily influenced by the culture of the entire organization in which it exists and by its relationships with other units.

The recommended steps for introducing partnership are defined by these questions that each step addresses:

Step 1. What is our business goal?

Step 2. Are we ready for this?

Step 3. What, exactly, do we want?

Step 4. Where are we now?

Step 5. What are the major aspects of the organization that need to be changed to get us from where we are to where we want to be?

Step 6. How should the plan be communicated to the workforce?

Step 7. How do we decide on the specific changes that need to be made and how they should be implemented?

Step 8. How should managers be trained for the implementation of partnership?

Step 9. How do we assess how well we have done?

These steps are abstracted from our own experience and that of many other practitioners as to how this kind of culture change can most effectively be introduced. Although the steps appear neat and sequential, in practice, considerable overlap will exist among them and you might move back and forth as the situation dictates. Before we describe the steps, here are four principles that should govern their application:

- **Don't lose sight of the business goal.** This chapter is largely devoted to process in two ways: partnership itself is a process because it defines *how* people can best work together in a business organization; we now describe *how* that process can best be introduced and sustained (in other words, another process). In all this discussion about how things should be done, we might lose sight of *why* they are being done. The effort can disintegrate into "collaboration for the sake of collaboration," which is a parody of the concept. Such process-infatuation is not too different from the way a bureaucrat over-focuses on the means (the procedures and rules) rather than the ends that the means are designed to accomplish.

  Although having a clear business goal for the effort does not guarantee the success of partnership, neglecting this certainly assures its failure. In a short time, the organization turns its attention to its business objectives, and the means familiar to it for achieving those, which will almost definitely not be partnership. Partnership then atrophies into a sideshow. *The business goal must be an integral part of the way an organization defines partnership for itself, and the way it will assess its value once introduced.*

- **Where partnership has worked best, the primary business goal has almost invariably been improved products or services for the customer.** Collaboration—up, down, and across— is fostered to better meet the needs of the customer and usually to delight the customer. This goal works wonders because it is in the direct service of the business and employees can really get enthusiastic about achieving it.

- **Introduce change using partnership principles.** The use of the principles of partnership should not be limited to the goal of the effort (the partnership organization), but should also govern *how* that goal is reached. Inconsistency in ends and means opens the credibility of the entire effort to question, "Does management really believe this stuff?" Furthermore, change that is essentially positive and that affects many people is best achieved by working collaboratively. It doesn't have to be designed in secrecy and forced on workers. Just as people welcome partnership, they welcome the opportunity to participate in its development and implementation as long as they feel it is serious business and not just another exercise. The basic structure of the process that we will suggest is that senior management be primarily responsible for setting the overall objectives and rationale of the effort. That is a requirement of leadership, and employees want to know the basic objectives come from the top. But the translation of that statement into detailed policies and practices and their implementation is the responsibility of task forces composed of individuals from throughout the organization. For most issues, "diagonal slices"— people selected across levels and functions—are the best way to form the task forces. To help assure that they continue to receive the support and attention they need, most task forces should be chaired by a senior-management member.

  If the organization is unionized, the union's active participation needs to be sought. Labor-management cooperative efforts have almost always been run by a joint labor-management steering committee.

- **Avoid assuming that people naturally resist change.** This assumption about resistance to change is another pessimistic assumption about people that we discuss throughout this book, such as that people are naturally lazy. People resist changes that they see as harmful to them or the organization, and they gladly welcome changes that they see as helpful. When was the last time anyone saw a worker turn down a salary increase? Or upset because his new manager treated him more respectfully than his previous manager? Or complain about management adjusting the work pace to allow workers to turn out higher quality work? Those *are* changes and if workers naturally resisted change, they would resist those changes, too. The notion that people have a difficult time with change is a way to explain "psychologically" why workers often don't want to do what management wants them to. They don't want to do those things because they consider them harmful! Does a worker resist a new technology that will replace him because he "resists change?" Is he upset about a transfer to a less interesting job because he resists change? He resists getting hurt.

The belief that people naturally resist change causes managers to act in counter-productive ways, such as secretly developing plans and springing them on workers at the last minute; not listening to the genuine and specific concerns that people have about changes (after all, why listen, if they're "just resisting change"?); needlessly overselling changes to workers; and, not doing the necessary planning to buffer the ill effects that change might bring ("they'll complain whatever we do"). Because of these behaviors, people do, indeed, act as if they resist change. It's the self-fulfilling prophecy at work again: employees' behavior reflects the way they are treated. Therefore, our advice is to largely ignore the assumption of "natural resistance" and, as we have said, assume that most employees welcome the changes that partnership will bring. Proceed with its development and introduction in ways consistent with that belief.

- **Maintain continual senior management attention and involvement.** We cannot emphasize enough the importance of visible senior management commitment to the change process. The change must emanate from the top and be continually sustained by it. Everyone in an organization wants to know what the top wants, especially in an effort as untraditional and innovative as the introduction of a partnership culture. The forces that tend to militate against partnership—the inevitable frustrations of the workplace and the tendencies of organizations to pull people and units apart as they focus on their own objectives—make essential reinforcement of the importance of partnership from those in power. That support must be communicated in word, and especially in deed, including the way rewards and recognition are distributed. If recognition is given irrespective of people's performance as partners, the partnership values will begin to appear hollow.

Here are the suggested key implementation steps to introduce partnership into an organization:

Step 1. What is our business goal?   The primary reason that partnership is introduced in an organization must be the achievement of key and specific business objectives. It can't be just that "things will be better this way" or "employees will be happier." As we previously mentioned, the most successful partnership efforts that we have observed have been those where improved products and services for the customer has been the primary goal. But whatever it is, the business objective must be an integral part of the way the organization thinks about partnership and the way it will evaluate its effects.

Step 2. Are we ready for this?   The decision to move to a partnership culture to achieve business objectives should be deliberate and thoughtful, with full understanding that culture change is a long and demanding process; the biggest pitfall is the temptation to do it superficially. The easy way is to avoid grappling with basic issues and changes and transform the effort instead into a "program" with catchy slogans, slick communications, and committees upon committees—all quite unrelated to the mainstream of the business and what goes on in the daily work lives of employees.

In this initial step, senior management requires two things: a good understanding of what partnership is and what it does, and a good understanding of themselves. The former is achieved through reading, and discussions with experts in the field, with managers, and employees in organizations that operate with a partnership culture. Visits to those organizations to see partnership in action—including its performance impacts—are especially useful. Our experience is that the greatest impact on executives' thinking comes from observable facts—seeing something actually working—and those facts explained and verified by other executives they respect and trust.

Self-diagnosis should follow immediately; for this, we suggest using a diagnostic questionnaire to assess readiness (such as one provided in

Appendix E, "The Readiness Questionnaire"). The questionnaire should be completed by all top management personnel, which usually consists of the chairman, the president, and their direct reports. It is critical, of course, that these people be asked to complete the questionnaires as they *genuinely* feel, not what they believe is the socially acceptable answer or what their bosses want them to say. Individual answers must be kept completely confidential, so it is best that the completed questionnaires be sent to an outside party or some other trusted source for scoring. Appendix E includes the method for scoring the Readiness Questionnaire.

The results of this self-diagnosis need to be reviewed thoroughly and critically by senior management. This is best done in an off-site setting where full and frank discussion is possible and encouraged. The questionnaire results are not precise measures of readiness, but stimulate discussion so that a decision about whether to go forward, and in what respects, can be thoughtfully made.

Step 3. What, exactly, do we want?   The next step, preferably at the same off-site meeting, is to formulate a clear, specific, and comprehensive statement of what the organization wants to do and why. It is best to integrate this with the organization's "purposes and principles" or vision statement (see Chapter 6), if one exists. It is that part of the statement devoted to the kind of relationship the organization wants to have with its workforce and should include the business rationale for partnership, that is, how a partnership culture will help the organization achieve its business goals. Tying it publicly to the business makes the statement—in fact, the entire process—more credible in employees' eyes, and credibility is further enhanced by being specific and avoiding platitudes. For example, it might include items such as "we will pay a wage that is fully competitive" and "we will organize into self-managing teams that will be delegated the authority they require to get the jobs done effectively." Credibility is also enhanced by including limits on what the organization is prepared to do, such as "we cannot guarantee lifetime employment" (but stating what it will do, such as handling workforce surpluses, to the extent possible, with normal attrition and with the retraining and redeployment of workers).

It is critical that the statement be developed by senior management and be identified to the workforce as the product of senior management's thinking and intentions.

At this stage, the statement will be in draft form and will be finalized and distributed in step 6.

Step 4. Where are we now?   Having decided on the basic direction, it is now necessary to get a good reading on the condition of the organization in relation to the partnership goals set forth in the statement. It is not sufficient to depend on senior management's views of this. Senior managers might think that they know where an organization stands, but they are often incorrect; the bias can be either positive or negative.

The best way to find out where an organization stands is a combination of subjective measures, such as how employees see their pay, and objective measures, such as their actual salaries compared to other relevant companies. On certain issues, it is impossible to obtain data other than through an attitude survey, such as the respect with which employees feel they are treated.

It could be argued that the employee survey measures are the most important; if, for example, the salary survey data show that the company pays competitively, but large percentages of employees disagree, does it really matter what the salary survey data show? Recall that our surveys do not confirm the widely held view that workers will always be unhappy with their pay. When they are unhappy, but the salary survey data say they shouldn't be, it is likely that the criteria employees use to judge the fairness of their pay differ from those used in the salary survey. Employees might be comparing their pay to that of workers in a different set of companies (perhaps nationwide instead of locally). At the least, a discrepancy should cause management to investigate why it exists rather than, as is usually the case, relying solely on the objective information to measure where the organization stands and then "educate" employees as to why they are wrong.

The survey should also include items from the Readiness Questionnaires so that views of partnership policies and practices can be assessed. This is especially helpful for middle- and lower-management populations where attitudes toward certain aspects of partnership might be unfavorable. These views will need to be addressed in communications to them and in their training.

We have been referring to organization-wide results. But, a survey should be conducted so that information is generated not just on employee views overall, but for various units, occupations, and levels. This provides a veritable X-ray of the organization, not only *what* the views are, but *where*—enabling greater precision in the development and application of action. It may be, for example, that blue-collar workers feel much less respect is shown them than for professional workers; or employees in particular departments might report much less cooperation with other departments than is true elsewhere in the organization. Thus divided, the data at a later stage of the process can provide individual managers with an assessment of how their own employees score on the various dimensions of partnership, including how they view their manager's behavior. This is extremely useful for self-analysis and for the training and coaching of managers. The use of the survey questionnaire for individual manager feedback is discussed more fully later in this chapter.

The survey instrument, which is developed to provide direction at the beginning of the process, is also a means—in conjunction with objective data—to assess the impact of the actions taken and, more generally, to evaluate the organization's progress over time toward a partnership organization.

Step 5. What are the major aspects of the organization that need to be changed to get it from where it is to where it wants to be?   Having at least tentatively determined the kind of partnership the company wants and where the organization stands now, senior managers are ready to be more definitive about the major changes that need to be introduced and the ordering of their introduction. These three principles can help guide those decisions:

- **View partnership as a total system.**   As previously noted, many elements of a partnership culture are interdependent: changing one element without considering the others can reduce the impact of a change and even have negative consequences. Management must be especially cautious about changing the non-financial aspects of its relationship with workers without first attending to equity deficiencies, if they exist (such as pay and job security) or at least declaring its serious intention of so doing. There is no way that the value of, say, informal recognition or greater job authority can be substantial or long lasting if people feel mistreated on the basic equity issues. And don't expect increased collaboration if one of its consequences is increased productivity that results in surplus workers and the danger of layoffs. It is not a matter of which element is more important, but which comes first.

- **Do something visible fairly quickly.**   Despite management's best intentions, the early stages of the change process are likely to be met with some skepticism by many employees. This is because they will probably have had prior experience with programs that sounded great but went nowhere. Therefore, it is helpful if, after proper consideration of the way the different elements of partnership relate to each other, one or two significant and highly visible actions be decided upon and introduced. These are, in effect, expressions of management's good faith. The diagnostic survey data can provide important clues as to what these steps might be. For example, one company learned from its survey that the "executive floor" was a major obstacle to performance and timely decision-making because it made interaction between employees and the senior leaders of their units difficult. (In truth, management didn't need the survey to uncover this complaint; they had heard it for years. The survey brought it to the surface and made it difficult to avoid this issue.) It was decided to relocate the managers to offices near their employees, which was a heartily welcomed change by most of the managers themselves. It is a good illustration of an action that is important, visible, consistent with the partnership concept, and relatively easy to quickly implement.

Another category of important changes where implementation can be started fairly quickly are those concerned with inter-unit relationships. Most surveys reveal damaging conflicts between specific units that lend themselves to the type of partnership-building intervention described in Chapter 10, "Teamwork."

- **Give the development and introduction of most of the changes the time they deserve.**   Some changes can be introduced quickly, but most require considerable time to analyze and implement. Take self-managed work teams, for example. That is a fundamental structural change that must be thought through carefully and that involves not just creating the teams themselves but also other supporting actions, such as the training of managers and employees to prepare them for it. Self-managed teams, and other such major initiatives, are often best introduced on an experimental basis in one or two areas of an organization; that way, they can be carefully observed and modified as needed to get them right for the business and the people in it. Although the introduction of a new culture is an undertaking that never really ends, a large organization should consider three to four years as the approximate amount of time it needs to achieve what most everyone will come to see as a genuinely participative culture.

- **Modify the action plan over time.** The initial plan of action is just that: initial. It is meant to be a dynamic plan that will be added to, subtracted from, and otherwise modified as the effort proceeds. Some changes will be a result of oversights during the planning phase, but others will be caused by changing business conditions or new, creative insights that are gained with experience. The evolutionary nature of the plan needs to be communicated to employees with encouragement, and a mechanism, for their participation in suggesting how the plan can continually improve.

Working with these principles, the statement of purpose and business goals, and the measures of where the organization currently stands, senior management identifies the initial changes it wants to see undertaken. At this stage, the action plan should not be too detailed. Here are verbatim excerpts of this kind of action plan from one company. The business goal of the effort in this company, which is a large financial-services company with large numbers of clerical employees, was "to dramatically improve customer service":

Actions to Achieve Partnership—Initial Plan

1. **Job security.**   Assure employees that no layoffs will occur as a result of actions taken through this program; develop a system to minimize layoffs for any reason (explore rings of defense).

2. **Compensation.**   Investigate and correct pay inequities where they exist in specific departments; study the impact of placing all employees on salary.

3. **Start organizing by customer.**   Investigate setting up teams, where feasible and on an experimental basis, to service specific groups of customers (by product and industry); organize measurements around these teams; consider team-based bonuses (but prevent inequities to rest of company); train managers in team and participative management and team members in working cooperatively with each other; learn from the teams the obstacles in the way of providing the best possible service to customers.

4. **Team building.**   Initiate team-building program between staff and line departments, especially between [several departments named].

5. **Formal communication.** Initiate regular communication of business results (including customer service and satisfaction measurements) to entire workforce.

6. **Operating committee [senior management] visits with employees.** Develop schedule and method for all O.C. members to visit and interact informally with employees at all the company's facilities.

7. **Dress code.** Institute informal dress code (with exceptions, as appropriate, for example, customer meetings).

8. **Status distinctions.** Eliminate reserved parking spaces for executives—make it first come, first served for all employees; eliminate separate dining facilities for officers.

9. **Physical working conditions.** Correct problems in departments [several departments named].

10. **Recognition.** Investigate means for giving special recognition for outstanding individual and team performance.

The changes that senior management said should be started immediately were the elimination of status distinctions and the introduction of an informal dress code. These were what they felt would be important and visible changes that would build early credibility with the workforce.

It is our experience that steps 1 through 4 of the action process we have recommended can be accomplished in two off-site senior-management meetings of two to three days each. Obviously, a significant amount of supporting staff work is required, such as preparing educational materials, speakers, and conducting and analyzing the survey.

To this point, the program has pretty much been the province of the senior management group. It is now appropriate to vet the ideas in meetings with other management levels, usually the next one or two levels down. The products of senior management's thinking are presented to the managers—the action steps tentatively decided upon and the process by which the effort will be introduced—and their reactions are obtained. At this time, it's especially important to address how the effort is likely to affect *the managers themselves* (for example, the nature of their jobs under a team approach and the training they will receive for it). Some might feel resentment at some of the changes, such as the loss of the status symbols that, as a manager in one of the meetings put it, "I've worked all these years to achieve." Their role in the process, such as serving on the task forces that will turn the broad partnership plan into specific actions, also needs to be described. The way these matters are addressed can be guided, in part, by the results for this group of the questions in the attitude survey pertaining to management "readiness."

It is critical that the strong commitment to partnership of senior management be affirmed in these meetings. Equally important is that, at that time, the managers have an opportunity to voice their concerns, suggestions, and what they foresee their needs will be to make the program work in their areas. Senior management needs to listen and, as appropriate, act on what they hear. They will not act on suggestions that would significantly weaken the effort (such as maintaining status distinctions) but the bulk of what will be suggested will be useful, and the plan should be modified accordingly.

Step 6. How should the plan be communicated?   The plan should be fully communicated to all employees and, in that communication, a balance must be struck between management's high hopes for the partnership approach and realism about the time and hard work that will be required for its success. In their eagerness to get employees "on board," in their communications organizations tend to overplay the benefits of this kind of effort, they treat it as a sort of miracle drug and understate what is required over an extended period of time to make it happen and the possible snags along the way. There is no need to convince most employees that partnership is a good idea; the convincing they need is of management's sincerity and that will be accomplished only through *action*. The purposes of the communication are to let people know the rationale for a culture of partnership, especially the impact expected on the success of the business and the job satisfaction of employees; what its major components are; the involvement that will be required from employees throughout the organization to make it work; and its limitations and potential pitfalls. That is, management must convey its excitement for the partnership approach, but do so in a way that is informative and realistic. Conviction and credibility—not salesmanship—are the keys. After employees are informed, they don't have to be sold on anything except that management means it.

The plan should be communicated both through the organization's formal media as a message from the CEO and in small group meetings of managers with their employees. To accomplish the latter, it is first necessary to meet with managers up and down the line to fully brief them on what is being planned and why, to answer their questions and concerns, and to prepare them for their meetings with employees.

Step 7. How do we decide on the specific changes that need to be made and how they should be implemented?   After senior management develops the basic plan, its translation into specific action steps should, as we have said, in most cases be the province of task forces composed of representatives from throughout the organization. The "diagonal slice" method is useful for selecting task-force members: the members are chosen from across levels and across functions. We strongly suggest that each of the task forces be led by a senior-management member. That type of leadership structure will not be resented by employees; on the contrary, it is an additional signal of the seriousness with which the organization is undertaking the effort. If a senior-management member does not have a management style or point of view that's appropriate for this kind of leadership role, he should not be chosen for it, of course.

The major exceptions to the task-force approach are those instances where the issues are best discussed and decided upon by management, and usually senior management. Pay is a good example of that. Unless there is a union and a formal bargaining process, it is inappropriate and awkward for employees to be involved in decisions about their salary structure. They might have to be queried about their views of pay—for example, why they believe their pay is not competitive when a salary survey indicates that it is, or how they might view variable pay—but the recommendation about what to do should reside with management. The benefits package is another example. Here, too, however, useful information can be gained from employees regarding benefit preferences and trade offs.

After being fully oriented about its mission, each task force is responsible for the following:

- Defining the assigned issue thoroughly.

- Learning all it needs to know about the issue, including the way other organizations deal with it.

- Developing a recommended action plan.

- Delineating responsibilities, resources needed, timetables, and so on for implementing the plan.

- Suggesting how the effectiveness of what is being proposed can be assessed.

The entire task force and implementation effort should be coordinated by an organization-wide steering committee that, on average, will probably meet about once a month and to which the task forces will regularly report their progress. The committee will suggest modifications in the individual task-force plans and will approve, or seek approval for, the actions that are finally decided upon. The steering committee also serves as the mechanism for airing and doing something about the concerns and suggestions emanating from the workforce as the change process proceeds. It is our view that this steering committee be chaired by a high official of the organization, preferably the CEO or COO.

By this point, you might feel that we demand a lot of senior management's time. You're right; a lot *is* required of them. If this was just "another program," little of their time would be taken, probably just to approve the overall objectives and plan, to hear an occasional, formal progress report, and to give an occasional speech. That is, it wouldn't be serious business. Here, we are talking here about a fundamental change in the culture of an organization. The CEO or COO should also consider himself or herself the Chief Change Officer (CCO). If that level of seriousness is not present, the organization should reconsider whether it wants to go forward.

Step 8. How should managers be trained for the implementation of partnership?   In addition to the preparation managers receive in the basic tenets of partnership and how to communicate the implementation plan to their employees (in step 6), they require training in the implications of a partnership culture for their own behavior. In this book, we have recommended policies and practices at the broad organization level, such as policies concerning job security and formal recognition programs. But, we have also discussed matters relating to individual managers, such as how to treat employees respectfully and provide day-to-day recognition for good performance. These should help any manager that seeks to improve the morale and performance of his employees, but they are especially useful for managers working in a partnership organization or an organization seeking to become one. Because the culture and policies of an organization profoundly impact employees, it is often difficult for individual managers to have nearly as much positive effect as they would like when working in a non-partnership environment. However, the reverse is also true: a partnership culture will obviously not have nearly the desired impact on employees whose managers do not behave in conformity with partnership principles.

A number of manager-training methods are available. One that is particularly relevant and effective for our purposes is "behavior modeling," where managers learn in part by observing and then emulating models of good managerial behavior.[2] Training must, of course, be adapted to the circumstances and objectives of the organizations in which it is applied and to the needs of individual managers. The adaptation can be governed in large measure by what the attitude survey results reveal about the strengths and weaknesses of the organization's managers and their readiness for partnership. Broad issues might pertain to all managers, but there are invariably differences between managers that are revealed by dividing the survey data into an organization's units. The survey data thus provide direction for the content of the training that is needed and, when employee attitudes are reported to a manager, they can be a powerful driver of change because they confront the manager with a mirror image of his behavior—the mirror being the views of his employees. The combination of individual survey data feedback with behavior modeling training therefore offers a particularly useful tool for bringing managerial behavior into line with an organization's partnership culture.[3]

Step 9. How do we assess how well we have done? In addition to its complexity, culture change is a long journey because it is never done perfectly, even after a careful experimental introduction. After all, we are dealing with human beings, and they never fail to surprise. A manager of a self-managing team might, under pressure from his boss who is concerned about serious and immediate business issues, revert to his prior autocratic style. A crucial support function can turn out to be uncooperative with the team. A new pay system introduced to reward team performance might provoke questions about the validity of the measurements being used. These kinds of things happen in the real world and the organization must regularly ask, "How are we doing?," and be prepared to act on what it has learned. Regular meetings need to be scheduled with employees that are devoted to surfacing and dealing with these issues. We also advise that employees be formally surveyed periodically to obtain a quantitative measure of their views that can be tracked over time and reviewed in conjunction with performance results. After all, a major purpose of partnership is to enhance the employee morale that underlies performance; that should be measured as systematically as the performance. If the organization has indeed made significant changes and has made them well, the impact will be readily seen in surveys. Poorly conceived or implemented changes show up as no change, or a decrement, in attitudes. This is true both at the organization-wide and individual-manager levels.

• • •

It's ironic that among the most satisfying aspects of organization life—as of life in general—are those that can be achieved only by hard work. This is especially true of attempts to change relationships: how people treat one another in their pursuit of earning a living. We refer both to the way differential power is used, which are the "vertical" relationships, and the "lateral" relationships among individuals and groups of relatively equal power. A key theme of this book is that the overwhelming majority of people in organizations act in simple pursuit of equitable treatment, a sense of achievement (for themselves and their organization), and camaraderie. They don't want to do either the organization or their colleagues harm, but it often appears that way or, at the least, that they don't care whether the organization or their colleagues succeed or the organization improves. That occurs because of what happens to people when they join organizations, a combination of the daily on-the-job frustrations that cause people to act in ways not in their better nature, the way management treats them as sources of problems, costs, and resistance rather than as assets, and the behavior of the tiny, often highly visible minority of employees that really doesn't care, or even does harm, and so reinforces management's pessimistic view of the workforce.

Partnership organizations emerge when senior leadership—in most cases, it has been the CEO—has the foresight to see what can be and not just what is. This requires not only insight into human nature (especially that people want to do good for a good organization) and not just eloquence in communicating the partnership philosophy, but also perseverance and hard work over a period of years to translate the philosophy into specific policies and daily management practices—the kinds that we have described in this book. It requires seeing and treating employees as genuine allies in achieving change.

PART VI

Appendices

APPENDIX A

Survey Administration and Population Composition

Administration

This book's data are taken from questionnaire surveys administered by Sirota Consulting from 1994–2003. The surveys are self-administered and use three different methods: the web, paper and pencil, and Interactive Voice Response (IVR). (IVR is an automated call-handling system where respondents are guided through a survey on the phone. A computer asks the questions and the respondent enters his or her answers using the telephone keypad or by communicating the answers orally.) The approximate percentages of respondents using these three methods over the decade are as follows:

Web-based method	65 percent
Traditional paper-and-pencil method	30 percent
IVR method	5 percent

The percentage employing the web continually increases. In 2003, it was about 75 percent.

On average, the questionnaires consist of about 100 questions, and almost all of them are multiple choice. About two to three questions are open-ended (that is, the respondent answers the questions in his or her own words). The respondents are guaranteed complete confidentiality for their answers; no one at the organizations in which they work can access an individual employee's responses.

Sirota surveys are nearly always administered to all employees in an organization. Samples are rarely used because one of the major purposes of the survey is to provide individual department managers with data that shows how their own employees respond to the survey. Although a sample of, say, 10 percent of the 20,000 employees of a company would be entirely adequate to provide a measure of the total population, 10 percent would be entirely inadequate for a manager of a 20-person department. Two employees (which is 10 percent of 20) tells the manager effectively nothing about the views of his or her 20 people. A premise of the Sirota approach to feedback is that action needs to take place at both the broad organizational level and at the individual department levels. Data are, therefore, required for both levels.

The average response rate for Sirota surveys is about 80 percent.

Population Composition

Table A-1 shows the distributions of the surveyed population by various parameters.

Table A-1   Distributions of the 1994–2003 Surveyed Population

Total Number of Organizations	**237**
Total Number of Respondents	**2,537,656**[*]
By Sector	
Computer related	5%
Education/research	3%
Financial services/real estate	14%
Government/public sector	5%
Hospital/healthcare	9%
Manufacturing	14%

(continues)

Table A-1   Distributions of the 1994–2003 Surveyed Population   *(continued)*

Total Number of Organizations	**237**
Total Number of Respondents	**2,537,656**[*]
By Sector *(Continued)*	
Oil/gas/mining	10%
Other services (hospitality, placement, consulting, etc.)	6%
Pharmaceutical	9%
Print publishing	5%
Retail	11%
Transportation/communication/utilities	9%
By Size of Organization[**]	
< 1,000	29%
1,000–4,999	35%
5,000–9,999	15%
10,000–24,999	8%
25,000+	13%
By Sex	
Female	53%
Male	47%
By Race	
Caucasian	74%
Black	12%
Hispanic	8%
Asian	6%

(continues)

Table A-1   Distributions of the 1994–2003 Surveyed Population   *(continued)*

Total Number of Organizations	237
Total Number of Respondents	**2,537,656***

By Tenure	
0–2 years	26%
2–5 years	22%
5–10 years	19%
10–20 years	20%
More than 20 years	13%
By Level	
Management	13%
Non-management	87%
By Region	
North America	78%
Europe	14%
Other	8%

*Some of the individual analyses described in this book are performed on subsets of the population. This is especially the case for the comparative correlational analyses where we require that identical questions be asked in a number of different populations. Nevertheless, the numbers of respondents used for those analyses are in the many thousands.

**These are the sizes of the actual organizations surveyed. The smaller ones are usually segments of much larger organizations (divisions, business units, and so on).

APPENDIX B

Reliability and Validity of the Data

Two basic kinds of tests are applied to data to determine their soundness. One kind of test measures *reliability*, and the other test measures *validity*. This appendix is a small sampling of the tests that have been applied to our data.

Reliability

Reliability refers to the consistency or dependability of a measure, and you can test for reliability in a number of ways.

One method of testing for reliability is called *internal consistency*. It is the extent to which questions that are designed to measure the same attitude—say, attitude toward the work itself—correlate with each other. (This is similar to an ability test, where the questions designed to measure mathematical ability should, if they are reliable, correlate with each other.) If the questions are reliable, they should not only correlate highly with each other, but significantly more so than with questions that measure other attitude areas (just as two mathematical ability questions should correlate more highly with each other than with two verbal ability questions).

In most of our surveys, we intentionally ask more than one question about the same subject area. This is not to "trick" the respondents, but to get at the area from a number of angles. When we do this, we *invariably* find that these questions correlate highly with each other, significantly more so than they correlate with other questions on the questionnaire. Here's a small, typical example of what we mean: Table B-1 shows two pairs of questions from a survey; the two questions in each pair are designed to measure the same attitude area, more or less. The areas are the attitude toward the work itself and the attitude toward the immediate supervisor. Table B-1 contains the correlations among all four questions. Notice that the correlations within each of the pairs are all high (coefficients in the .60s to .70s range)—demonstrating high reliability—and, as expected, considerably higher than the questions in one pair are with questions in the other pair (coefficients in the .40s range).

Table B-1   Correlations of Job and Immediate Manager Items

	Supervisor Is Honest	Trust My Supervisor	Sense of Accomplishment on the Job
Trust Supervisor	(.78)		
Sense of Accomplishment on the Job	.44	.45	
Use of Skills on the Job	.45	.44	(.66)

The reason that the questions across the two attitude areas still correlate significantly with each other—albeit lower than within the attitude areas—is that they are not completely independent. For example, a supervisor who employees trust is also likely to give them latitude to use their skills and abilities on the job (that might be one reason employees trust him). When more independent attitude areas are related, we find low correlations. For example, the correlations between attitudes toward the work itself and attitudes toward pay fall between .10 and .25, those between pay and equipment are .05 to .15, and so on.

Of course, we never find perfect correlations, even between questions that are designed to measure the same attitude area. For one thing, the questions tap somewhat different aspects of that area. Second, there is always "measurement error," such as an employee misinterpreting a question or making a mistake in the marking of her answer.

We once made a mistake in designing a questionnaire. We inadvertently asked two identical questions on the same very long questionnaire, once at the beginning of the questionnaire and once toward the end. This mistake turned out to be fortuitous in that it provides us with a terrific additional test of reliability, namely, "test-retest" reliability, which measures whether individuals provide consistent responses when they answer the very same questions after a short time interval. The correlation between the two was .92, which is just about as high as correlations in our work get. This clearly demonstrates that people do not answer questions randomly or haphazardly.

Validity

Validity is a measure of the extent to which the questionnaire measures what it purports to measure. For example, attitudes toward pay might be consistent (reliable), but they might not be actually measuring attitudes toward pay (just as a thermometer might always give the same reading, but it might be the wrong reading).

We have innumerable tests of the validity of our data. Here's a small sampling:

1.   **Demographics.**   Let's not start with attitude questions, but with what are termed demographics. In almost all of our surveys, we ask respondents for their length of service, sex, race, and so on. We do this so we can divide the data by these variables and determine whether any attitudinal differences exist between the groups (such as between men and women). These are actually very sensitive questions to ask in an "anonymous" survey because employees often feel that their answers to these questions can identify them. But, in every case where we have achieved a high response rate (more than 80 percent), the distributions we obtain on the surveys are almost identical to the actual demographic distributions provided to us by the organization. Apparently, the employees, despite their misgivings about identification, tell us the truth. Table B-2 shows an example from one company.

Table B-2 Demographic Distributions: Survey Responses Versus Actual

	Percentage of Respondents in Survey	Actual Percentage in Workforce
Classification		
Full-time	92%	91%
Part-time	6%	7%
Per diem	2%	2%
Sex		
Male	53%	55%
Female	47%	45%
Tenure		
0–2 years	23%	21%
2–5 years	11%	10%
5–10 years	21%	23%
10–20 years	28%	27%
More than 20 years	18%	19%

2. **Response to change.**   We usually survey very large populations. Individuals might have all sorts of quirks—an employee may, for example, be happy with his pay when, by all objective standards, his pay is low—but these quirks should not make a big difference when surveying large numbers of employees. If pay questions are valid, they should, on average, reflect actual compensation in the way compensation is normally evaluated (for example, what employees are paid compared to what they might earn in similar jobs in other companies). Therefore, if pay is significantly raised for a workforce and the answers to our questions on pay do not, on average, show increased satisfaction, we would doubt the validity of those questions. But, the fact is that when employee pay is significantly raised, their attitude toward pay *does* move up markedly.

For example, in a company with five plants, the employees in one plant ("E") expressed much less satisfaction with their pay on a survey than did the employees in the other four plants. The reason was that the company did not differentiate in its pay scales between areas of the country and "E" was in a much higher wage and cost-of-living area than were the other four plants. This policy of no "area differentials" was changed as a result of the survey, which led to an average wage increase of about 15 percent over the next two years for "E" employees. In the other plants, the wages increased an average of 7 percent. Table B-3 shows the satisfaction with pay data from the five plants in two time periods.

Table B-3   Percent Satisfied with Pay in Five Plants in Two Time Periods

Plant	Time 1	Time 2	Difference (Time 2 – Time 1)
A	45%	46%	+1
B	53%	54%	+1
C	53%	51%	–2
D	43%	46%	+3
E	32%	49%	+17

Satisfaction with pay increased markedly in Plant E and only marginally, if at all, in the other four plants. You might ask, "What is so surprising—what would you expect?" That is precisely the point: these common-sense tests—nothing esoteric, nothing "psychological"—applied to attitude results give us great confidence in their validity.

The pay data bring us to a broader point: our surveys are performed so that the information is *used*; they are not for academic interest. When, for whatever reason, no action occurs after a survey, *no changes in employee attitudes are seen in the next survey* The data are remarkably stable because it takes action to change them. Furthermore, if action is taken in one respect, it shows up on the questions relating to that change, but not in other respects. Table B-4 shows the attitudes toward the work itself in the same five plants. These attitudes hardly changed at all.

Table B-4 Percent Satisfied with the Work Itself in Five Plants in Two Time
Periods

Plant	Time 1	Time 2	Difference (Time 2 − Time 1)
A	68%	67%	−1%
B	74%	74%	0
C	73%	72%	−1
D	66%	69%	+3
E	76%	77%	+1

Employees carefully differentiate between the various attitude areas: Plant
E markedly increased on attitudes regarding pay, but hardly at all regarding the work itself. This phenomenon of differentiation underlies the previously mentioned small correlation between attitudes toward pay and
attitudes toward the job itself. Most employees fill out the questionnaires
thoughtfully and carefully, noting what they're pleased with and what
they're not.

Take another example of the impact of management action on survey
data: an energy company laid off a large number of employees in two
consecutive years, even though it promised after the first layoff that there
would be no more. We conducted surveys after the first layoff and after
the second layoff. We have no data about attitudes before the first layoff,
but the results of our first survey indicated, as would be expected, that
employees were unfavorable about their job security (31 percent below
our norm). After the second layoff, the results, which were already very
low, got even worse: now 51 percent below the norm. Table B-5 shows
the data.

Table B-5 Satisfaction with Job Security

Time 1 (After First Layoff)	Time 2 (After Second Layoff)	Norm
29% favorable	9% favorable	60% favorable

Job security was the largest declining item in the second survey. Interestingly, with the loss of so many people and the subsequent demands placed

on those who remained, several items showed sharp *improvements*, especially job challenge and intra-department teamwork. This makes sense because the work became more challenging and the employees had to rally around each other to accomplish what needed to be done. Again, we see evidence of the sharp differentiation employees on surveys make between different aspects of work situations.

Take a third example of the impact of change as a test of the validity of the survey data: a particularly poor CEO (by everyone's standards, such as the board of directors, his direct reports, and the general workforce) was removed and replaced by a CEO strongly committed to improving performance and raising morale. Table B-6 shows the before and after survey results regarding the company's leadership after just one year with the new CEO at the helm.

Table B-6   Impact of New CEO on Attitudes Toward Company Leadership

	% Favorable		
	Under Previous CEO	Under New CEO	Difference (1 Year Later)
Leadership Question			
Sense of direction	44%	86%	+42%
Effective leadership	42%	80%	+38%
Listening to employees	37%	72%	+35%
Overall job being done by senior management	50%	84%	+34%
Interest in employee well-being	52%	81%	+29%

As you can see, the attitude changes were huge.

3. **Relationships with performance measures.**   Among the most important tests of validity is the way employee attitudes predict performance (just as many ability tests are supposed to predict academic achievement). Chapter 2, "Employee Enthusiasm and Business Success," details the strong positive relationships we and others find between employee morale and organization

performance. We can provide numerous other examples of the relationship between attitudes of various kinds and performance. Here is just one more: the relationship we almost invariably find between the perceived customer focus of an organization (measured by employee surveys) and customer satisfaction (measured independently by customer-satisfaction surveys). We consistently find that, across various industries, the more employees say a company is customer-focused, the greater customer satisfaction is. Again, you might ask, "What else would you expect?" Again, that is precisely the point: what common sense tells us should be found is found, thus reinforcing confidence in the validity of the survey. No, we didn't need a survey to tell most managers how critical it is for employees to see their organizations as customer-focused to achieve customer satisfaction. The survey serves to inform management just how customer-focused its organization is.

Table B-7 shows the correlations between customer focus and customer satisfaction in companies in various industries.

Table B-7   Correlations Between Perceived Customer Focus and Customer Satisfaction

Customer Focus Question	Type of Company	Correlation
The company strives for excellence in customer service	Retail	.57
Is committed to customer satisfaction	Telecommunication	.63
Makes exceeding customer expectations a priority	Hospitality	.64
Has a strong interest in patient well being	Hospital	.56
Places management emphasis on measuring customer satisfaction	Automotive	.68

APPENDIX C

Job Satisfaction: Demographic, Occupational, and Regional Breaks

Table C-1 shows job satisfaction broken into demographic, occupational, and regional groups.

Table C-1 Responses, by Demographic, Occupational, and Regional Groups, to the Question: "How Would You Rate Your Satisfaction with the Job Itself—the Kind of Work You Do?"

	Favorable	Neutral	Unfavorable
By Tenure			
0–2 years	76%	18%	6%
2–5 years	73%	19%	8%
5–10 years	75%	17%	8%
10–20 years	77%	16%	7%
More than 20 years	77%	17%	7%

(continues)

Table C-1   Responses, by Demographic, Occupational, and Regional Groups, to the Question: "How Would You Rate Your Satisfaction with the Job Itself—the Kind of Work You Do?"   *(continued)*

	Favorable	Neutral	Unfavorable
By Sex			
Female	76%	16%	8%
Male	75%	18%	7%
By Race/Ethnicity			
Caucasian	76%	16%	8%
Black	76%	15%	9%
Hispanic	79%	14%	7%
Asian	75%	16%	9%
Native American	75%	14%	11%
By Level			
Management	83%	12%	5%
Senior	88%	8%	4%
Middle	85%	11%	4%
First-level	80%	14%	6%
Non-Management	74%	17%	9%
Salaried	76%	16%	8%
Hourly	72%	19%	9%
By Region			
North America	77%	16%	8%
Europe	68%	23%	9%

(continues)

Table C-1   Responses, by Demographic, Occupational, and Regional Groups, to the Question: "How Would You Rate Your Satisfaction with the Job Itself –the Kind of Work You Do?"   *(continued)*

	Favorable	Neutral	Unfavorable
By Selected Industry Sectors			
Healthcare	79%	15%	6%
Retail	78%	16%	6%
Financial services	77%	15%	8%
Manufacturing	76%	17%	7%
Oil/gas/mining	71%	22%	8%
By Size of Organization			
< 1,000	77%	16%	7%
1,000–4,999	77%	15%	8%
5,000–9,999	76%	15%	9%
10,000–24,999	78%	15%	7%
25,000+	71%	19%	10%

APPENDIX D

Comparisons with Other Norms

Many employee attitude surveys are conducted, but the data from them are almost always proprietary. We have access, from time to time, to the results of surveys conducted by others, and while we cannot publish those, we can attest to the great similarity between their results and ours. A fortunate exception to the proprietary nature of normative data is found in the Federal Human Capital Survey 2002, which reports the results of a 2002 survey of the attitudes of more than 100,000 employees randomly selected from the 24 agencies represented on the President's Management Council. These agencies comprise 93 percent of the executive branch workforce.*

The U.S. Office of Personnel Management, the organization conducting the survey, was provided with "a set of private-industry norms drawn from an average of survey data from large, primarily U.S. corporations." We are familiar with those norms and can vouch for the care with which those data have been collected and compiled. Table D-1 shows the results

What Do Federal Employees Say? Results from the 2002 Federal Human Capital Survey. Published by the U.S. Office of Personnel Management (www.opm.gov).

for nine questions that are similar enough in wording to allow reasonable comparison. We point out, however, that even slight differences in wording can result in significant swings in the data, as we explain in the discussion that follows the table.

Table D-1 Comparisons of Sirota Normative Data with Federal Public and Private Sector Norms on Similarly Worded Questions

	Sirota Norm	Federal Study Norms	
		Public Sector	Private Sector
Job itself	76%	68%	67%
Teamwork within work unit	73%	80%	79%
Benefits	65%	63%	63%
Information to do job	62%	71%	67%
Opportunity to improve skills	59%	57%	59%
Training	57%	53%	58%
Company communications on important matters	52%	45%	54%
Recognition	51%	46%	48%
Amount of pay	46%	56%	44%

Considering the differences in a number of question wordings and in the types of organizations included (e.g., the exclusively large, well-known companies in the federal survey's private sector norms), the data are remarkably similar. We have ordered the questions by the percentage favorable in our norms and the orderings are close. The rank-order correlations between the sets of norms are as follows: between our norms and the federal private sector norms, .95; between our norms and the federal public sector norms, .80; between the federal public and private sector norms, .83. The norms we have seen from elsewhere—often using identical questions and with populations similar in composition to ours—are even closer to ours.

Among the larger discrepancies we see are satisfaction with the job and with pay. The Sirota job satisfaction norm is higher than either of the other two (the latter are still 2/3 favorable), but we attribute the discrepancy almost entirely to a wording difference: we ask very specifically about "your job—the kind of work you do," while the other surveys ask the respondents: "Considering everything, how satisfied are you with your job?" We have found that many respondents tend to include attributes in addition to the work itself when the question is worded in terms of "job satisfaction," especially "considering everything." Support for our assertion comes from data in response to another question about the job in the federal survey that is worded more similarly to ours: "I like the kind of work I do." The positive response to this question is 82 percent! Unfortunately, this wording was not used for the private sector norm.

In contrast, our question on pay is worded almost identically in both other surveys. Our data are very close to the private sector results, but both are significantly below the satisfaction with pay expressed by public sector employees. We believe this to be a real difference.

Appendix E

The Readiness Questionnaire

The Readiness Questionnaire is a short instrument that can help a management team come to terms with its views of partnership policies and practices. Often, there will be verbal agreement with a concept, such as partnership, but managers might have serious reservations about it (reservations they are reluctant to express publicly). The Readiness Questionnaire data help get these views "on the table" so they can be discussed and informed decisions made as to whether and how to move ahead in the implementation of partnership.

The Readiness Questionnaire covers key partnership policies and practices. An organization can add or subtract questions to the instrument to make it more relevant to its needs.

It is best that the completed questionnaires be sent to an outside party, or some other trusted source, for scoring. This appendix contains instructions for scoring.

The following is a suggested Readiness Questionnaire that can be used with appropriate modifications to fit the organization.

The Readiness Questionnaire

This questionnaire is designed to measure your basic views of employee relations. The results of the survey will be thoroughly discussed by the management team to determine whether, and in what respects, the organization is ready to move ahead in modifying its approach to managing people. The results will be reported in a way that will make it impossible to identify individual answers. Here are a few guidelines and instructions for filling out the questionnaire:

- The questions ask about employee relations. In answering the questions, think of the people who constitute the bulk of the employees in your organization. We want to know what you feel policies and practices for these employees should be.

- Obviously, some of the answers are more "socially acceptable" than others, and you might be inclined to answer that way. Try to answer the way you genuinely feel. The only "right" answer is the one that expresses your views. As previously mentioned, you are the only one in your organization who will see your individual answers.

- Each question will be answered on a 7-point scale, and the endpoints of the scale are defined. For example, take question 1:

  Question 1. If you had your way, would it be your policy or practice to:

| Pay employees no more than what you have to, even if it's below what other companies pay for similar work. | 1 2 3 4 5 6 7 | Pay as much as you can afford, even if it's considerably more than what other companies pay for similar work. |

If you are the type of manager who wants to pay rock-bottom wages, you would likely circle "1." If it is—or would be—your practice to pay as much as you possibly can, even if that means your employees would earn considerably more than what they could get elsewhere for similar work, you would likely circle "7." If you are somewhere between those poles, you would circle a number in between "1" and "7," depending on where you felt your attitude fell. The midpoint of this scale is "4."

Let's begin. Remember to keep in mind the employees who constitute the bulk of your workforce and policies and practices for them *in general*. Please answer as you genuinely feel, not what might be "socially acceptable."

If you had your way, would it be your policy or practice to:
(Circle one number for each question.)

1. Pay employees no more than what you have to, even if it's below what other companies pay for similar work.

   1 2 3 4 5 6 7

   Pay as much as you can afford, even if it's considerably more than what other companies pay for similar work.

2. Provide no more in the way of benefits (medical, etc.) than what you have to, even if it's less than the average of other companies.

   1 2 3 4 5 6 7

   Provide as much in the way of benefits as you can afford, even if it's more than the average of other companies.

3. Provide safety conditions that meet the minimum required by law.

   1 2 3 4 5 6 7

   Provide the utmost in safety conditions.

4. Lay off employees as soon as they are no longer needed.

   1 2 3 4 5 6 7

   Do whatever you can reasonably do to not lay off people (retraining them for other jobs in the company, etc.).

5. Do no more for laid-off employees than what you have to do (severance payments, etc.).

   1 2 3 4 5 6 7

   Do as much for laid-off employees as you can afford.

6. Insist that employees throughout the organization are treated with courtesy and respect.

   1 2 3 4 5 6 7

   Not be at all concerned about this.

7. Have employees—even if they are experienced—supervised closely.

1 2 3 4 5 6 7

Have experienced employees supervised only generally and instead depend on their own initiative and motivation to perform well.

8. Make extensive use of recognition for employees, even when performance is not extraordinary (just satisfactory).

1 2 3 4 5 6 7

Recognize only those employees whose performance is extraordinary—well beyond what is expected.

9. To the extent possible, divide the work so that each employee does just a small piece of it.

1 2 3 4 5 6 7

"Enlarge" or "enrich" work so that, to the extent possible, an employee does a "whole job" from beginning to end.

10. Invest in the best possible training for employees to do their jobs (perhaps even somewhat more than what they might need).

1 2 3 4 5 6 7

Do the bare minimum in this respect.

11. Provide development opportunities for employees to prepare them for higher-level assignments.

1 2 3 4 5 6 7

Do little or nothing in this respect.

12. Communicate to employees only what they have a "need to know" to do their specific jobs.

1 2 3 4 5 6 7

Communicate as much as possible to employees (the reasons for decisions, state of the business, etc.).

13. Insist that communications to employees be completely honest.

1 2 3 4 5 6 7

Not be at all concerned that communications be honest.

14. Insist that employees at all levels share financially in the achievements of the business (through bonuses, or higher base pay, or better benefits, etc.).

1 2 3 4 5 6 7

Not be at all concerned that they share financially in the achievements of the business.

15. Insist that employees not be exploited in any way (for example, working extremely long hours without extra compensation or time off).

1 2 3 4 5 6 7

Not be at all concerned about this.

16. Insist that employees have a reasonable workload that will not harm their health or personal or family lives.

1 2 3 4 5 6 7

Get as much work as you legally can from them.

17. Provide as pleasant physical working conditions for employees as you can afford.

1 2 3 4 5 6 7

Provide no more than what you have to in order to get the work done.

18. Make sure that employees get reasonable time off to take care of their personal and family needs.

1 2 3 4 5 6 7

Allow this only in the most extreme circumstances (such as a medical emergency).

19. Assure that, if employees have complaints, they are given a full and fair hearing.

1 2 3 4 5 6 7

Not be at all concerned about this.

20. Insist that, when business dips, sacrifices are made at all levels, from senior management on down.

1 2 3 4 5 6 7

Not be at all concerned about this.

21. Work cooperatively with the union. (If there is no union, answer as if there were one.)

1 2 3 4 5 6 7

Fight the union every chance you get, including having it decertified, if possible.

22. Eliminate status distinctions between levels (reserved parking spaces, separate eating facilities, etc.).

1 2 3 4 5 6 7

Fully preserve status distinctions.

23. Stimulate an atmosphere of cooperation and teamwork between individuals and between departments.

1 2 3 4 5 6 7

Not be at all concerned about this.

24. Stimulate competition between individuals and between departments.

1 2 3 4 5 6 7

Not do this at all.

25. For promotions, give strong preference to people inside the organization (rather than hire from the outside).

1 2 3 4 5 6 7

Give no such preference.

26. Insist that senior-management personnel periodically visit with employees at all levels.

1 2 3 4 5 6 7

Do little or nothing in this respect.

27. Discourage employees from conversing with each other on the job if the conversation is not work related.

1 2 3 4 5 6 7

Not be at all concerned about this.

After you complete the questionnaire, make a copy to keep for yourself and send the original to {insert the scorer's name}. When the group meets to discuss the group results, bring your copy with you so you can compare your responses to those of the group.

Instructions for the Scorer of the Questionnaire

The scoring is simple. Each question is based on a 1 to 7 scale. For some questions, 1 is the highest partnership score while for others, it is 7. Which is which is indicated on the scoring sheet (see the next section, "Scoring Sheet"), although for most questions, it should be obvious (nothing is hidden or tricky).

You will obtain average scores for the group surveyed on each question and for combinations of questions. To get these averages—where we always want 7 to be the highest average partnership score—you need to convert the questions where 1 is the highest partnership score. To do this, first calculate the average for each question, which is done by taking the sum of the answers given by all respondents to the question divided by the total number of respondents to the question. Then, subtract from 8 the averages for the questions where 1 is the highest partnership score.

For example, here are the answers for a group of 12 people on question 10, where 1 is "Invest in the best possible training for employees to do their jobs (perhaps even somewhat more they might need)," and 7 is "Do the bare minimum in this respect."

Invest in the best possible training for employees to do their jobs (perhaps even somewhat more than what they might need).

1 2 3 4 5 6 7   Do the bare minimum in this respect.

Number of respondents giving each answer.

2 4 3 1 2 0 0

Calculate the average by multiplying the number of respondents giving each answer by the answer weight (2×1, 4×2, 3×3, etc.), adding those products ($2 + 8 + 9$, etc.) and dividing that sum (33) by the number of respondents (12). In this example, doing this yields an average of 2.75. Because question 10 has 1 as its highest partnership score, it must be subtracted from 8. The average that will be used, then, is 5.25 ($8.00 - 2.75$). (Remember: You would not subtract from 8 the averages to those questions where 7 is already the highest partnership score.)

You now have calculated usable averages for each question. Enter those averages on the scoring sheet. That form also contains lines for the following "averages of averages:"

- **Total partnership score.** This is the average of all of the questions: simply add up all of the averages and divide by the number of questions (27).

- **Equity score.** This is the average of all of the questions relating to equity.

- **Achievement score.** This is the average of the questions relating to achievement.

- **Camaraderie score.** This is the average of the questions relating to camaraderie.

The scores can easily be graphed (as bar graphs with the vertical axis ranging from 1 to 7). Two pages of graphs are desirable. One page would show the total partnership, equity, achievement, and camaraderie averages. The other page would show each question's average, ordered by equity, achievement, and camaraderie.

The maximum possible score is 7, and the group discussion should focus on how far its scores on the various questions and averages are from that maximum. There is no precise criterion as to what constitutes a score that should be considered "far" from the maximum. A rule of thumb is a difference of 2.00 or more (i.e., an average score of 5 or below).

Scoring Sheet

Equity Questions	Average	Usable Average[*]
1		
2		
3		
4		
5		
6[*]		
13[*]		
14[*]		
15[*]		
16[*]		
17[*]		
18[*]		
19[*]		
20[*]		
21[*]		
22		
26[*]		
Total Equity Score (Sum of the Usable Averages)		
Equity Average (Total Equity Score Divided by 17)		

[*]*For the questions with asterisks, the usable average is 8.00 minus the average. For the other questions, the usable average is the average.*

Achievement Questions	Average	Usable Average*
7		
8*		
9		
10*		
11*		
12		
25*		
Total Achievement Score (Sum of the Usable Averages)		
Achievement Average (Total Achievement Score Divided by 7)		

For the questions with asterisks, the usable average is 8.00 minus the average. For the other questions, the usable average is the average.

Camaraderie Questions	Average	Usable Average*
23*		
24		
27		
Total Camaraderie Score (Sum of the Usable Averages)		
Camaraderie Average (Total Camaraderie Score Divided by 3)		

For the questions with asterisks, the usable average is 8.00 minus the average. For the other questions, the usable average is the average.

Total Partnership Score (Sum of All 27 Usable Averages)		
Partnership Average (Total Partnership Score Divided by 27)		

Endnotes

Introduction

1. Some anecdotal material is derived from our recollection of comments made in focus groups, interviews, and observations over the years; some write-in comments have been modified to protect the confidentiality of the respondents.

2. We try to present quantitative information in a way that will make sense to readers unfamiliar with, or not particularly interested in, complicated statistical analyses. The latter are primarily "multivariate" analyses through which a number of variables are manipulated simultaneously. We employ such analyses in most of our work—especially multiple regression analysis and structural equation modeling—but reserve reporting and discussing them for other researchers. A major benefit of those analyses is to test the conclusions we reach with simpler methods (e.g., whether the correlation between two variables holds up when other variables are added). Most of the statistical results shown in this book have been subjected to these tests. We have been unable to do this when the data did not lend themselves to it, such as a number of the relationships with objective performance measures. In those instances, the number of units for which measures are available for all of the variables is insufficient.

3. Likert, R. *The Human Organization*. New York: McGraw Hill, 1967; Maslow, A. H. *Motivation and Personality*. New York: Harper and Row, 1954; Mayo, E. *The Human Problems of an Industrial Civilization*. New York: Macmillan, 1933; McClelland, D.C. *Personality*. New York: Dryden Press, 1951; McGregor, D. *The Human Side of Enterprise*. New York: McGraw Hill, 1960.

Part I
Chapter 1

1. Munk, N. "The New Organization Man." *Fortune*. March 16, 1998. *137*, no. 5, pp. 62–68.

2. Gross, D. M. and Scott, S. "Proceeding with Caution." *Time*. July 16, 1990, pp. 56–62.

3. O'Toole. J., et. al. *"Work in America: Report of a Special Task Force to the Secretary of Health, Education, and Welfare."* Cambridge, USA: MIT Press, 1973, pp. xv–xvi.

4. Herzberg, F., Mausner, B., and Snyderman, B. *The Motivation to Work.* New York: Wiley, 1959.

5. Rothschild, E. "GM in More Trouble." *New York Review of Books.* March 23, 1972. *18*, no. 5, p. 19.

6. Equity has been studied by one group of organization psychologists under the designation "organization justice." The researchers make a host of fine distinctions between different forms of justice—much more than we feel important for our argument or managers' practical use—but their basic conclusions are the same as ours: a feeling of being treated fairly is extremely important for workers and for their contribution to the organization. For an overview of the research, see Colquitt, J. A., Conlon, D.E., Wesson, M. J., Porter, C., and Yee Ng, K. "Justice at the Millennium: A Meta-Analytic Review of 25 Years of Organizational Justice Research." *Journal of Applied Psychology.* 86, 2001, pp. 425–445.

7. The correlations with camaraderie tend to be lower than that with achievement largely because of a technical reason, namely, the significantly smaller variance in response to the camaraderie question.

Chapter 2

1. Pfeffer, J. and Sutton, R. *"The Knowing-Doing Gap."* Boston: Harvard Business School Press. 2000.

2. Goleman, D. *Working with Emotional Intelligence.* New York: Bantam Books. 1998, pp. 118–119.

3. Wylie, A. "How You Can Unleash the Power of Storytelling." *The Rostrum.* Feb. 2000; found at http://debate.uvm.edu/NFL/rostrumlib/WylieStorytellingFeb'00.pdf.

4. Pfeffer, J. *"The Human Equation."* Boston: Harvard Business School Press. 1998, pp. 31–56.

5. This finding is from a thus far unpublished analysis of the relationship between employee satisfaction and defect rates in 182 units of the Credit and Risk Group of a large financial institution surveyed by Sirota in 2003.

6. Rucci, A. J., Kirn, S. P., and Quinn, R.T. "The employee-customer-profit chain at Sears." *Harvard Business Review.* January-February 1998, pp. 82–97.

7. Smith, S.B., Del Duco, S.M., and Mischkind, L.A. "The impact of social/cultural factors on tornado warning performance." Presented at

the Society for Industrial and Organizational Psychology 18th Annual Conference, Orlando, FL, April 12, 2003.

8. Eskildsen, J. and Dahlgaar, J. "A causal model for employee satisfaction." *Total Quality Management. 11*, no. 8, December 1, 2000, pp. 1081–1094; Maister, D. *"Practice What You Preach: What Managers Must Do to Create a High Achievement Culture."* New York: The Free Press. 2001; Oliver, J. "Invest in people and improve profitability and productivity." *Management Today.* March 1998, pp. 90–91; Ostroff, C. "The relationship between satisfaction, attitudes and performance: An organizational level analysis." *Journal of Applied Psychology. 77*, 1992, pp. 963–974; Schneider, B., Hanges, P. J., Smith, D. B., and Salvaggio, A. N. "Which comes first: employee attitudes or organizational and market performance?" *Journal of Applied Psychology. 88*, 2003, pp. 836–851.

9. Reichheld, F. F. *"Loyalty Rules!"* Boston: Harvard Business School Press. 2001; Reichheld, F. F. *"The Loyalty Effect."* Boston: Harvard Business School Press. 1996.

Part II
Chapter 3

1. Sloan A. "Jobs—The Hit Men." *Newsweek. 127*, no. 9, February 26, 1996, p. 44.

2. Results of a 2001 online survey of telecom employees conducted by TeleCareers.net; quoted in Broadband Week Direct, 10/9/01; found at www.broadbandweek.com/newsdirect/0110/direct011009.htm.

3. Cascio, W.F. "Downsizing: What Do We Know? What Lessons Have We Learned?" *Academy of Management Executive. 7*, no. 1, 1993, p. 95–104; Lehrer, S., "Effectively Coping with Downsizing." *The Government Accountants Journal.* December 1997, p. 12–13; Cascio, W.F., Young, C.E., Morris, J.R. "Financial consequences of employment-change decisions in major U.S. corporations." *Academy of Management Journal. 40*, no. 5, 1997, pp. 1175–1189; Hitt, M., Keats, B., Harback, H., Nixon, R. "Rightsizing: Building and Maintaining Strategic Leadership and Long-Term Competitiveness." *Organizational Dynamics. 23*, no. 2, 1994, pp. 18–32.

4. Mishra, K.E., Spreitzer, G.M., and Mishra, A.K. "Preserving Employee Morale During Downsizing." *Sloan Management Review.* Winter 1998, pp. 83–85.

5. Thurow, L. *USA Today.* March 21, 2001, p. 15A.

6. Parker, J. "Where Layoffs Are a Last Resort." BusinessWeek Online, Oct. 8, 2001.

7. Sharplin, A. D. "The Lincoln Electric Company." Northeast Louisiana University, Lake Charles, Louisiana. 1981, p. 4.

8. Iverson, K. "How Nucor Works." *New Steel.* November 1997 (newsteel.com), excerpted from Iverson, K. and Varian, T. *"Plain Talk: Lessons from a Business Maverick."* New York: John Wiley & Sons, Inc., 1997.

9. Levering, R. and Moskowitz, M. "Best Companies to Work For: The Best in the Worst of Times." *Fortune. 145*, no. 3, February 4, 2002, p. 72.

10. Business for Social Responsibility (www.bsr.org). Issue Brief: Downsizing:Layoffs/Closings (last updated October 2001).

11. As reported on WKPRC. See Click2Houston.com. "Thousands Furloughed at Continental Airlines—International Layoffs Still to Come." Posted: 1:13 P.M. CDT, September 21, 2001. Updated: 6:44 P.M. CDT, September 21, 2001.

Chapter 4

1. Levine, D. I. "Can Wage Increases Pay for Themselves? Tests with a Production Function." *Economic Journal.* Royal Economic Society. *102*, 1992, pp. 1102–1115.

2. Pfeffer, J. *The Human Equation.* Boston: Harvard Business School Press. 1998, p. 200.

3. Abowd, J., Kramarz, F., and Moreau, A. "Product Quality and Worker Quality." NBER Working Paper # w5077, 4/95; Policy Brief— Prevailing Wage Laws. January 7, 2000; found at www.lbo.state.oh.us.

4. Near, J. W. "Wendy's Successful 'Mop Bucket Attitude'." *The Wall Street Journal.* April 27, 1992, p. A16.

5. "Lawler, E.E. III. *Strategic Pay: Aligning Organizational Strategies and Pay Systems.*" San Francisco: Jossey-Bass. 1990, p. 57.

6. Whyte, W. F. *Money and Motivation: An Analysis of Incentives in Industry.* New York: Harper and Row. 1955, pp. 41–44.

7. Our norm for attitudes on the fairness and accuracy of appraisals is 66 percent.

8. Lawler, Edward E. E. III. *The Ultimate Advantage.* San Francisco: Jossey-Bass. 1992, p. 177.

9. Lawler, E. E., III. *Strategic Pay: Aligning Organizational Strategies and Pay Systems.* San Francisco: Jossey-Bass. 1990, p. 125.

Chapter 5

1. Kilborn, P.T. "Strikers at American Airlines Say the Objective Is Respect." *The New York Times.* November 22, 1993, A1, A8.

2. Witness, for example, the characterization by Kathryn Jones in her March, 2001 *Texas Monthly* "Biz" column, *American Flyer*: "Crandall was the hot tempered, cutthroat CEO who built Fort Worth–based American into an industry juggernaut by the sheer force of his competitive thirst for blood. Nicknames like Fang and Darth Vader stuck for good reason."

3. American Airlines is reported to have recently begun a major initiative in its relationship with its employees, seeking a true "partnership"— rather than adversarial—relationship with them. "A Profile: American Airlines changes its business operation to move on workers' ideas." National Public Radio, All Things Considered. September 13, 2004.

4. For a comprehensive description of Nordstrom policies and practices, see Spector, R. and McCarthy, P. D. *The Nordstrom Way: The Inside Story of America's #1 Customer Service Company.* New York: John Wiley and Sons, 2000. Also see Peters, T. J. *Thriving on Chaos.* New York: Knopf, 1987, pp. 378–379.

5. Peters, T. J. and Austin, N. *A Passion for Excellence.* New York: Warner Books, 1985, p. 207.

6. Caudron, S. "The New Status Symbols." *Industry Week. 248*, no. 12, June 21, 1999, p. 44.

7. Peters, T. J. *Thriving on Chaos.* New York: Knopf, 1987, p. 381.

8. We say "typically," because there are numerous variations on these practices for salaried employees. For example, in some organizations, a salaried employee can lose pay if he is absent beyond an allotted number of "sick" or "personal" days. Also, certain salaried employees—those whose work resembles that of hourly workers—are not exempted from the legal requirement to be paid overtime. Furthermore, we do not address the legal distinction between "exempt" and "non-exempt" workers. Although the U.S. fair labor laws tend to speak to the same kind of status distinction that we describe, the law's purpose is to protect workers from owners who might otherwise impose harsh compensation rules based on arbitrary time restrictions and definitions. Here, we are concerned with the effect of maintaining wage status distinctions—primarily salaried vs. hourly—on the culture of the employment environment and, hence, on worker enthusiasm.

9. Public Employees Federation (PEF), President's message (Roger E. Benson). November 1999; found at www.thecommunicator.org/comnovember1999/prezmez.htm.

10. Taken from the *Sirota Consulting* handbook.

11. Muoio, A. "The Truth Is, The Truth Hurts." *Fast Company Magazine*. April 1998, Issue 14, p. 98.

12. A full treatment of Stack's philosophy can be found in: Stack, J. and Burlingham, B. *The Great Game of Business*. New York: Doubleday and Company. 1994.

13. Peters, T. J. and Waterman, R. H. Jr. *In Search of Excellence*. Harper Row, New York. 1982, pp. 121–134.

14. Sherman, S. "Stability: Donald Graham's Washington Post." *Columbia Journalism Review*. Sept./Oct. 2002, p. 42.

Part III
Chapter 6

1. The correlations range from .389 (pride in efficiency) to as much as .644 (pride in products and services).

2. For years, Merck has been a highly respected company, known for its integrity, generosity, and professionalism. George Merck's commitment to 'medicine for people not profits' is in pointed contrast to other companies that focus primarily on share price. In the 1980s, Merck achieved the number-one spot on *Fortune's* list of Most Admired Companies for seven straight years. No company is even close to that record. For example, Merck is credited with saving millions of people annually from the debilitating disease of river blindness by donating its drug Mectizan to tropical nations. Do recent events, however, spell the end of an era for Merck—have priorities shifted so markedly to short-term profitability as to seriously damage the company's reputation for integrity and its long-term business prospects? We refer to the withdrawal of Merck's drug Vioxx from the market amid allegations that information about serious side effects of the drug on the heart were suppressed by the company.

3. Collins, J.C. and Porras, J. I. *Built to Last*. New York: Harper Business Books. 1997.

4. In their calculation, all dividends were reinvested and appropriate adjustments were made when the companies became available on the stock exchange.

5. Collins, J.C. and Porras, J. I. *Built to Last*. New York: Harper Business Books. 1997, p. 55.

6. Ibid., (p. 57).

7. Ibid., (p. 57).

8. Waddock, S.A. and Graves, S.B. "The corporate social performance-financial performance link." *Strategic Management Journal. 18*, no. 4, 1997, pp. 303–319.

9. Cited in Business for Social Responsibility Web site, White Paper, "Introduction to Corporate Social Responsibility"; found at www.bsr.org/BSRResources/index.cfm.

10. Frooman, J. "Socially Irresponsible and Illegal Behavior and Shareholder Wealth." *Business and Society. 36*, no. 3, September 1997, pp. 221–249.

11. Wayne, L. "Designee Takes a Deft Touch and a Firm Will to Treasury." *New York Times* (Late Edition (East Coast)). New York, NY: Jan. 16, 2001, p. A1.

12. Vogel, D. "Recycling Corporate Responsibility." *The Wall Street Journal.* August 29, 2002 (in Manager's Journal), p. B2.

13. Schultz, H., Yang D.J., and Conger, E. *"Pour Your Heart into It: How Starbucks Built a Company One Cup at a Time."* New York: Hyperion. 1997.

14. Kahaner, L. "How Their Mission Statement Helped Johnson & Johnson Survive the Tylenol Crisis"; found at www.kahaner.com, excerpted from Jones, P. and Kahaner, L. *Say It & Live It: 50 Corporate Mission Statements That Hit the Mark*, First Edition. Currency Books. May 1, 1995

15 The Malcolm Baldrige National Quality Award was created by Public Law 100-107, signed into law on August 20, 1987. The Award Program, which is responsive to the purposes of Public Law 100-107, led to the creation of a new public-private partnership. Principal support for the program comes from the Foundation for the Malcolm Baldrige National Quality Award, which was established in 1988.

16. Hude, H. "Quality in the Service Sector, Proceedings of the 1991 Making Statistics More Effective in Schools of Business (MSMESB)." The Wharton School, Univ. of Penn., 1991; See also Smith, F. "Customer Satisfaction: A Job That's Never Really Done." J. D. Power & Associates Customer Service Conference. Santa Monica, California. November 13, 2003.

17 "'Baldrige Index' Outperforms S&P 500 by Almost 5 to 1." National Institute of Science and Technology (NIST) press release. February 25, 2000

Chapter 7

1. For a sophisticated defense of hierarchy, see Jacques, E. "In Praise of Hierarchy." *Harvard Business Review.* Jan.-Feb., *68*, no. 1, 1990, pp. 127–133.

2. One of the best-known and instructive investigations of the effects of different leadership styles was conducted in the 1930s by Lippitt and White. Known as "Leadership and Group Life," the study was conducted under the direction of Kurt Lewin. The study involved directing groups of schoolchildren in the production of arts and crafts artifacts in four different clubs. They had three types of leaders assigned to them: 1) autocratic: aloof, used orders, no consultation with group; 2) democratic: offered guidance, encouraged group participation; 3) laissez-faire: gave knowledge but did not do much else. The key results were: in the democratic group: morale high; group members friendly; good relationship with leader; when leader left room, operated independently; fair amount of originality; and, although they produced less than the authoritarian group, the quality of production was much higher. In the authoritarian group: two kinds of behavior, aggressive and apathetic. Aggressive were rebellious, demanding of attention from leader, blamed each other when anything went wrong. Others were submissive. The group's productivity overall was higher than the democratic group, but the quality was much poorer. The laissez-faire group was the worst group with poorest productivity and quality; lowest morale; most demands placed on leader; least independent work; and least cooperation. See Lewin, K., Lippit, R., and White, R.K. "Pattern of Aggressive Behavior in Experimentally Created Social Climate." *Journal of Social Psychology. 10*, 1939, pp. 271–99.

3. Lawler, E. E., III. *The Ultimate Advantage.* San Francisco: Jossey-Bass, 1992, p. 33.

4. Morse, J. J. and Lorsch, J.W. "Beyond Theory Y." *Harvard Business Review.* May-June 1970, pp. 61-68.

5. Pfeffer, J. *"Competitive Advantage Through People."* Boston: Harvard Business School Publishing. 1994, p. 43.

6. Peters, T. J. *Thriving on Chaos.* New York: Alfred A. Knopf. 1987, p. 291

7. Excerpted from Tom Peters Company web site; found at www.tompeters.com.

8. Tomasko, R. M. *Downsizing: Reshaping the Corporation for the Future.* Amacom. 1987, p. 143.

9. Peters, T. J. *Thriving on Chaos.* Alfred A. Knopf, New York. 1987, p. 355.

10. Peters. T. J. *Thriving on Chaos*. New York: Alfred A. Knopf, 1987, p. 359; and Lawler E. E., III. *The Ultimate Advantage*. San Francisco: Jossey-Bass, 1992, p. 62.

11. For research evidence on SMTs, see Manz, C. C., and Sims H. P. *Business Without Bosses: How Self-Managing Teams Are Building High-Performing Companies*. San Francisco: Jossey-Bass, 1995; Orsburn, J. D., Moran, L., Musselwhite, E., and Zenger, J. H. *Self-Directed Work Teams*. Homewood, Ill.: Business One Irwin, 1990; Katzenbach, J. R. and Smith, D. K. *The Wisdom of Teams: Creating a High Performance Organization*. Boston: Harvard Business School Press. 1992; Yeatts, D. E. and Hyten, C. *High-Performing Self-Managed Work Teams: A Comparison of Theory to Practice*. Thousand Oaks, California: Sage Publications, Inc. 1998.

12. "I'd be the first to agree that if the performance level of (these) self-directed work teams were close to that of Toyota, then it would be worth sacrificing a little performance to have more fun at work—but it's not close; it's not even in the ballpark." Interview with Dr. Paul Adler, Prof., Marshall School of Business at USC, by David Creelman, on HR.com. May 14, 2001.

13. Milkman, R. *Farewell to the Factory: Auto Workers in the Late Twentieth Century*. Berkeley: University of California Press. 1997, p. 171.

14. The Profit Professionals of Business Solutions—The Positive Way; found at www.profitpro.us/profit__ideas.htm; see also the federal government's *User's Guide to Successful Suggestion Programs, the Interagency Advisory Group Committee On Performance Management and Recognition, Suggestion Program Working Group, Office of Personnel Management* (1995 Edition).

15. Katzenbach, J. R. and Smith, D. K. *The Wisdom of Teams: Creating a High Performance Organization*. Boston: Harvard Business School Press. 1992; Fandt P. "The Relationship of Accountability and Interdependent Behavior to Enhancing Team Consequences." *Group and Organization Studies. 16*, no. 3, 1991, pp. 300–312.

16. Clemmer, J. *Pathways to Performance: A Guide to Transforming Yourself, Your Team, and Your Organization*. Canada: Macmillan. 1995, p. 215.

Chapter 8

1. In Greek mythology, Ponus, who represents the drudgery of toilsome labor, is the child of Erebus (darkness) and Nox (night). Not a pleasant allusion.

2. Keep in mind that we are discussing *job* satisfaction, not *overall* satisfaction. These two terms are easily confused. The latter is the global concept: how, *in general*, people feel about their employment situation—their "morale," as it were. Overall satisfaction is the product of a number of specific factors, such as attitudes toward job security, pay, leadership, ability to get the job done, and the work itself. The last of these—attitudes toward the work itself—is "job satisfaction" and is just one of the specific factors that go into overall satisfaction. It is distinguishable from those factors, as in, "I wish I could stay here because I really love the kind of work I do, but I can't live on what they pay me."

3. As described in Peters, T. J. *On the Nature of Work*. May 7, 1993; found at www.tompeters.com.

4. Employees also prefer managers who stress quality. The correlations between managers being seen as stressing quality and satisfaction with those managers are in the .70s. The correlations between managers stressing quantity and satisfaction with them are slightly negative.

5. Sirota, D. and Greenwood, J. M. "Understand Your Overseas Work Force." *Harvard Business Review*. 1971, pp. 53–60.

Chapter 9

1. For an overview of the research, see Hellervik, L.W., Hazucha, J.F., Schneider, R.J. *Behavior Change: Models, Methods, and Review of Evidence in* Dunnette, M. D. Hough, L. M. *Handbook of Industrial and Organizational Psychology*, second edition, Palo Alto, California: Consulting Psychologists Press, 1990, pp. 823–895.

2. Employees who are inordinately sensitive to criticism need a lot of attention, praise, and reassurance. The guidelines we propose should be followed quite literally with them to keep a difficult situation psychologically from getting even worse.

3. Lepsinger, R. and Lucia, A. D. *The Art and Science of 360° Feedback*. San Francisco: Jossey-Bass, 1997; Sederburg, M. E. and Rogelberg, S. G. "Informed Decisions: Research-Based Practice Notes. 360 Degree Feedback: Methodological Advice from Multiple Sources." *The Industrial-Organizational Psychologist*, 1998, *36*, pp. 67–76.

4. See, for example, Smith, G. P. "People Need to Feel Appreciated": found at www.businessknowhow.com/manage/appreciate.htm. See also, Smith, G. P. *Here Today, Here Tomorrow: Transforming Your Workforce from High-Turnover to High-Retention*. Chicago: Dearborn Publishing. November 2001. Smith prescribes praise over cash when it comes to retaining "the best and brightest." "People have a basic human need to feel appreciated, and recognition programs help meet

that need," notes Smith. "Money might attract people to the front door, but something else has to keep them from going out the back." Also, see Bob Nelson, writing in the *Quality Digest*: "Salary raises and bonuses are nice, but they seldom motivate people to do their best on the job on an ongoing basis...Having learned that employees are motivated by intangible rewards, companies would be wise to consider the power and possibilities of no-cost job recognition when trying to motivate employees to do their best." ("Secrets of Successful Employee Recognition." *Quality Digest*, QCI International, 2004; published at www.qualitydigest.com.)

5. Collins, J.C. and Porras, J. I. *Built to Last*, New York: Harper Business Books. 1997, pp. 173–176.

Part IV
Chapter 10

1. Among the more interesting explorations of "social capital" and its importance is Don Cohen's and Laurence Prusak's, *In Good Company: How Social Capital Makes Organizations Work.* Boston: Harvard Business School Press. 2001.

2. Mayo, E. *The Social Problems of an Industrial Civilization.* New Hampshire: Ayer. 1945, p 111.

3. See Hill, G.W. "Group Versus Individual Performance: Are N+1 Heads Better than One?" *Psychological Bulletin.* May 1982, p. 535. See also Morgan, J. and Blinder, A. "Are Two Heads Better than One: "An Experimental Analysis of Individual Versus Group Decision Making." *National Bureau of Economic Research.* September 2000, No. 7909.

Part V
Chapter 11

1. Ross, A. "Boarding Houses." *Journal of Antiques and Collectibles.* March. 2003; found at www.journalofantiques.com/Mar03/hearthmar03.htm.

2. U.S. Department of Labor, Bureau of Labor Statistics, Mass Layoff Statistics (MLS); found at www.bls.gov/mls/home.htm.

3. Farber, H. and Krueger, A. "Union Membership in the United States: The Decline Continues." Working Paper No. 4216, National Bureau of Economic Research, 1992. These conclusions were reached on the basis of an analysis that controlled for the effects of structural changes in the economy, such as the increasing proportion of service workers.

4. The improvement in employment conditions is by no means universal. In fact, there is evidence that, for certain segments of the workforce, there might be a return to earlier sweatshop-like conditions. For example, in 1996, the U.S. Department of Labor estimated that out of 22,000 U.S. garment shops, at least half were in serious violation of wage and safety laws.

5. Katz, H. C., Kochan, T. A., and Weber, M. A. "Assessing the Effects of Industrial Relations Systems and Effort to Improve the Quality of Working Life on Organizational Effectiveness." *Academy of Management Journal. 28,* 1985, p. 519; Ichniowski, C. "The Effects of Grievance Activity on Productivity." *Industrial Relations Review. 40,* 1986, pp. 75–89.

6. See, for example, Adler, P. S. "The 'Learning Bureaucracy': New United Motor Manufacturing, Inc." *Research in Organizational Behavior. 15,* 1992, p. 120; Bohlander, G. W. and Campbell, M. H. "Problem-Solving Bargaining and Work Redesign: Magma Copper's Labor-Management Partnership." *National Productivity Review. 12,* no. 4. 1993, pp. 519-533; Eckel R., Eckel, P. F., and Herman, A. "Lean Manufacturing, Worker Empowerment and Labor-Management Collaboration at Ford Cleveland Engine Plant #2"; found at www.fmcs.gov (search on Ford Cleveland Engine Plant).

7. Gittell, J. H.. *The Southwest Airlines Way: Using the Power of Relationships to Achieve High Performance.* New York: McGraw-Hill. 2003, p 165.

8. Ibid., (p. 165).

9. "A Profile: American Airlines changes its business operation to move on workers' ideas." National Public Radio, All Things Considered. September 13, 2004.

10. Gittell, J. H. *The Southwest Airlines Way: Using the Power of Relationships to Achieve High Performance.* New York: McGraw-Hill. 2003, p. 183.

Chapter 12

1. "At Continental, Morale Is Everything." *Human Capital: Strategies and News*; found at www.octanner.com/news/HumanCapital.

2. Goldstein, A. P. and Sorcher, M. *Changing Supervisory Behavior.* New York: Pergamon Press. 1974.

3. The "360" technique described in Chapter 9 is also an effective way to provide feedback to managers on their own behavior. Here, managers receive data from a number of sources, not just their employees.

Index

F

Q-R

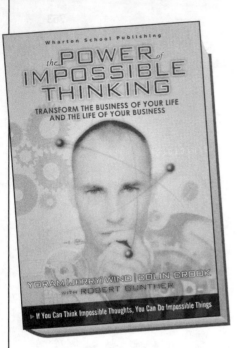

The Power of Impossible Thinking

You don't live in the real world. You live in the world inside your head. We all do. Our invisible mental models shape everything we do. Often, they keep us from seeing what's right in front of us, and prevent us from changing our companies and society...even our *lives*. *The Power of Impossible Thinking* is about fixing your mental models, so you can *see* reality and *act* on it. Based firmly in neuroscience, it shows how to develop new ways of seeing...understand complex environments...even how to do "mind R&D" to keep your models fresh and relevant. Whether you need to beat the competition or lose weight, your mental models may be the problem...and *The Power of Impossible Thinking* is the solution.

ISBN 0131425021, © 2005, 336 pp., $24.95

Failsafe Strategies

In the 1990s, in the name of "revolutionary business models," businesses took on massive risks almost without concern. Today, many companies have become powerfully averse to taking the risks that are essential to long-term success. Now, there's a whole new way to think about risk: one that liberates you to act, while protecting you against danger. Dr. Sayan Chatterjee shows how to identify high-risk, high-return opportunities, and then systematically manage and reduce those risks up front, as you design your initiative... not after you operationalize it. Using his techniques, you can safely pursue opportunities your competitors will walk away from—and sustain profit growth far into the future.

ISBN 0131011111, © 2005, 312 pp., $26.95